DU

The l
reade

26·9·

BLOOD ON THE THISTLE

BLOOD ON THE THISTLE

The heartbreaking story of the Cranston family and
their remarkable sacrifice in the Great War

STUART PEARSON
AND
BOB MITCHELL

JOHN BLAKE

Published by John Blake Publishing Ltd,
3 Bramber Court, 2 Bramber Road,
London W14 9PB, England

www.johnblakepublishing.co.uk

www.facebook.com/Johnblakepub facebook
twitter.com/johnblakepub twitter

First published in hardback in 2014

ISBN: 978-1-78219-906-9

British Library Cataloguing-in-Publication Data:
a catalogue record for this book is available from the British Library.

Design by www.envydesign.co.uk

Printed in Great Britain by CPI Group (UK) Ltd

1 3 5 7 9 10 8 6 4 2

© Stuart Pearson and Bob Mitchell 2014

The right of Stuart Pearson and Bob Mitchell to be identified as the Authors of
this Work has been ~~asserted by them in accordance with the Copyright~~, Designs
~~and Patents Act 1988.~~

Papers used by John ~~Blake Publishing are natural, recyclable products~~ made from
wood grown in susta~~inable forests. The manufacturing processes conform~~ to the
enviro~~nmental regulations of the country of origin.~~

Every attempt ~~has been made to contact the relevant copyright-h~~olders,
but some were unc~~ontactable. We would be grateful if the appropriate~~ people
~~could contact us.~~

'The Cranston family was one of a few who made such a great sacrifice and suffered such a significant loss' – Lieutenant-Colonel Roger Binks, the Scottish National War Memorial, Edinburgh

Dedicated to the memory of a most remarkable Scottish family and to the families of an estimated 125,000 Scottish soldiers, sailors and airmen[1] who lost their lives in the Great War.

---

1 Figure quoted by the Commonwealth War Graves Commission in its booklet, 'The Work of the Commonwealth War Graves Commission in Scotland' (2012).

CONTENTS

ACKNOWLEDGEMENTS   IX
INTRODUCTION   XIII
CRANSTON FAMILY CHART   XV
PROLOGUE (SYDNEY, AUSTRALIA, 1921)   XVII

PART ONE (1881–1912)

THE FLITTIN' (1881)   3
THE SANDS (1894)   21
WATCH THE BIRDIE (1908)   45
HOGMANAY (1911)   55
AGNES'S FAREWELL (1912)   67

PART TWO (1914–20)

1914   77
1915   113
1916   153
1917   219

1918   239
1919/1920   269

PART THREE (1927–9)
A PLACE OF SAFETY   287

PART FOUR (THE AFTERMATH)
SCOTLAND   297
CANADA   301
AUSTRALIA   303
CONCLUSION   307
BIBLIOGRAPHY   309

ACKNOWLEDGEMENTS

I wish to express my sincere gratitude to the many Cranston descendants who contributed anecdotes, memories, photographs and memorabilia pertaining to the Cranston family of Haddington. Assistance came from America, Australia, Canada, England, New Zealand and Scotland.

From Australia, I would like to expressly thank Christine Leader (granddaughter of Angus) and Alison Mackey (granddaughter of Agnes McDowall, née Cranston). In Canada, I received wonderful support from Don Chapman in Mission, British Columbia. Don is married to Connie (granddaughter of Mary Weir, née Cranston) and his efforts in producing a family register as well as enhancing numerous images has single-handedly made this biography possible.

Connie's sister, Shayron, in Toronto, has played a hugely significant role in investigating and unravelling the fragmented and almost forgotten history of Mary Weir's time in Canada. Shayron would make a great detective, if she ever wanted to take up that profession.

In Scotland, I wish to express my appreciation and gratitude in particular to brothers Colin and Robert (Rab) Cranston; Ian and Margaret Cranston, as well as Stewart and Moira Cranston.

But in truth, almost every descendant contributed something to the production of this family history. Even my daughter, Anna, presented me with a folder of information that she had independently assembled during years of research.

Then there are people who are not related to the Cranston family that I want to thank. In Scotland, Margaret O'Connor and Craig Statham from East Lothian Council were both outstanding in their assistance. Margaret organised and approved many Cranston related activities, including access to Council archives and Craig was unstinting in his research of the files. He constantly uncovered information that had a direct and positive impact on the story.

However, there is one person who deserves more praise and acknowledgement than any other. Bob Mitchell is an amateur historian and author who resides in Haddington and we have collaborated on this book as co-authors. Bob has lived and breathed the Cranston story for the past few years and has come to know them as well as anyone could. We have corresponded regularly and I can say without any shadow of doubt, I would not have been able to produce this book without his crucial assistance.

There are a number of images included in this book. The majority are my own copyright or that of other Cranston descendants who have given me their permission to use the images. However, there are a few images that came from other sources. In every instance I have endeavoured to find the copyright owners of these images to seek their permission to use the photograph. If I have omitted to do so in every case, please contact me and I will remedy the oversight in subsequent editions.

Most importantly, I want to thank my patient and supportive

ACKNOWLEDGEMENTS

wife, Ingrid. Without her constant encouragement, I might have lost my enthusiasm for this project long ago. Without her eye for detail and insistence on accuracy, the finished book would have been a much poorer product. If it were not for her love, I would be a very lonely old man.

STUART PEARSON, May 2014

INTRODUCTION

This book is based on a true story about the Cranston family of Scotland. They lived, loved and in some cases died in the East Lothian town of Haddington, from the late 19th century into the early part of the 20th century. Even though there is no one alive today who can give an eye-witness account of the daily life of the Cranston family, they still existed.

This story has been recreated from a number of sources. First, were the primary and secondary documentary sources, which the authors found were surprisingly abundant. Second, the recollections and received stories of descendants. And thirdly, the reconstruction of events in order to prove or disprove the veracity of these anecdotes. The times and events they lived and died through were real and have been recreated from painstaking research.

However, some fictional characters, including Effie Fairgrieve and Sandy Pow, have been created to enhance the telling of the story. There are also a few events which have been included for dramatic effect, without detracting from the accuracy of the narrative.

Given that it has been over 90 years since the original Cranston family ceased to reside in Haddington, the authors have attempted to recreate the history of the family as faithfully and as truthfully as possible, set in the social context of its time.

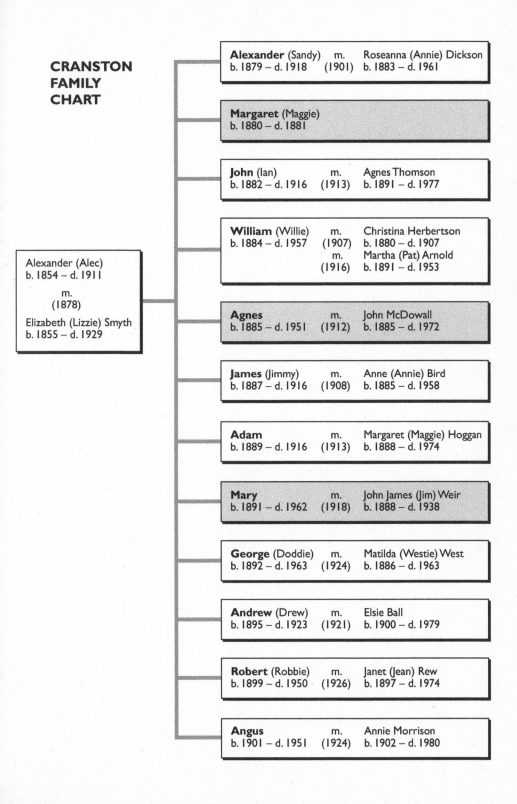

CRANSTON FAMILY CHART

Alexander (Alec)
b. 1854 – d. 1911

m.
(1878)

Elizabeth (Lizzie) Smyth
b. 1855 – d. 1929

Alexander (Sandy)   m.   Roseanna (Annie) Dickson
b. 1879 – d. 1918   (1901)   b. 1883 – d. 1961

Margaret (Maggie)
b. 1880 – d. 1881

John (Ian)   m.   Agnes Thomson
b. 1882 – d. 1916   (1913)   b. 1891 – d. 1977

William (Willie)   m.   Christina Herbertson
b. 1884 – d. 1957   (1907)   b. 1880 – d. 1907
                            m.   Martha (Pat) Arnold
                            (1916)   b. 1891 – d. 1953

Agnes   m.   John McDowall
b. 1885 – d. 1951   (1912)   b. 1885 – d. 1972

James (Jimmy)   m.   Anne (Annie) Bird
b. 1887 – d. 1916   (1908)   b. 1885 – d. 1958

Adam   m.   Margaret (Maggie) Hoggan
b. 1889 – d. 1916   (1913)   b. 1888 – d. 1974

Mary   m.   John James (Jim) Weir
b. 1891 – d. 1962   (1918)   b. 1888 – d. 1938

George (Doddie)   m.   Matilda (Westie) West
b. 1892 – d. 1963   (1924)   b. 1886 – d. 1963

Andrew (Drew)   m.   Elsie Ball
b. 1895 – d. 1923   (1921)   b. 1900 – d. 1979

Robert (Robbie)   m.   Janet (Jean) Rew
b. 1899 – d. 1950   (1926)   b. 1897 – d. 1974

Angus   m.   Annie Morrison
b. 1901 – d. 1951   (1924)   b. 1902 – d. 1980

PROLOGUE
(SYDNEY, AUSTRALIA, 1921)

The heat is stifling and the cicadas[2] are screaming their mating songs across the northern suburbs of Sydney. The oppressive temperature hovers over Eastern Australia like a heavy blanket, smothering most human activity. The leaves on the gum trees hang low and vertical to avoid the scorching rays of the sun. Dried bark and leaves are scattered over the ground, ready to be crunched underfoot by the first passer-by.

It is the summer of 1921, yet one proud lady is dressed as if she was still living in the freezing northern hemisphere. She wears a heavy black dress down to her ankles, with a matching black jacket over a white blouse.

This 66-year-old, grey-haired woman wanders erratically up the dirt street towards Gordon railway station on Sydney's semi-rural North Shore. When she passes one of the few houses, which are built sporadically along the track, she stops, gesticulates and

---

2 Cicada: a small tree-living insect that is slightly larger than a cricket and has a unique mating sound or song.

mutters incoherently as if talking to imaginary friends. If anyone were present to hear her, they would not know what she is saying, because her broad Scottish brogue disguises her ramblings completely. She walks beside wooden post and rail fences that surround partially cleared fields and past the workers' cottages of men who were clearing them. She slowly makes her way up the hill towards the main road that runs adjacent to the railway line.

It is Sydney in the middle of a hot summer's day at a time when most people of the sparsely populated North Shore are either at work or taking refuge inside their cool houses from the midday heat. No one sees her.

As yet, nobody knows she has wandered off from her family home in Ryde Road, but soon her married daughter will return to the residence and start frantically searching for her mother in the nearby bush. The old woman's name is Elizabeth and she is mentally ill. Only she does not know it.

As she continues to meander her way up the long hill, strands of white hair become detached from the neat bun at the back of her neck and beads of sweat start running down her forehead.

Elizabeth crests the top of the ridge at the Pacific Highway and she sees a train approaching Gordon railway station. The rising white plume of steam spewing out of the locomotive's engine seems to draw her towards the platform. She walks past the few wooden shops that are situated along the unpaved road and down the other side of the slope towards the station. As she nears the station entrance the passenger train is pulling away from the platform to continue its journey north. Elizabeth, still talking to herself, passes the two passengers who have alighted from the train.

They barely give her a second glance. It is too hot to be bothered with an inappropriately dressed old lady. Down on the platform the station assistant who had collected the passengers' tickets returns to slowly sweeping the platform.

Elizabeth sits down on a railway bench and starts to rock gently and rhythmically on the seat muttering to herself.

The station assistant is a young, conscientious chap and it does not take long for him to notice this old lady's erratic behaviour. He studies her for a few minutes while he continues to sweep, moving inconspicuously closer and closer to her.

He is now standing next to her and with a pleasant smile asks if she is all right. At first he can only hear incoherent ramblings, but as she continues talking he begins to detect the same words repeated. As he struggles to cut through the strong Scottish accent, the words eventually become more distinct to him.

The lady sitting on the railway bench, rocking back and forth is saying, 'I'm waitin' for ma boys tae come hame.' Over and over.

The station assistant is unfamiliar with people who are mentally disturbed, but he is convinced he is seeing one now. He takes her out of the sun and sits her down in the relative coolness of the station's waiting room. He gets a glass, fills it with water and offers it to this woman. She accepts the drink with indifference, but as she is sipping the water Elizabeth looks up into the railway employee's face and says, 'Adam, is that you?'

The assistant knows that the over-dressed, grey-haired woman is confused and for several minutes tries to find out her identity and why she is at the railway station. He is not successful. The woman will not engage him in a logical conversation. She just keeps muttering about her 'boys'.

He notices that she is carrying a small handbag and hopes there might be some form of identification inside. She does not seem to notice him taking the bag from her. The young man looks inside for anything that will help him get this peculiar person off his platform. In the handbag are some personal papers and a note that carries a surname and an address nearby in Gordon. The young man is satisfied he has found the old lady's name and address and is about to close the bag when he comes across an official looking letter that has been folded and refolded many times. He knows he must ring the local police to escort the woman away but something about the letter looks unusual and important. He decides to open it and have a look.

He is shocked. There on the top left hand corner is the Royal Coat of Arms and on the top right hand corner are the words, 'Privy Purse Office, Buckingham Palace'.[3]

The young man's hands start to tremble. He has never seen a letter from royalty before. Slowly, it dawns on him that something unusual must have happened to this person. He reads the contents silently to himself:

Madam,

I am commanded by the King to convey to you an expression of His Majesty's appreciation of the patriotic spirit which has prompted your five sons to give their services at the present time to the British Armed Services.[4]

Five sons! This lady had five sons in the Great War. He looks up from the letter and slowly his attitude towards the woman begins to alter.[5] She is no longer a deranged nuisance. He returns to the letter.

The King was much gratified to hear of the manner in which they have so readily responded to the call of their Sovereign and their country, and I am to express to you and to them His

---

3 Privy Purse is the Financial Secretary to the Sovereign.
4 The original of the royal letter to Elizabeth Cranston has been lost over time, but the words reproduced here are taken directly from a copy in the Royal Archives.
5 The King's letter was written in 1915. Two more Cranston sons would enlist – one each in 1916 and 1917 – making a total of seven sons who served in the Great War.

Majesty's congratulations on having contributed in so full a measure to the great cause for which all the people of the British Empire are so bravely fighting.

On behalf of His Majesty, His Royal Highness King George V, I have the honour to be, Madam, Your obedient servant.

[Signed] F. Ponsonby.[6]

The station assistant folds the royal letter closed and respectfully returns it to the lady's purse. Here, on his station, is someone who has actually received a letter from the King!

Then he notices items on her clothing that, in his haste to get rid of this woman, he had completely overlooked before. On the lady's sleeve are four small black velvet strips of material that have been sewn onto her black crepe jacket. He suddenly realises that these are widows' and mothers' mourning ribbons. He has seen a few women dressed in mourning, some of them even wearing a ribbon to signify the loss of a soldier, but it is now three years after the Great War ended and in Australia it is rare to find women still wearing mourning dress.

On top of that, the young station assistant has never seen four mourning ribbons before. He is stunned. It means that out of the boys who had gone to war, four had died. The young lad is now completely in awe of this lady. Not only has the King thanked her for sending so many of her boys off to war, but so many of them had died.

This is going to be one of those occasions in his life about which he will tell his grandchildren. But in the meantime, he will make her as comfortable as possible until the police arrive to take her home.

While he is fussing around her, this lady keeps mumbling to

6 Lieutenant-Colonel Frederick Ponsonby, 1st Baron Sysonby, GCB, GCVO, PC, was Keeper of the Privy Purse at Buckingham Palace 1914–35.

herself, 'Ma boys, ma boys. Where are ma boys?' There is a faraway look on her face as she stares fixedly into the distance.

In her mind, however, she is half a world and a lifetime away dreaming of people and places the young station assistant will never know.

PART ONE
(1881-1912)

THE FLITTIN'
(1881)

The old cart carrying the meagre Cranston possessions creaked doggedly forward against the icy, driving wind. It was in the depths of winter, but the sun was gamely trying to pierce the dirty skyline. The little family huddled in the cart was leaving behind them the seaport of Leith and a barrow-load of disappointment. In front of them was the sprawling county of East Lothian, and their future.

Elizabeth, Lizzie to everyone who knew her, stole a glance at Alec Cranston, her husband of three years. He was holding the reins of the old borrowed horse and gently coaxing it to move up a slight rise in the road. He gazed straight ahead as Portobello merged into Joppa, his flat cap pulled firmly down on his head against the freezing cold wind, his ever-present pipe dangling from his mouth.

Physically strong and concentrating on the task at hand, Alec looked confident, glad to see the back of the grime, the disease and the grinding poverty that infested Leith. Lizzie seemed reassured by her husband's strength of character and resolve. Despite everything, she had chosen wisely. Not that there had been a great deal of choosing if she was perfectly honest.

She pulled the thin woollen blanket tighter around her to protect the two-year-old child sleeping quietly against her bosom. Soon the horse's hooves striking the gravel road set up a soft, rhythmic beat and Lizzie began to reflect on recent events in her still young life.

She pondered if womanhood was always so dramatic. A few years ago she had been a carefree lass living with her grandparents in the country and now she was a married woman who had already given birth to two children and was pregnant with another. She could scarcely believe what was happening to her. But the simple truth of Lizzie Cranston's life was that she had always experienced both the highs and the lows that fortune and fate can deal out.

It had commenced in the most inauspicious circumstances in that part of Edinburgh of which rural Scotland knew nothing. St Cuthbert's in the Pleasance was built precisely to cater for the needs of women in the dire straits that her mother, Margaret, had found herself: alone, pregnant and far from home. The nuns of St Cuthbert's provided charity that was basic and care that seemed grudging, but mother and child survived and for Lizzie, at least, things were about to take a turn for the better.

She was never quite sure how her mother made her way back to her native Banffshire some 280 kilometres to the north of Edinburgh, or how her grandparents had welcomed the arrival of their illegitimate granddaughter, but perhaps it had been with calm resignation. Their circumstances were hardly unique. Lizzie was thankful her grandparents truly loved children. After they had raised a dozen children of their own, Lizzie became part of a clutch of grandchildren that several other unwed daughters had brought back to Keith to be looked after by the grandparents. It was as if it was yesterday that they had lived and worked together and she had been truly happy.

It was her grandfather, John, that she had especially come to love. He had taught her the rudiments of farm work from the day that she had first walked and she had always preferred it to being cooped up indoors. He had taught her to find birds eggs in hedgerow and field, he had shown her how to tell the time with a dandelion clock and secretly, because he would have admitted it to no one, he had used his huge, calloused hands to make her daisy chains.

If Lizzie had ever felt different in those days, it had never caused her any upset. She was not the only child to be brought up by her grandparents and she was vaguely aware that she was lucky. She was seldom hungry and always listened to. For a good 10 years, she had thought only fleetingly of her mother, and of her father, who was never mentioned, she thought nothing at all. By the time she reached her teens she had become a country girl at heart and owed her allegiance to the people and places of Banffshire.

It was impossible for Lizzie not to feel ambiguous towards her mother. For years she had wished for nothing more than for her grandparents John and Janet McLeay to be her real parents but that, she knew, could never be the case. If nothing else it would have sorted out the issue of her surname once and for all. The older she had become, the more Lizzie thought about her real identity and the 50 per cent of herself about which she knew nothing.

For most of the people with whom she had grown up she was known as 'Muggie McLeay's quine',[7] but at school if ever she did anything wrong she was called 'Elizabeth Smith' – surely the most common girl's name in the world. Then there was the letter she had accidentally stumbled across a couple of years ago addressed to 'The Parents or Guardians of Miss Elizabeth Smyth'.

---

7 girl

5

'Smyth' had momentarily seemed an attractive option for the young Lizzie, but her best pal had quickly vetoed that.

'Smyth!' she had echoed with all the scorn and incredulity that a 10-year-old can muster, 'Whit kind o' name is that? It's nae a name at a' as far as I ken.' Lizzie said nothing, but the seed was sown.

At 15 years of age, Lizzie Smith had long considered herself to be a woman. Where she came from there were no in-between stages: you were a girl, or a woman, and there were only so many of the first that could be carried in any rural family.

History was about to repeat itself and she was heading for Edinburgh and a position in service, the lowest rung on the employment ladder. She was to be met at Waverley Station by the mother she barely knew: the mother who, a short generation ago, had completed that self-same journey.

Smith it may have been in Banffshire, but as the train crawled beneath the shadow of Edinburgh Castle on that particular day in 1870, it was Elizabeth Smyth who prepared to disembark at Waverley Station.

The countryside of the North-East may have had nothing to recommend it as a finishing school, but it had a deserved reputation for producing people who were not afraid of hard work. Despite her lack of street wisdom, Lizzie had quickly settled at her first place of employment and would have stayed there indefinitely but for a strange encounter at the church some 10 months later.

As a child, Lizzie had not given a great deal of thought to religious matters, but had attended the Kirk in Keith as a matter of course throughout her young life. Now that she was in Edinburgh, the offer of a couple of hours off on a Sunday to attend to her spiritual needs was too good to miss, even though the minister did go on a bit once he got cranked up. She began to regularly attend the nearby Kirk o' Field Parish Church at 140 Pleasance, just a few doors away from her mother's tenement.

'Miss Smyth?' The Reverend Bennie looked enquiringly as he spoke to Lizzie for the first time. His head was slightly averted to cover up both his shyness and last night's encounter with a half bottle of whisky, but his general demeanour was kindly.

'I have been asked to pass on a message to you from someone with your best interests at heart,' he said. 'Are you happy at your present place of employment?'

'Very happy,' spluttered Lizzie, suddenly called upon to use her best English, 'and very grateful. Thank you, sir.'

The Reverend ignored her answer.

'I am sure you will have noticed how some of the houses are very grand in the new part of the town. I understand that the owner of one of the houses in York Place has a vacancy for a domestic assistant and has a great preference for young women from the North-East. If you were interested in this superior position he would be available to see you at 3.30 this afternoon.'

Reverend Bennie paused long enough for the information to sink in. He then finished with a sternly delivered caution, 'His name is Mr Melville and he is a Writer to the Signet.'

Lizzie did not know what a Writer to the Signet was, but correctly imagined it was an important position that carried a great deal of wealth and influence.[8] She blushed slightly and asked timidly, 'Has my employer recommended me?'

The Reverend shook his head. 'It is perhaps better that they know nothing about it at this stage.' He turned quickly away, thoughts only on the remainder of his whisky. Talking to young women, he realised, was not his strong point. If all young males were like him, he pondered, it would take a spate of virgin births to save mankind from extinction.

As Lizzie started to walk away from the church still puzzled by

---

8 Writer to the Signet is a uniquely Scottish description of a judicial officer within the legal profession. The Society of Writers to the Signet is almost 500 years old. Today, they are an independent professional body of solicitors.

the conversation with the Reverend, she happened to look back and saw him deep in conversation with a well-dressed overweight man who had suddenly appeared.

The interview with Mr Melville was a success and she was appointed to the position of upstairs domestic assistant in the largest house in which she had ever been, 43 York Place. It had 12 rooms in all.

Her mother's response had been shattering. Far from sharing her young daughter's happiness, she seemed decidedly unimpressed.

'Well, it hisnae taken his nibs long to get his interfering nose in. Congratulations, the sky's the limit now you have Auld Smythie pullin' your strings.'

Lizzie was puzzled and a little upset at her mother's reaction.

'But Ma, I got the job on my ain merit, and because Mr Melville likes lassies frae the North-East. Whit can possibly be wrong with that? Naebody will ever pull my strings!'

'Oh grow up, I could see it coming a mile awa',' Margaret replied abruptly. 'The auld bugger was more than happy tae have you rinnin' aboot the hills o' Banffshire without as much as a pair o' drawers on your erse, but nae sooner are you doon here than he has to start moving you up the social ladder. It widnae dae if he was discovered tae hae a daughter bidin' in the Pleasance!'

Her mother had well and truly burst Lizzie's bubble; although frankly she hadn't a clue about what she meant. The talk of drawers by which her mother presumably meant underwear seemed particularly puzzling.

Lizzie knew of no one back home who wore such things and those who did, she was well informed, were only doing so to ape the Queen herself who had only recently adopted the fashion. The fact that they were rumoured to have been popular with a certain class of lady in Paris for some time impressed Lizzie not a whit. What happened in far-off France could have no bearing on her life!

Her new position proved to be something of an eye-opener. Lizzie's day started early and finished late. Her work, on the whole, was back breaking, but it had its advantages. Her room, which she shared with only one other servant, was in the attic but it was dry, clean and considering what she had been used to, almost luxurious.

The house of Archibald Melville WS was a far cry from the only real home Lizzie could recall, her grandparents' cottage in Keith, and for the next six years she was exposed to a lifestyle about which she could only dream.

Lizzie was paid a little more than the going rate and wore a uniform the cost of which was deducted from her wages. She learned the etiquette of upstairs living and related in an easy manner to her superiors.

Occasionally she met the mysterious Mr Smyth, whose face seemed vaguely familiar. Might he be the man she saw talking with the minister in the churchyard? She was not sure. A Law Clerk, he often brought documents to and from the house bound in thin red cotton tape.

Thomas Smyth, for that was his name, did not appear to be old nor calculating, but somewhat gregarious and with the jolly disposition of a man who had not needed to work physically hard at any point of his life. From time to time he stopped to chat to her, but the conversations were short, courteous and innocuous. Lizzie suspected Mr Smyth to have been her father, but she could not turn to anyone to confirm it. Apart from a sarcastic comment or two, her mother refused to discuss it further.

Back in the cart Lizzie smiled to herself and pulled the worn blanket a little tighter about her body. Sensing her movement next to him, Alec was brought back from his own faraway thoughts. He squeezed her exposed hand and enquired, 'Aw richt, lass?' Alec took his eyes off the road ahead and turned momentarily to look into his wife's face. 'You ken we're daein' the richt thing,' he smiled reassuringly, searching for confirmation in her eyes.

'Aye,' said Lizzie, 'I'm glad to see the back o' that place.'

Alec looked around and noticed that they had entered the Royal Burgh of Musselburgh. He could not resist the temptation to lapse into verse.

> Musselburgh was a Burgh
> When Edinburgh was nane
> Musselburgh will be a Burgh
> When Edinburgh is gane.

Alec recited the ancient rhyme with which the honest town[9] folk loved to assert their imagined superiority over their overbearing city neighbours. Lizzie and Alec snuggled closer against a freezing blast off the Firth of Forth and the horse stoically continued to plod eastwards. Soon Lizzie was back with her thoughts again.

Two events happened in 1877 which were to change Lizzie's life for ever, and if her mother Margaret was to be believed, they were very much related.

Mr Smyth stopped attending York Place. When this happened exactly was uncertain, but Lizzie could vaguely recall that his visits had become less and less frequent until it became apparent that they were a thing of the past. Mr Melville himself informed her that his friend had died of something called Bright's disease[10] and Lizzie was surprised at how desolate the news made her feel. Her mother showed little emotion when Lizzie passed on the news to her.

---

9 The 'Honest Toun' (or Town), an affectionate nickname for Musselburgh.
10 A kidney disease that would be described in modern medicine as chronic nephritis.

'Well, well, he brought maist o' it on himsel' I'll wager. Too good tae himsel' by half, he was. You will have worked oot that he was your faither, I'm sure,' she remarked almost casually, 'Smyth is no a very common name doon here either.'

Mother and daughter never spoke about the subject again. Two months later Mr Melville muttered something about 'tightening belts' and without quite looking Lizzie in the eye announced that he was 'letting her go'.

And so it was that Lizzie went to stay with her mother, stepfather and her half-siblings in the Pleasance, where she secured a succession of poorly paid domestic work.

At one of these jobs she befriended the matronly Margot MacPherson whose brother, a carter,[11] enjoyed Scottish Country music.

'Ma, I need tae pee.' Sandy's urgent plea startled the couple from their separate reveries. Lizzie had adhered to the Cranston tradition of calling the first-born son Alexander, but to differentiate between the two men in her life she had shortened the son's name to Sandy.

They had now reached the outskirts of Longniddry and everyone, including the old horse, required some respite and nourishment. Bruised oats and chaff for the horse and oatcakes and cheese for the humans. All were beasts of burden and all were reliant on oats.

After a few minutes for everyone to empty their bladders and replenish their stomachs, it was time to go. 'Come awa', lass. It's dark early at this time o' year,' said Alec, indicating the dying sun.

The Cranston family climbed back on the cart and the horse announced it was about to recommence the journey with a very audible and smelly fart. 'Naughty beastie!' admonished the two-

---

11 A person who transports material and people with horse and cart, for pay – once an important service in rural areas, but not a common practice or term nowadays

year-old. Lizzie prepared to reprimand him but noticing his father's barely concealed grin, she relented and the family laughed together as the horse pulled away eastwards.

From the very first night they met, just off the Canongate, Alec had seemed to be instinctively sensitive and appreciative of her background.

'What hiv we got here,' he had asked impishly, 'a richt teuchter?'[12] But she sensed that he was not poking fun at her northern ways. Although the best part of 400 kilometres apart, the North-East and the Borders had much more in common with each other than with anywhere in between.

It had been Alec's first attempt to introduce his band of musicians to the braw[13] townsfolk of Edinburgh and he had accepted an invitation to play at the Carters' soirée just off the so-called Royal Mile. For Alec it had been the chance to put his alien lifestyle as a grain warehouseman in Leith behind him for one night at least, while he played lead fiddle with a group of three mixed-ability musicians whose hearts were all in the countryside.

The evening had not started well. The Quadrille band had not been formed long and therefore their repertoire was limited to a small number of well-known dance tunes. The scattering of carters and their guests were slow to warm up, attracted perhaps more by the promise of a mince pie at the interval rather than by any great appreciation of the band. Sensing the crowd needed something different, Alec chose a lively set with which he was familiar and which crucially included 'The Bonnie Lass

---

12 A mildly contemptuous term originally used by Lowland Scots to describe Highlanders, but its usage spread to occasionally describe any rural dweller.
13 Very good; smart; splendid.

o' Fyvie' and 'Barnyards o' Delgatie', two staple tunes of the North-East.

'Have you ony idea where Delgatie is?' Lizzie asked shyly as the couple met over the eagerly awaited and bitterly disappointing mince pie a few minutes later.

Alec had to admit that he had no idea, but any embarrassment his ignorance may have caused was more than compensated for by the fact that it had thrown him and this attractive young woman together. He had spotted her when she had arrived with a slightly older companion and had sensed that, despite her slight air of detachment, this was someone he could get to know better.

'Aboot 20 miles frae whaur I bide in Keith,' she beamed, 'As the craw flees. An' I've niver heard it played better, this far sooth.'

This had prompted the 'teuchter' remark but Alec was quick to make amends. 'I was gaun tae ask if I could walk you hame but nae if you bide in Keith.'

At the end of the evening, her companion was deep in conversation with her brother, thereby conveniently allowing Alec to escort Lizzie home. The Pleasance, despite being in the opposite direction from Leith, was only a short walk from the Canongate, and Lizzie, although trying not to look too keen, had readily agreed to be walked home.

The Pleasance had long since seen better days, but it did not matter. The overcrowding, the filthy public houses, the wretchedness and above all, the smell, were entirely recognisable to Alec and no different from that of Leith. It was life in the city.

After saying their farewells, Alec reflected on her unusual surname, which he had never heard before. He hoped that this girl with the unusual name of Smyth might not be too grand to bother with the likes of him. Yet they had agreed to meet on the following Sunday, at the bottom of Arthur's Seat. He was glad that Lizzie was not the kind who spent all of her Sundays in monastic reflection.

Events had taken their course. In spite of a distinct absence of soft lights and sweet music and Lizzie's hitherto strict adherence to her grandmother's puritanical advice, that summer had precipitated an exciting carnal exploration and by its end the couple found themselves to be in an all too familiar predicament.

Lizzie could recall by heart, the first letter she had written to her grandmother after she had married and moved to Leith. After the initial pleasantries, she had dropped her bombshell.

I'm mairried noo. To a right handsome man from the Borders. I'm sure you will hae worked oot that I am in what Granda ca's 'the faimily wye' bit please brak it tae him gently. When he gets ower the shock he'll be pleased tae ken that Alec is an honourable man who couldna' wait tae mairry me when he found oot.

Despite the forced timing of the wedding, it was no surprise to Lizzie that matrimony itself suited her. Rather than toiling tirelessly for others, she could see a higher purpose in working for the greater good of the family. She threw herself into cooking, cleaning, polishing, sewing, mending and the other hundreds of tasks called housework and secretly admitted to herself that she loved it. Alec loved it, too.

After getting over the shock of being informed he was to be a father, Alec knew he had no other choice but to marry the lass. It was not such a burdensome task either, because Alec had genuinely fallen in love with her and would have asked for her hand in marriage in any event. It was just that nature advanced the timetable somewhat.

Alec had advertised in *The Scotsman* for engagements with his

Quadrille band and for the time being, financial matters were surprisingly manageable.[14]

The cart suddenly hit a deep rut in the gravel road and Lizzie looked up to be told by Alec that they were passing eastwards through Aberlady in what was fast becoming the twilight, or 'mirk' as Granny McLeay used to call it. Sandy was now fast asleep on the Indian rug, snugly surrounded by furniture and covered with an old coat. If today was anything to go by, East Lothian was going to be cold.

The cart was not overloaded with goods because the young couple had not had the time or the money to accumulate many possessions. Apart from the odd chair and table there were, however, a few items that held special significance for both of them. The first was an Indian rug that had been bought new.

Alec had been inordinately proud of this purchase, which he had made at the Leith dockside from a man of swarthy complexion who guaranteed that it had come all the way from India and was of the highest quality. Alec had called it his 'magic carpet' and Lizzie blushed involuntarily when she recalled what had happened next after he had ceremoniously spread it out on the well-scrubbed floor of their flat. Her memory was playing tricks on her. Would that have been the present pregnancy, the one who was making his or her tiny presence known at this very moment? No, it was longer ago than that. It must have been their wee Maggie. Their bonnie Margaret Cranston.

The second important item was a clock, which was a family heirloom, and the third was Alec's old battered violin, because it had brought them together in the first place.

Marriage had started out well enough. Alec was already working as a grain warehouseman at the Carpet Lane Mill, the largest and

---

14 Advertisement of Wednesday December 11, 1878 reads *'Engagements wanted for Quadrille Band. Terms moderate. Alexander Cranston 192 Bonnington Road, Leith.'*

oldest flour mill in Leith. The position involved Alec collecting grain from the Leith docks and then after the Mill had processed it through the enormous stone grinders, distributing the flour to various bakeries in and around Leith. It was good work at the Mill and it paid decently enough so that, together with income from the occasional band engagement, it had allowed the young growing family to move into a two-room flat at a newly-built tenement located at the corner of Great Junction Street and Bonnington Road.

The tenement boasted all the latest modern conveniences such as running water, inside toilet and coal-fired stove. It housed tradespeople and shopkeepers who were all good folk with drive and ambition. Just a few months after moving in, Elizabeth gave birth to their second child, Margaret, named in honour of Lizzie's mum. Inside this safe cocoon, the Cranstons felt protected from the rabble and human detritus that infested the streets of Leith.

It was about this time that Alec gave Lizzie another gift that she would treasure the rest of her life. It was a pebble brooch made of green agate, red cornelian stone and silver. It had the Scottish lion on a shield as well as the St Andrew's Cross and was of a type much sought after at the time. It was expensive too, having cost Alec almost a week's wages. But it was not the price that made it special, it was the emotional sentiment invested in the brooch that set it apart in Lizzie's eyes. The ornament had been purchased to celebrate the birth of the family's first daughter, Margaret.

Then something completely unexpected happened. Out of the five flour mills operating in the Leith area at the time, the Carpet Lane Mill was the oldest and the least profitable. It was no longer competitive and was forced to close in 1880, with the loss of about 160 jobs, including Alexander Cranston's.

Unfortunately for Alec, none of the other mills were hiring and he was obliged to take a lowly paid job as a street labourer to feed the family. At the same time, income from the band's engagements started to fall away and soon they could not afford the high rent they were paying at 6 Bonnington Road. They moved out of their pleasant flat into a one-room tenement in a nearby slum. Lizzie recalled how Alec had been extremely disappointed at losing his job and being forced to give up the flat. However, instead of letting it get him down, Alec had shown his responsibility by quickly securing another job, even if it was such a poorly paid labouring one. To have continuous employment when so many others in Leith were without work was a strong indication of Alec's worth as a man and provider.

Suddenly, it struck her, out of the blue, that dreadful day a few months earlier. Maggie had never been a naughty toddler, but she had been naturally inquisitive. Her screams as she pulled the pot of boiling soup from the stove would remain with Lizzie for ever.

Margaret died an agonising death when she was just 16 months old. She suffered extreme scalding to her face, neck and chest.

Lizzie recalled the false hope she had felt when Margaret appeared to rally at one point only to be replaced by feelings of devastation when the whimpering infant finally became silent. It had been the 15 blackest days in Lizzie's young life. At that point she vowed never to part with the pebble brooch that Alec had bought for her. For Lizzie the brooch would always symbolise a precious life lost.[15]

Silent too, was Alec, apart from the occasional sob, as he lay next to her side, but in an impenetrable world of his own. Did he blame her for the accident? Lizzie could not tell. But she most definitely blamed herself and as the darkness refused to lift, she

---

15 The pebble brooch still exists today and 140 years later is currently in the possession of one of Lizzie's great granddaughters in Australia.

wondered fleetingly if her two men might not be a whole lot better off without her.

Following Maggie's death, there had been days that stretched into weeks where she had no memory of what she did, who she spoke to and how she felt. It scared her that she had lost control like that, but thank goodness for the nameless, sexless little bundle of potential life that now flickered inside her.

Lizzie gradually shook off her despondency and became the protector of this defenceless baby to be. To others, it was obvious that it was a role to which she was perfectly suited.

Living in the city had been a cruel failure and now all that both parents wanted was to remove themselves from this wretched place as quickly as possible. Life in the country was preferable, even if Alec was only able to secure a poorly paid position as an itinerant forester.

An involuntary shiver ran down her spine, but Alec mistakenly thought the cause was the buffeting cold. He leaned across and gave her a reassuring pat on the shoulder.

'We must be getting afa close noo lass, Cover that licht for a minute and see if there's anyone aboot.'

After a brief pause while Alec searched in the gloom, he suddenly pointed ahead and said, 'There he is, he said he wid be waiting for us! Jockie, Jockie Lugton, is that you?' Alec's shouts were aimed at a flickering paraffin[16] light some 30 metres or so ahead, precisely where, according to his reckoning, the gate to the estate at Dirleton should be. His calculations were right on every score.

'Mister Lugton to you,' boomed an amiable sounding greeting from the direction of the solitary lamp, 'and you should consider yoursel' privileged, Cranston. Its nae everybody that gets a personal welcome frae the grieve. The last person I came doon here to meet

---

16 Outside Britain, paraffin is more commonly known as kerosene.

was the Lord Lieutenant and he was on the Queen's business'. As the cart grew closer he could see there was a passenger rugged up in a threadbare blanket. 'This will be the good lady then?'

Lizzie warmed instantly to the cheerful Jock Lugton. He was the grieve of the estate, a position somewhere between foreman and estate manager and the person who oversaw the day-to-day running of the enterprise.

It was he who had employed Alec after meeting him only once over the course of a forestry job in a Morningside estate in Edinburgh. The two estates had a family connection and Alec had impressed.

He was also the man who trusted Alec enough after that meeting to allow him to borrow the estate's horse and cart for the move. As the two men eyed each other up again, both hoped and felt that they had made the right decision.

'We've seen a lot waur,' Alec grimly affirmed once the grieve had given them the keys to their new home and made to take his leave. 'It's wind- and damn near waterproof, lass. What mair could we expect?' Indeed, Lizzie had expected no better than this most basic of shelters and there was no denying that she had just left a place that was a lot worse. They had two rooms and a fireplace, and their spare bucket would easily accommodate the drips from the roof at the far corner of the smaller room. She must remember not to put their bed over there.

All she needed was a match for the paraffin lamp and directions to the well; then she could get started. Yesterday she had scrubbed that 'orra hole o' a flat' of theirs until her hands had been red raw; knowing full well that whoever went in afterwards would most likely not appreciate it. Tonight she could get started on their own wee country house. Alec knew exactly how his wife's mind worked.

'Dinnae even think aboot it,' he smiled, not unkindly. He then carefully unwrapped from an old working jacket his pride and joy, their eight-day clock that his mother had given him as a wedding present and placed it gently on the mantle shelf.

Lizzie lay awake long into the night, her mind racing with the tasks ahead of her. The baby inside her kicked from time to time, almost half-heartedly it felt, while the two men folk in her life slept contentedly by her side. She must make it clear that this was for one night only. It was freezing and wee Sandy had used his charming smile to wheedle his way into her bed where he promptly made the best of things.

It was Lizzie's turn to smile now. Just like his father, she thought.

THE SANDS

(1894)

It had been over two years since their last move and Lizzie had a feeling that her ever-increasing flock was beginning to put down roots. This was one of the longest periods the young family had remained in the same location since their arrival in Haddington nine years earlier. The work at Dirleton estate had been limited and Alec moved the family to Haddington after a year or two where there were more opportunities for full-time employment.

Not having to flit every year or two had allowed Lizzie the opportunity of turning their little cottage, centrally located between the river and the main street of the town, into a proper home for her brood. She dug up a fair portion of the tiny back yard and planted a vegetable patch so that the Cranstons could become as self-sufficient in food as possible.

She grew seasonal vegetables, such as tatties,[17] beetroot, cabbage and peas. Lizzie was disappointed that the small space did not allow her to construct a chicken run as well, like her grandparents had taught her back in Keith, but the setback was easily overcome.

---

17 potatoes

She was able to barter eggs and poultry off friends and neighbours, with an abundant supply of wild game hunted and fished in the nearby hills and rivers. She was happy whenever her husband took the boys out and returned with a pigeon or hare, or a fat trout from the river. Her man was a good provider and he was teaching her sons to be the same.

The Sands in 1894 was not a salubrious address and the move had not brought about an improvement in their living standards. The rooms were inadequate and too few; sanitation was non-existent and, while an unreliable flicker of gaslight illuminated the cobbled street, inside lighting was by paraffin. And it was Scotland: the walls were always damp.

Nevertheless, Lizzie was happy residing in The Sands. The cottage was one of a number of terraced cottages tied to the estate where Alec worked as a forester.[18] Work was as secure as it could ever be in his line of business. And her family was growing up. Sandy, the oldest, had long taken his position in the family seriously and although he had only started as an apprenticed cartwright,[19] his employer had already described him as having the makings of a craftsman. From an early age he strove to augment the family's income and look out for his mother, whose constant child-bearing and occasionally erratic behaviour perplexed him.

It was only four years earlier that the Cranston family had made what would be their first trek across the Tyne to the Nungate side of Haddington, which was regarded as colourful in polite conversation, or downright seedy in more forthright discussions. There they had stayed at a terrace house at Bridge End on the east side of the Nungate Bridge for two years until it was time to flit

---

18 Accommodation was part of the wage package offered to rural workers, allowing employees the opportunity of supplementing their meagre income with growing fruit and vegetables, sometimes even raising an animal or two. The accommodation was tied to their length of employment. After one or two contractual cycles, many families would move on.

19 Builder of carts and in particular the highly-skilled maker of wooden spoked wheels.

again, this time back across the Tyne to their current address by the ancient bowling green in The Sands.

With an ease that would have surprised many longer-established Haddington families, the Cranstons quickly took to life in the Nungate with the rest of the assorted specimens of humanity who made up their neighbours. Their status as new arrivals scarcely seemed to matter.

Residents of the Nungate were known to be close-knit and loyal, descended it was said from Romany stock and not used to receiving any favours. They could look after themselves and were ever ready to do battle for one of their own. Although strangers, the Cranstons were somehow acceptable – they had no airs and graces, could fend for themselves and were, by and large, good neighbours.

The Tyne itself, not one particular bank of it, became the backdrop to the family story. Alec's involvement with the Nungate side of the river continued. Once a week after the evening meal he changed into his uniform of the 7th Volunteer Battalion of the Royal Scots[20] and attended the Drill Hall in the Nungate for band practice. Alec regretted the fact that the military band was a pipe and drum outfit, because it did not allow him to show off his skills as an accomplished fiddler. But he was content to play his part as a drummer in the band while he continued to perform with a small group of musicians once a month in the Nungate's Golf Tavern.[21]

There, he enjoyed playing his new fiddle, which replaced his old one, and the more he played the more proficient he became. He

---

20 In the mid-1890s the uniform of the 7th VBRS was a rifle-green tunic and trousers with the cuffs, collars and piping of the tunic being scarlet, black belts and the newly introduced 'Astrakhan' fur busbies with red-and-black plumes.

21 The public house at 5 Bridge Street, Haddington has been officially known as the Golf Tavern for well over a century, except for a brief period from 2001-2011 when it was renamed the Toll Bridge Hotel. However, unofficially it has always been known affectionately as the 'Long Bar'. (Reference: Lynn Gordon, publican, www.golftavernhaddington.co.uk/.html)

would also make a few coppers out of the night and that was always handy to put on the table in front of Lizzie when he got home.[22]

There were few things in his life that Alec could say with absolute determination he would defend with his life. His wife and children were certainly the most important, but what most people did not know was that his newly acquired violin came a close second.[23]

Late one night in May while on his way home from a session at the Golf Tavern he happened to come across a number of men standing around the Nungate Bridge in their shirt sleeves and waistcoats, smoking, spitting and looking for some amusement. It was Saturday night and the lads were fuelled by a large quantity of alcohol they had consumed during the evening. Prominent among a small group of them standing at the far end of the narrow bridge was 'Luggie' Wilson and his younger brother 'Shitey'.

Luggie owed his nickname to the unfortunate shape of his right ear that hinted darkly at some long forgotten bar-room brawl but which was, in fact, the product of a long and difficult birth, which had also left him somewhat slow on the uptake.

Shitey had experienced an unfortunate accident in his trousers on his first day at school some 20 years earlier and had attended only occasionally thereafter. Perhaps this stranger approaching them from the shadows offered them the prospect of some sport.

'Whaur dae yi' think yir gaun?' demanded Luggie in what, for

---

22 Over time, Alec earned a reputation as a well-known local musician (Source: *Haddingtonshire Courier* March 1915 article.)

23 The violin was made in 1894 by William Nisbet, a Scottish East Lothian fiddle-player of high regard. He was more importantly considered a 'genius' maker of violins. William Nisbet (1828-1903) lived most of his life in Preston Kirk, East Lothian, Scotland (about 9km from Haddington). Nisbet was self-taught in wood-carving and violin making and produced about 120 violins in his life, of which the latter models show continual improvement in quality and sound. The violin obtained by Alec Cranston is believed to have been among the last 20 or so Nisbet made and is considered one of his finest pieces. It is now owned and lovingly restored by Sheila Sapkota, a professional fiddle player who can be contacted at www.riddellfiddles. co.uk/contact.htm

him, was a lengthy sentence. His question acted as the perfect cue for Shitey.

'Aye,' he grunted, 'Whaur dae yi' think yir gaun?' The other two characters looked on, expectantly. Alec Cranston ignored the challenge from men half his age. As he stepped out of the shadows the brothers could see he was carrying something in the crook of his arm.

'Whit dae yi have there?' Luggie said, pointing to the object lodged under Alec's arm. 'Aye, whit dae yi have there?' chimed in Shitey as the boys started to gather menacingly around Alec. Alec may not have been a big man, but a life of hardships had toughened his small physique into all bone and muscle. Chopping and sawing wood six days a week for the past 14 years had also given him unexpected strength in his upper-body. And then there was the difficult time he had spent in the dockyards of Leith. The uncertain nature of employment there literally meant fighting other men for a job. In Leith, the alternative to working was to starve and Alec Cranston had never starved.

Alec placed the violin case gently on the ground and rushed at the two ringleaders with such suddenness and force it took the lads completely by surprise. Before they could react, Alec had taken hold of the brothers by the front of their shirts and propelled them backwards into the stone wall of a building behind them.

Their heads struck the solid wall with an audible crack that caused the other two youngsters to wince. Then for good measure he pulled the two boys off the wall and knocked their heads together again with sufficient force to have an immediate effect.

'Aaah ya bast ….' groaned Luggie as he crumbled to the ground dazed and confused. 'Aye, aah ya ba,' echoed Shitey before collapsing beside his brother and starting to cry. The other two lads stood back a respectful distance from Alec praying that he would not mete out the same punishment to them.

Alec scooped up his treasured fiddle and strode off into the darkness, leaving behind four lads who were under no illusion that this particular fiddle player was a man they should never trifle with again.

The Tyne River was central to everything that happened in the Cranstons' daily life. Its water supplied the brewery and the tannery; the old bridge stood as both a pathway and barrier between the Nungate and the Burgh proper with the sinister-looking iron ring in the bridge still visible, from where felons had been hung until fairly recently. St Mary's, the historic and semi-ruined parish kirk had been built, according to legend, at a spot where the river bent like a shepherd's crook. It was an intriguing tale.

It was a few kilometres upstream by the village of Pencaitland that Alec and his third son Willie were to experience a wondrous day in each other's company that summer. Willie was still only ten at the time and with eight children, the Cranston family was already a large one. The simplest of calculations suggested that such days would have been a rare occurrence. Alec had little spare time to allocate to each child. And yet the reality was that this pair had become increasingly likely to seek out each other's company whenever their schedules allowed. Alec was an expert countryman and Willie a desperately keen pupil. Young Willie had already become something of an expert with the rifle and more than competent with his home-made fishing rod, but there was one country skill he craved above all others: he longed to guddle trout.[24]

Far above the town, the father had been in his element that

---

24 To guddle trout (also known as tickling trout) is the country art of catching fish with bare hands.

day. The weather was passable, the grass dry and Alec had the satisfaction of knowing there was plenty of work to keep him busy on the nearby Coulston Estate for a while yet.

Lizzie had long sung Willie's praises to anyone who would listen. On this fine day, she turned to her husband and said, 'He's a right laddie, that yin. He'll brak a few herts once he starts noticing the lassies.'

'Never mind herts,' replied the proud father, 'by the end of the day I'll hae him guddling troot!'

Alec found an ideal spot, a spot where the water flowed swiftly past and around a number of sizeable boulders. The water was much cleaner here than downstream around Haddington, where the discharge of industrial waste and raw effluent had, at times, almost turned the Tyne into an open sewer. There was not a hint of a trout's presence, which was just as well since it meant that there were no birds nearby to compete against in the art of catching fish.

'This is it,' whispered Dad, 'and remember, you're going to get wet.' Just in case the prospect of a soaking might put Willie off, Alec promised him that they would clean, cook and share the spoils right there on the banks of the river. It would be a rare treat indeed.

Willie was belly down on top of the largest boulder, a metre or so from the bank, and his father was right, he was going to get wet. Willie knew that under the ledge of that boulder there was every chance that a trout might be waiting, facing upstream and ready to snatch at any morsel propelled in its direction. And he also knew that if he could silently immerse his fingers in the water, searching noiselessly for where he thought the tail of any trout might be, a miraculous thing might happen.

It was there, as if it had been waiting for him! Willie's finger cautiously made contact with the fish's belly. This was the make or break moment, one false move and the fish would be gone. But it stayed! Gently, as his father had showed him, he started to rub the fish's belly, gradually moving towards its head. He had never felt anything like it. The fish was actually allowing Willie to stroke its belly as if it was in some form of euphoric trance, and stealthily, almost guiltily, his hand moved towards its gills.

Remembering his father's expert tuition, Willie chose his moment carefully. His fingers were in the gills when suddenly he grasped the head tightly, and with a deft flick their illicit treat was on the bank of the river.

His father's congratulations were as understated as they were appreciated. 'Weel done, laddie, you've just mastered the art of guddling. We'll mak' a poacher o' you yet.' Willie decided to make the most of the magic moment.

'When can a get anither shot o' yer fiddle, Da?'

Alec promised his musically gifted son that he could have another lesson when they got home and cleaned up.

Alec was proud of the six boys he had fathered so far, especially their woodsmanship skills. He had taught each one to fish, trap and shoot. He had taken them up to Garleton Rifle Range, just outside the boundary to the north of the town, to hone their skills with the rifle. At first he taught them to shoot with a .22 calibre small bore rifle. This allowed them to hunt in the nearby countryside without causing too much alarm or damage, except to rabbits and the occasional bird. Then he graduated them onto more powerful rifles, such as the .303 calibre rifle all volunteers possessed when they enlisted in the Volunteer Battalion. Alec made sure that every son could shoot competently and some even showed a high level of proficiency. Sandy and Ian[25] would be able

---

25 The Cranstons second son, John, was routinely called Ian, as was customary then and now in many Scottish families. This is similar to other European derivations such as Jan, Johannes, Gianni and Ioannes.

to hold their own in any contest, Alec thought, but William, well, he was rapidly developing into an expert shot.

Alec could hardly wait until Willie was old enough to join him in the Foresters' Association Shooting Team against the teams from the Oddfellows, Gardeners and the Freemasons in the annual Friendly Societies Trophy. With Willie at his side in the near future, Alec could dream of winning the coveted cup for many years running.

That summer was warm and dry and Lizzie was eternally grateful. The sun and clear skies helped her dry out her ever-growing piles of washing, made the house more comfortable to live in and reduced the pain in her arthritic hands. At the age of 34, Lizzie was pregnant with their 10th child and even though she loved having children she secretly knew each pregnancy was taking a little more out of her than the last. Lizzie did not regard herself as old, just a little worn out at times.

As some of the children raced out the door to play with friends, Lizzie reflected that the long summer days had provided another unintended benefit. She barely saw her older children from dawn to dusk. But for their need to eat, she would hardly see them at all.

For the Cranstons, one particular highlight of the summer was the annual Agricultural Show. The town stood in the middle of some of the finest agricultural land in the whole of Scotland, and irrespective of how close any family was to the soil, the show, which had been held in Haddington since 1881, was a red-letter day for everyone.[26]

---

26 Information from *Weel Speed the Plough: A Souvenir Photographic Album celebrating the 200th Anniversary of the United East Lothian Agricultural Society*, ed., Chris Tabraham, D. & J. Croal, Haddington, 2004.

For once, despite the fact that plenty of work was available, Alec Cranston was not going to work that Saturday and his leisurely breakfast was taken with the full blessing of his employer who held some position of importance on the Show's organising committee. To be fair, he had spent the whole of the Friday evening until dark hammering in fence posts on various parts of the showground, for which he received as wages three-dozen eggs and the promise of all the beer he could handle on the Saturday afternoon.

Lizzie had been mildly outraged that her husband could not have held out for hard cash as a reward for his labours, but welcomed the addition of so many eggs and her mind started spinning with the possibilities of what she could cook for her family.

By midday Alec had walked his neighbour's whippet round the Tyne and exchanged pleasantries with Sandy Pow, the postman, who was hurrying to complete his deliveries in record time. 'See you ower by,' shouted Alec as the younger man sped past his doorway. The Cranstons might not have received mail often, but everyone in the town still knew who Sandy Pow was.

Lizzie wasted little time in considering a response to her husband's request that she accompany him to the show.

'Aye, sure', she said sarcastically, 'I've got a huge pile o' claes tae be getting on wi'. I'll be in the steamie[27] till teatime.'

Alec shrugged his shoulders in resignation as he left for the show. He was secretly relieved his pregnant wife would be saved the long walk to Amisfield on the outskirts of town where the show was held. As far as the bairns were concerned, the older ones could look after themselves while the younger four would be in the care of nine-year-old Agnes.

The long driveway to Amisfield house was full of individuals and

---

27 Public wash houses were known by this sobriquet across Scotland and the building in Haddington was no exception (reference Craig Statham (2007), *Old Haddington*, Stenlake Publishing, Ayrshire Scotland, at page 38).

families making their way, mainly on foot, to the spot where the main ring had been constructed by Alec Cranston and his fellow volunteers. All kinds of animals had been washed and groomed and were standing in an assortment of odd-sized pens waiting to be judged and paraded in front of the onlookers.

The show, which had been established over a long number of years, was not without its controversy. A few years earlier in 1890 the Agricultural Society had caused a sensation by allowing a balloonist to attend, but other attempts at modernisation were not so welcome. Nearer the front entrance a number of stalls had been hastily erected and a variety of mongers were loudly trying to attract attention. The recent addition of vendors to the festivities was considered by some to lower the tone.

Alec had to make his way to the ringside where he and his fellow woodsmen were entered in the tug-o-war, a hotly contested competition in which honour and a fair smattering of Nungate beer was at stake.

Back at the wash house, Lizzie was convinced that the family wash was becoming heavier every week. She sensed that the problem lay within her. A few years back she would have tackled all this toil in half an hour then run over to the show and taught that man of hers how to tug on a rope! But sadly she realised those days were now behind her.

For those Cranstons at the show ground, the afternoon had been a modest success. Ian had triumphed at the shooting gallery and had won an assortment of under-ripe crab apples that had obviously come from a nearby tree. Ian mused that the fruit was not even worth stealing, but he was well satisfied considering he was one of the youngest competitors. Willie and Agnes were convinced they would have won the wheelbarrow race but for the furious argument over who was to be the barrow, which meant they missed the start. The woodsmen had finished a creditable third in the tug-o-war and Alec and his pals had retired to the beer tent. As the afternoon drew to a close, someone produced a paper and comb and started to make music.

For those like the Cranston children who had no direct involvement in agriculture, the festivities were drawing to a close and the crowds were rapidly thinning. Willie and Agnes, their dispute long forgotten, found themselves heading together in the direction of the Nungate Bridge and home. Agnes, like the bulk of the smaller children on this summer day, was in her bare feet and skipped easily across the grass; Willie was beginning to secretly curse his decision to wear a pair of hand-me-down boots. It was a decision made as a statement that he was growing up, but they were starting to hurt his feet.

As the brother and sister rounded the corner by the Long Bar they sensed that something was not quite right. Fortunately, the sizeable smattering of youths gathering on the Nungate side of the river with an air of purposeful menace had not spotted them and they quickly ducked out of sight. Agnes was fearful, and Willie had no desire to be her bodyguard. Their eyes met and simultaneously, they mouthed the word 'ford'. The Nungate Bridge was not the only, nor indeed the oldest, crossing in the vicinity.

Like all but the most timid of the children who lived close to the Tyne, the pair had used the ford on many a river crossing in the past but they knew it was fraught with danger. It was not the theoretical risk of drowning or the threat of catching some horrible disease from the effluent that polluted the Tyne that most worried them as they prepared to enter the water. It was the fact that they would be disobeying Ma's strongly expressed orders and if discovered they would be in sore trouble.

Such risks, however, seemed much less immediate than facing the gathering on the bridge. Agnes hitched up her dress and Willie slung his boots, now carefully tied together by their laces, round his neck. Still unobserved, they slipped into the river, which was up to their knees, and started to wade across. But it was not Lizzie that was waiting for them on the other side. Sandy, their oldest brother, strode towards them looking 'keyed up' and authoritative.

'Agnes,' he instructed, 'go and look efter the wee ones this minute. Willie, we need you at the brig. Now!'

The masterful tone of his voice meant that both obeyed him immediately. Something was definitely afoot.

Lizzie was quite alone in the wash house with a huge pile of washing. The building was old, humid, and full of noise and steam. Lizzie, with her sleeves rolled up, had already started to form beads of perspiration on her brow when an irate stranger burst through the door.

'Oh, I thocht you was somebody else but I see noo your no,' she half shouted, quite unhelpfully. 'That's the last time I iver go near that show, the bloody gentry have got it a' carved up among theirsels. If you have stayed here for lang your bound tae have heard aboot ma tomato chutney – the best in the toon, but I didnae even get a mention among the also rans. And listen tae this...'

Lizzie was sorting out the piles of clothing for washing, but she tried to listen. The woman was incredibly ugly, she decided.

'And here's a' the proof you need. See my rhubarb jam? Well, I was too busy tae mak ony this year, so I bocht twae pund frae the grocer and swapped the labels. And they still didnae gi' me a mention!' Suddenly another explanation entered her head. 'If that scrawny bugger o' a grocer has been sellin me shite, I'll ...' But Lizzie never heard what might happen to the unfortunate grocer.

For the first time the ugly woman paused to take in her surroundings. 'Michty me, lass, are you in the faimly way?' she nodded to the bump on her stomach. Her voice seemed almost kindly. 'How mony will this mak?'

When Lizzie told her, she responded sympathetically, 'You must be a right glutton for punishment. I put my fit doon efter five. The last two were twins and I telt ma Geordie, if they're comin' oot in pairs there'll be nae mair! The last I heard o' him he wis bidin' ower the brush wi' some fish wife frae Eyemou'. Can you imagine the stink in that hoose? He wis nivver hard on the soap, ma Geordie.'

For no particular reason she could think of, the burden of the daily grind rose up to overwhelm Lizzie while this other lady prattled on about her own troubles. A tear formed in the corner of Lizzie's eye and trickled down her clear, pale cheek. The stranger's attitude changed immediately.

'My name's Effie Fairgrieve,' she explained, 'and I ken how life can get too much for wives and mothers like us.' She put a reassuring arm round Lizzie's shoulder and said, 'Come on, lass. Let's finish this washing together and then I'll get you hame.' Lizzie meekly allowed herself the luxury of having some help with this chore. She seemed unusually at ease with this grotesquely rotund stranger. She felt they could get on.

But just as the washing was almost completed the heavy wooden door of the wash house burst open and a wide-eyed, petrified Agnes screamed, 'Ma, Ma oor boys are in a terrible fight!'

Lizzie followed her daughter out of the building, with Effie close behind. There above them on the Nungate Bridge were eight or nine Haddington lads brandishing sticks and throwing stones and rocks at about the same number of males on the opposite side of the bridge. Each side was sending over as many projectiles as they were receiving. Both groups were yelling insults at each other that were not supposed to be shouted in public, but what alarmed Lizzie most was that at least half the people above her on the Haddington side of the bridge were her children! From what she could see, they appeared to be the aggressors in this fight.

Unfortunately, locked away in the thick-walled wash house

with the loud sound of steamers, boilers and mechanical washing devices, Lizzie had not heard the fight start. Otherwise she would have intervened at the beginning. But now that missiles were flying back and forth across the Tyne and the lads from both sides had their blood up, she could see that any moment someone would get seriously hurt. From her brief observation she concluded that her eldest son Sandy was leading the Haddington contingent.

She saw one of her youngest children, Adam, just five years old, supplying his two brothers Ian and Willie with rocks and stones he had gathered from near the old bowling green. Mary, not yet out of infancy, was standing close by, fascinated by the activity around her, but Lizzie could see her youngest daughter was dangerously exposed to the occasional flying object.

Without a moment's hesitation she raced around to the start of the bridge and strode up the incline towards her eldest sons. As she neared Sandy he was yelling out, 'You're a' fou o' shite. She's no a hoor and you're no comin' ower this brig, ever!'

Lizzie called out to get her son's attention, but his gaze and anger were firmly directed towards the opposite end of the bridge. She then stood next to Sandy and ordered him to stop, but he was still in a rage. He looked at his mother and shouted in her face, 'They're no gaunae tak' this brig.' Lizzie was momentarily taken aback, for the first time she was seeing her 14-year-old son displaying the steely determination of a man.

Before anything else happened, a stone the size of a potato whizzed between mother and son, narrowly missing Lizzie's abdomen. Lizzie had momentarily forgotten she was expecting a baby, but Effie had not. The reaction of Effie Fairgrieve was as immediate as it was unstinting. She reached over and took the stick from Ian's hand like it was a child's toy. He made no protest or move against this formidable woman he had never seen before. With rocks, pebbles and sticks still being hurled in her direction she strode fearlessly over the bridge. She walked straight up to one of the lads she knew and said, 'Tommy O'Brien, I ken you. Get hame before I lose my temper.' Then she gave him a solid clip across the back of the head with the stick for good measure.

Effie then turned on the other lads and yelled, 'You almost hit that wimman,' jabbing her stick in the direction of Lizzie for emphasis, 'and her in nae state tae look efter hersel'. I pray to Mary and Joseph that she is nae hairmed. Now bugger off the lot of you before I call the Stardies.'[28]

The intensity of the fight had now left the Nungate boys, to be replaced by the fear of serious repercussions. No one needed any further discussion. The boys just faded away back to their respective residences. There would always be another day to fight with other people for one reason or another.

Later, Alec and Lizzie tried to get to the bottom of what had transpired but it seemed they got a different version of events depending on who was questioned. Sandy said he was defending the honour of a girl from the lads across the river who had called her a 'hoor'. Ian and Willie claimed they were only present to support Sandy.

The younger children really did not understand what had transpired, but even so from this day on they would refer to this event as the 'Battle of the Nungate Bridge'. In their minds, their three heroic brothers had fought off and defeated a horde of invading 'barbarians' from across the river.

This skirmish would soon have been forgotten but for one entirely unexpected and far-reaching outcome. Everyone agreed that Effie Fairgrieve had behaved courageously and was the main person responsible for defusing the fight. Without her timely intervention, someone could easily have been hurt. It was from

28 police

36

this unpromising beginning that Lizzie started thinking she may have found a friend.

It was a warm mid-summer's night in Haddington and, as usual, Ma and Agnes were washing up after the evening meal while the men folk relaxed outside in their shirts and waistcoats enjoying a quiet smoke. Lizzie and Agnes were left to their own thoughts as the pile of plates, cups and cutlery slowly progressed from one side of the bench through the washing basin full of soapy water to the other side and then into Agnes's hands for drying.

Lizzie recognised that life could sometimes be harsh on her oldest daughter. Like girls everywhere she had been introduced to the daily grind of endless domestic chores at an early age. For the working poor, life was hard, unrelenting and even cruel at times. But it was very much worse if you were a woman. Men could get out of the house, earn money, possess property at law, vote and if they wanted, commit sins of the flesh that were condoned by many as a positive sign of their virility. On the other hand, most women were confined to unpaid domestic work looking after the men folk of the house, producing babies, and being seen but not heard. In most Scottish households, women were regarded as being slightly above children but a long way below men in the totem of life. It was cynically said that in some residences the family dog was more highly valued than women, particularly if it was a working dog.

However, Lizzie did not waste time dwelling on this issue. The simple truth for her was that she had started working before she was seven back in Banffshire. Inside the house, it was helping her Granny weave rugs from coarse carpet wool on a primitive cottage loom. Outside the house, she and Granda spent hours tending the garden, milking the cow and looking after chickens.

But as easy as it was for Lizzie to imagine the sights and sounds of her youth in rural Banffshire, she realised that her thoughts should be about the young child beside her. She refocused her attention on Agnes and the wonderful surprise that she had planned for her.

'Lass', she said, 'Have you iver been tae Musselburgh?'

'Of course not, Ma,' her daughter replied, incredulous that her mother would not know this fact, 'but Pa has promised tae take me one day.'

'Weel,' said Lizzie, stretching out the reply for dramatic effect, 'How would you like to go the morn?' A smile beamed from Agnes's face, but before she could utter a word, Lizzie cut her off with the all important explanation.

'The herring season is in full swing, but I dinnae trust those fish mongers who come tae Haddington for the Friday merkets. The fish are on the turn and the price they charge is highway robbery. The morn you and I are going to Fisherrow by Musselburgh to get some fresh herring for oor meal.'

'Oh Ma, that's grand, absolutely grand, but I've got naething tae wear. My good claes are filthy frae the rain and mud last weekend that Adam and Mary splashed ower me. I ... I ... dinnae ken whit tae dae,' she started to stutter in anxiety.

'Och lass, dinnae concern yoursel'. As a reward for being such a good girl, I've managed tae find some bonnie floory cloth and mak' a new frock for you. It's hinging up on the back of my bedroom door if you'd like to try it on.' Agnes started to race away, but checked herself after a few paces. A little sheepishly she ran back to her mother, flung her arms around her midriff and said, 'Oh, Ma I'm so lucky. Thanks for everything.' Agnes then scurried off to inspect the new dress leaving her mother standing at the washbasin bursting with pride and feeling very pleased with herself.

Mother and daughter were up early the following morning and worked furiously to have the rest of the household fed, washed, clothed and ready for the day. Alec and Sandy had gone to their respective workplaces. Ian had volunteered to look after the young children if he, instead of Willie, could get some extra practice on his dad's fiddle.

The only person not happy about this arrangement was young Mary. She cried and fussed all morning begging to go with the other two, but there was no way Lizzie was going to take the almost four-year-old with them all the way to Musselburgh. She left the house promising Ian they would be back by early afternoon.

An hour later, mother and daughter stepped off the train at Musselburgh station near the town centre after diverting along a short branch line from Newhailes Junction. It was mid-morning and they both took off to the nearby fishing port on the other side of the River Esk determined to enjoy themselves and to strike a bargain. Just as they neared the recently constructed fish market at Fisherrow, Lizzie steered her daughter away in another direction.

'The fish is too dear in there, lassie. We're gaun where the fish is straight aff the trawlers and a' half the price.'

Agnes had been barely able to contain her excitement all day, now she was intrigued as well. She tagged along beside her mother eager to see what would happen. The two women passed a row of stone cottages and when they turned a corner they were suddenly presented by a view of the wide Firth of Forth stretching out into the North Sea. Directly in front of them across the road was a little muddy beach where a sizeable crowd of people were hovering over wicker baskets full of herring.

A slight sea breeze was blowing on shore and bringing with it what Agnes thought was an exotic collection of smells. She could detect salt, fish, something she thought might be the smell of sand and finally the more usual acrid stench of unwashed clothes and bodies.

The two women stepped around the fly-blown rotting corpse of a stray cat lying in the culvert of the road as they made their way to the beach. The stench of decaying flesh made pregnant Lizzie's stomach turn. As they crossed the road, Agnes could see some of the women were wearing clothing similar in style and colour to each other. They were obviously the fisherwomen of the area she had heard so much about. As if to confirm her observations one of the more weather-beaten females called out, almost singing,

Wha'll buy my caller herrin
They're bonnie fish and halesome farin,
Wha'll buy my caller herrin,
New drawn frae the Forth.

Mother and daughter drew closer and could see that there were more types of fish for sale than just herring. On mats and groundsheets placed in front of the buyers were a scattered collection of fish such as sole, haddock and cod, freshly caught the night before. But it was the herring that Lizzie was here to buy, so she ignored the other tempting offerings and scanned the dozen or so wicker baskets, called creels, for the one that contained the freshest. When she was satisfied on that point, Lizzie started bargaining with the fisherwoman who claimed ownership of the creel.

Nine-year-old Agnes was amazed at how the two ladies went from exchanging pleasantries to arguing in a matter of seconds. She watched and listened as her mother expertly pointed out deficiencies in the fish and therefore demanded a lower price. Initially, the fisherwoman seemed to be holding her own in these negotiations, but little by little the price started to come down. Finally the fisherwoman brought the negotiations to a halt with an ultimatum on price. She was prepared to sell the herring at her latest 'gie awa' price, but would go no further. Lizzie could either agree or leave and she sensed correctly the fisherwoman could not be pressured to lower the price beyond this point.

'I'll take twa dozen,' Lizzie said, 'but I want them gutted and scaled for that price!'

'You what!' exploded the seller and another argument followed that was even more heated than the first.

Agnes was taking everything in, absorbing it all and learning in the process what it meant to be a good housewife with little money to spend but many mouths to feed. As they walked away over the bridge back towards the station at Musselburgh, Lizzie allowed her daughter to carry the herring, gutted and scaled for the price agreed. Mother and child were pleased with themselves and Agnes had newfound admiration for her mother's negotiating skills.

With the money that Lizzie had managed not to spend, she had one more surprise in store for her daughter. Just outside the entrance to the railway station stood an ice-cream shop.[29] It was here that Lizzie steered her daughter for the second part of her reward. Agnes had never been in such a place and was amazed by the whole ambience. The truth was that Lizzie had never entered an ice-cream shop either, but she was certainly not going to look around wide-eyed and mouth agape like her daughter. You never know what advantage these foreigners would take of two women inexperienced in the world of ice-creamery!

To take the weight off her tired feet while they waited for the ice creams to appear, Lizzie sat on a chair. Mother and daughter looked at each other and both instantly knew this part of the trip would remain their special secret. As they ate their ice creams in

---

29 These establishments were a rarity in Scotland at the time and had not yet arrived in Haddington at all. They were overwhelmingly operated by immigrant Italians who had brought the concept with them from their homeland.

silence back on the train to Haddington, Lizzie knew that the bond between them would never be as strong as it was at that moment.

Back home, Lizzie and Agnes set about making a special dinner for the family with the herring purchased earlier in the day. The backbones were removed, which entailed the vigorous use of a rolling pin to smash the skeletons. Then the heads and tails were cut off. The fish was seasoned with a little salt and pepper and then coated with oatmeal. At this point Lizzie showed Agnes how to press the oatmeal into the fish with her fingers to make sure it stayed in place. On the kitchen stove a dollop or two of lard had been heated in a large frying pan and the coated fish was then fried in batches until golden brown.

A few hours earlier Alec had gone outside to the backyard garden and dug up a bucketful of new potatoes, which were washed, scraped and were now boiling on the stove in salted water. A wonderful fried fish aroma filled the house and before the herring and potatoes had been cooked, husband and children started hovering around the kitchen entrance. After a splendidly satisfying meal of tatties and herring accompanied by plenty of butter the two females retired to the kitchen again and started washing up as they had the night before and as they would the next.

Agnes had observed that during the meal her mother had hardly eaten, even claiming that she was too full to eat her fair share. But she had managed to overfeed everyone else. Agnes had heard her mother make this excuse many times before, but it only now dawned on her what Ma was really doing. It was another of life's little lessons she was learning and she committed it to memory without comment. As she dried yet another night's set of dishes on another scrupulously clean piece of cloth, young Agnes looked around at the contented family; happy, well fed, healthy and determined to better themselves. Being a woman in Scotland may be one of the hardest and most thankless positions possible,

Agnes had concluded years before, but it was now beginning to dawn on her that it could have its rewards too.

Agnes was starting to learn that the only way a family like hers could survive was if everyone co-operated and pulled their weight. Everyone, even the smallest child, had jobs to do according to their age and ability. Sometimes it was necessary for a sharp word or a slap from mother to remind Agnes and her siblings of their duties. Occasionally, it would be necessary for father to take the extreme action of laying a strap across the legs of a defiant child, but thankfully in the Cranston household such actions were rare, even if frighteningly effective.

On this night Agnes started to realise that raising a family involved love and discipline, not one or the other. Furthermore, it was her mother that played a central role in imparting both affection and order and thereby making the family as content and prosperous as possible.

Agnes looked up into the face of her hard-working mother washing up next to her and resolved she would do everything necessary to grow up to be just like her.

WATCH THE BIRDIE
(1908)

'By the Lord Harry,[30] haud still Alec!' A sudden jerk propelled Alexander Cranston's head just about as far to the right as it could go. 'Breathe in!' The same head was jerked to the left. 'Why you had tae have a Cranston Adam's apple, I'll nivver ken.'

Alec had been the owner of his Adam's apple for 55 years and had not been aware that there was anything unusual about it. Neither had he been aware that his family was afflicted by a particularly objectionable kind of Adam's apple; but it was a point not worth making.

'There,' Lizzie said, and her whole demeanour changed as the stud finally clicked into place. Alec's savagely starched collar was now secured to his very best working shirt. 'One doon and eight tae go. Dinnae you move another inch, Angus, and come here this minute,' she yelled, but her youngest son had already scampered out of the crowded room.

Alec gingerly fingered the inside of his collar and found, slightly

---

30 A favourite exclamation of Lizzie, a veiled reference to Satan.

to his surprise, that he was still breathing. Why had he agreed to an expensive family portrait being taken? Sadly, he already knew the answer to that question.

His cancer was increasingly focusing his mind. It was the reason that he could run his finger along the inside of his previously tight collar and the reason why those once calloused fingers now resembled those of a shopkeeper or clerk. Or as Sandy Pow the postie had more colourfully put it, 'a baby's arse!'

It was Sandy Pow who had first diagnosed Alec's condition as an ulcer a year or two previously and being ever so knowledgeable had also suggested the cure. 'Plenty of bread and milk,' he said, 'and a little bit of boiled fish on pay night!'

Sandy was known throughout the town as a highly intelligent individual and his opinions, whether asked for or not, came free of charge. There were many in the town who believed that had Sandy ever known the identity of his father, he might well have become a doctor or maybe even a High Court Judge. As it was, he had been brought up solely by his tight-lipped mother and considered himself lucky to have obtained a position with the Post Office. On the delivery of letters and parcels he was undoubtedly an expert.

But Sandy Pow the postman was not an expert about everything and in the case of his friend, for Sandy considered himself a friend of the entire Cranston family, he was very wrong indeed.

When Alec Cranston continued to lose weight and feel poorly, he eventually found himself in the local doctor's surgery, a place he had avoided all his life. After a series of tests the doctor finally gave him the bad news – cancer, and it was inoperable.

Unfortunately, the doctor could not say whether Alec had six months or six years to live. It was at that point that Lizzie stepped in and decided the family needed to be gathered together before their father passed away. She sent a telegram to their eldest son, Sandy, who was at that time working in America on the reconstruction of San Francisco after the 1906 earthquake and fire.

As expected, Sandy had returned, but there was now something different about him. Even though he accepted his duty as the eldest son was to step into his father's shoes and look after the family, his mother sensed he was not happy about coming back. She suspected he might have become infatuated with America like so many other Scots had before him. Lizzie made a mental note to have a long conversation with her 29-year-old son and get to the bottom of his mood change.

Lizzie had been surprised that her husband had agreed to the idea of a family photograph. Borders people have their own ways, ideas and superstitions and whatever else he might be, he was definitely a Borderer. His grandmother Jeanie (some said she came of travelling folk) had been dead set against the newfangled art of photography.

'It's unnecessary and unnatural,' she had said. 'Why can't folk look intae a puddle if they want tae ken what they look like? Though goodness kens, some folk may get a terrible fricht!' But she was especially opposed to the taking of photographs of entire families.

'Just dinnae dae it, it'll steal the family's future,' she had said decades earlier when a travelling photographer turned up in her village of Linton, Roxburghshire, and offered to take images of the local families.

The thought had resurfaced again that very day, the day that the portrait was to be taken, but Alec quickly dismissed it. The Cranstons were a fine, upright family who deserved to be photographed together and there was no way that the ramblings of a suspicious old grandmother would prevent the taking of a family photograph that day, even if Alec shared some of the old woman's genes and, deep down, some of her misgivings.

Then he thought about Maggie. His dearest, first-born daughter, Margaret McLeay Cranston. If she had lived, she would have been turning 28 that year.

Coincidentally, Lizzie was having similar thoughts as she was getting dressed. Without telling anyone else why, Lizzie completed her outfit by pinning on her special pebble brooch that Alec had bought her when Margaret was born. Even though she was no longer alive, she would still be present spiritually at the family portrait.

By special arrangement it was agreed that the womenfolk would wash and dress themselves first before the men got up. This procedure, devised to protect modesty all round, required a good deal of forward planning as all ablutions had to take place in the cramped living room where the parents and eight-year-old Angus had spent the night, they in a bed partitioned off by a curtain, he on some bedding on the floor.

Angus, whose job it had eventually been to empty the dirty water on the street outside, had been amazed at the ridiculous lengths the women had taken in the name of cleanliness.

'They must have used at least a basin and a half o' water between them,' he told his incredulous big brothers.

For the older brothers there would be no basins. They grabbed what they could in the way of old rags and headed for the Steamie, only a short walk away. The building doubled as a public bath house as well as a private wash house, though in truth it was not very private. While the women washed in the seclusion of the home, the men scrubbed themselves in the nearby communal baths of the Steamie.

Unlikely as it would have seemed, by 10.30 that morning, the Cranston family assembled in their flat at No.23 Hardgate, all spick and span and ready. The walk to the studio was mercifully a short one. It was only a few metres along their street in what had long been the local newsagents. For the men, looking and feeling conspicuous in their Sunday best, it was a few metres too far; they were terrified that they would be accused of 'putting on airs and graces' or 'aping the gentry'.

For Effie Fairgrieve, who by now had become a regular visitor, this was a chance too good to miss. Much as she liked the Cranstons and secretly approved of the expedition, she quickly established herself as the social commentator. Her first target was the eldest son, Sandy, who had joined the family from his home in Musselburgh.

'Well, well Sandy,' she teased him, 'you've been busy! Nae two minutes back frae America and I hear that wife o' yours has got another bairn. It's mair than your scalp that they Red Indians should have been efter, I'm thinking!'

Raucously, she turned to the Cranston daughters.

'You're looking real bonnie, lassies,' she grinned, 'but let's hope you've got your clean drawers on! They tell me that fancy machine o' John Paton's can see richt through your skirts!'

The girls turned red, and Effie, determined that this was to be her day as well, cheerfully spat in the gutter before ambling to the Cranstons' fireplace to check on the contents of their teapot.

'Mr Paton,' Lizzie explained to the 31-year-old photographer,[31] 'I've brought my family for their 11 o'clock appointment. This here is my daughter, Agnes, she'll dae the speaking. She's used to folk like yer good self.' It had been agreed in advance that Agnes would be the family spokesperson as her position in service at the bank manager's residence required a degree of articulation and self-confidence that her mother did not have.

'Ah, come this way.' Mr Paton was obviously pleased to have the undivided attention of a pretty young woman. 'My studio is in the laft, er attic,' he smiled. 'What a charming family.' The Cranstons

---

31 Calculated from 1911 Census of Haddington.

49

carefully picked their way through the bundles of newspapers, the sale of which was still Mr Paton's main occupation, and headed for the studio.[32]

There was an audible gasp as the family first set eyes on the studio. The contrast with the pokey shop below was immense. One side of the sloping roof consisted almost entirely of a skylight type window, which seemed too large to have been an original. Some of the older boys ran their tradesmen's eyes over the construction and Sandy, the wheelwright and carpenter, whispered, 'Very impressive,' to no one in particular. 'I've never seen onything quite like it.'

'I have,' replied Ian, in equally hushed tones. 'The officers had something similar in their snooker room in China. Natural light, you cannae beat it. Gaslight just disnae have the same effect.' Mr Paton rubbed his hands together with the air of an old-fashioned minister about to deliver a sleep-inducing sermon.

'What we have got to do this morning is create a work of art. Just as surely as a renaissance artist would have done. The principles are exactly the same, but with a little bit of patience from you and a dash of inspiration from yours truly, I can guarantee that this fellow here' – he almost fondled his surprisingly ornate camera –'will reproduce a degree of accuracy that a renaissance artist could only dream aboot.'

Adam winked at his sister, Mary. Both had spotted the photographer's habit of occasionally lapsing into the unrefined local vernacular. Angus and Robert rolled their eyes. Patience does not come easily when you are only seven and nine years old.

'Hadn't we better get on with it?' enquired Agnes, 'my father could be doing with a seat, you know.' Seeing how the father was visibly exhausted from the climb up the stairs, John Paton quickly got down to business.

---

32 The studio was located upstairs at No.6 Hardgate, but the skylight has since been replaced by a closed roof.

'Ah, the guests of honour. Sir, Madam, sit right here in the middle, where everyone can see you. And you young man, we don't want you to get lost in the crowd,' he was addressing Angus. 'You stand right in between them.'

Agnes breathed a sigh of relief. If anyone could keep her mischievous youngest brother at peace it was her parents. She and John Paton then allocated the remaining two seats in order of seniority. On mother's left hand side sat Sandy, mercifully denuded of the American-style hat that he had teasingly assured his mother he would be wearing.

'There will be no 12-gallon hat in oor photo,' Lizzie had countered. 'I dinnae want ony o' my family looking like thon Buffalo Bill!'

On the father's right sat Ian, the professional soldier cum forester, his debonair appearance concealing enough adventures to last him a lifetime.

Things were in full flight now. Agnes and John Paton quickly identified the tallest of the remaining brothers who were allocated a place on the back row, positioned carefully to maximise the lighting from the large window.

'This is my brother, Willie, an ironmonger,' explained Agnes, 'and Jimmy, a stone mason.' If this information was of limited relevance to the photographer, the same could not be said about the third brother taking up his position in the rear. Adam, the baker, had just finished his shift at the co-operative and had presented Mr Paton with a couple of fancy cakes! The photographer frowned and adjusted his glasses then frowned some more. His gaze switched from the group to the ceiling and then back again.

'What we need is some contrast. Ladies, can you take your place with a brother on each side of you?' He seemed satisfied.

Robbie had been unable to take his eyes off the skylight since he had entered the room. The craftsmanship of the framework fascinated him, and the angle at which the frame was set was very cleverly done. How he wished that Sandy or Jimmy could have been down here with him instead of posing in the back row like the gentry in their Sunday best. They would have told him how it was done.

'Young man,' the photographer addressed Robbie, 'we need to make sure we get a good look of you. I want you to stand right in the middle there, just in front of your wee brother.' Robbie did as he was told and was rewarded with a kick on the back from the poker-faced Angus! Mr Paton recognised the two remaining brothers.

'Ah, the young workers,' he explained, for Drew and George, who was universally known as Doddie,[33] both did odd jobs around the town after school. 'I want you to sit on the rug here and for God's sake, smile. You look like a pair of turkeys in the week before Christmas.' The photographer, pleased with the positioning of all the family, then turned his undivided attention to a piece of paper he had retrieved from a nearby drawer. He held it aloft and counted slowly to himself.

'It's called dead match paper,' Ian whispered to his father, 'I saw them using it in South Africa. He's countin' how long it takes tae change colour and that will tell him how much daylight there is. He'll be getting under that blanket any minute noo.'

No sooner said than done. John Paton quickly disappeared under the dark blanket which covered the camera on its tripod, emerging again to address the family. It would take about five seconds for the photograph to be taken during which time the entire family must remain absolutely still. He looked sternly at the younger boys when making this announcement and warned them that they would need to be on their very best behaviour or else the parents' money would be wasted. He even offered a bribe.

---

33 In Scotland, Dod or Doddie is often used as a replacement for the name George.

'If you stay perfectly still and don't spoil the photograph you can each have a stalk of my rhubarb to take home with you,' he announced grandly. It was a lousy bribe, as Drew and Robbie had been part of a raiding party on Mr Paton's garden the previous night and knew firsthand that his rhubarb tasted foul!

It was then that their father interrupted by saying, 'How aboot a penny each tae spend on them boiled lollies you baith like?' The two lads smiled and sat perfectly still.

'Almost ready,' the photographer announced before disappearing once again.

'About time too,' yawned Willie to his equally fed up sister Mary. 'If Wellington had taken this much time setting oot his army at Waterloo, we micht a' be speaking French today.' Mr Paton issued his final orders from beneath the blanket.

'Now all stay perfectly still and "Watch the Birdie", as they say.' It was the longest five seconds that any of them could remember but finally John Paton announced that he was finished.

'A work of perfection, I am absolutely certain and well worth every penny, Mrs Cranston. Well done.'

The relieved family were already quickly disentangling themselves from the carefully choreographed formation in which they had found themselves and with the tension quickly disappearing they piled out onto the street.

'I look forward to seeing you all back here in 10 years,' yelled Mr Paton from his studio. Nobody said a word as every member of the Cranston family knew Alec Cranston, the patriarch of the Cranston family, would be dead soon. This was probably the first and last portrait of the family that would ever be taken.

To lighten the mood, Jimmy whipped out a penny whistle from under his jacket and said, 'Come on, we're goin' tae dance our way home.' Mary and Andrew turned red, and their parents averted their eyes, but Jimmy had plenty of takers. Willie burst into a passable version of a Highland fling, Adam hooked arms with Agnes, Ian hooted while Sandy attempted a tap dance. And then, to the amazement of the handful of onlookers and in the complete absence of alcohol, the Cranston family hopped, skipped and danced along the street in the wake of the penny whistle. The two youngest boys took off for their favourite lolly shop in the High Street, rewarded with a penny each from their Pa as promised.

As the rest of family approached the Cranston flat, they were met by the bemused Effie Fairgrieve, who emerged from the doorway with a wide grin on her face. 'I've seen it a' noo. Yer kettle's boiling. Come awa' in before ye get arrested!'

HOGMANAY
(1911)

Lizzie and Mary felt like they were at the point of exhaustion and there was still more than six hours of the old year left. It was a year that they would be glad to see the back of. The house smelled of bleach, which was remarkable considering the number of human bodies that were squeezed into its few barely adequate rooms. The floors were scrubbed, the walls were scrubbed and anything washable had been washed. The hearth in the back room had been cleaned and freshly laid while the big fire in the main living area blazed gamely on. It would be its turn next.

The coming of the New Year was celebrated like no other festival in the Cranston household. After all, it had been celebrated for much longer than Christmas ever had in Scotland and there was something uncomfortably English about Christmas.

The Cranston family had gone to work as usual on Christmas Day as the shops and businesses had remained open and the food on offer at the evening meal had been unspectacular. Although the churches had been busy on Christmas Eve and some attempt had been made to conjure up an atmosphere of goodwill, tonight was definitely what mattered.

Hogmanay and the welcoming in of the New Year on the stroke of midnight was originally a pagan festival, which was perhaps why it was shrouded in superstition and ritualistic practices. Such practices were adhered to with various degrees of enthusiasm depending on the individuals involved, and for Lizzie, they were sacrosanct. Her upbringing in the rural North-East of Scotland coupled with her time spent in Edinburgh and the Lothians meant that her knowledge of such things was extensive and her superstitions persistent.

For Lizzie, the number-one priority was to have everything spick and span. The New Year must be welcomed into a bright and sparkling environment. Despite the time of year, the fire must be allowed to go out before the bells of midnight struck and the hearth must be cleaned and reset, ready to be lit again in the New Year. But not all preparations were physical. It was deemed most unfortunate to carry any petty squabbles or disagreements into the New Year and real attempts were made to patch up quarrels before the old year finally vanished. Effie had her own slant on this: 'You could hae skelpt ma lug yesterday and ye micht kick my erse the morn, but the nicht we'll a' be freens.'[34] It was a splendid sentiment!

The food promised to be something special this year. A huge pot usually reserved for the laundry had simmered on the fire for most of the afternoon. It reminded Lizzie of her Granny who used to make a similar soup by putting virtually everything in it. The family recipe was not difficult to remember. To a base of barley and lentils were added ingredients that the family had acquired or scrounged over the previous few days.

Tatties and neeps,[35] which Willie had been given by a grateful employer, were added to a large meaty bone from the butchers. Some green vegetables of unknown pedigree had been removed

---

34 friends
35 turnips

from a field on the outskirts of the town and the remains of last night's rabbit were thrown in for good measure. The whole concoction was thick and rich and was described by the 12-year-old Robbie as being 'barrie scran', or a delightful repast.

Mary, who was already a professional cook and currently working for a wealthy farmer's family at Cramond on the outskirts of Edinburgh, was responsible for the *pièce de resistance*, the clootie dumpling. Considered by some to be Scotland's national dish, it consisted of a rich mixture of flour, suet, currants, breadcrumbs, sugar, raisins, cinnamon, an apple, eggs and golden syrup, wrapped in a piece of cloot[36] and boiled for three or four hours before being dried off in front of the fire. Tonight it would be served with custard, a rare dish and one fit for the recently crowned king.

There was still more to come. The main treat would be eaten after the New Year had been safely seen in and the mere prospect of it was enough to keep many a young Cranston in check who might otherwise overindulge in whisky. It was a genuine steak pie. Beef was not often on the Cranston menu until Doddie started his butcher's apprenticeship and it was still a rare occasion for him to return home with steak. But come the morning of the first, all would be eating in style.

The hiatus between the closing of the public houses and the coming of the New Year was traditionally a difficult one in Scotland, with men, who had already overindulged, desperate for more drink or somewhere to lie their heads. The Cranstons were no different to most other Scottish families at the time. Around every event in their lives was the constant presence and consumption of alcohol, usually in the form of whisky. Alcohol was consumed after work at the pub and sometimes at home into the wee small

---

36 cloth

hours of the night when there were celebrations to be enjoyed, or grief to be shared. The Cranston males considered their drinking habits to be quite normal. They worked hard and they drank hard. And this had been the way in Scotland for centuries.

At last the family was starting to gather and the younger children hoped that an odd copper or two might find their way into their pockets. And after 12 there was the prospect of draining a couple of their brothers' whisky glasses!

It was expected that other guests would arrive at any time after the bells,[37] including Klaus, who was Doddie's pal and fellow apprentice at the butchers, Sandy Pow and Effie Fairgrieve, who had become Lizzie's confidante.

In fact Doddie, for whom this was the second New Year in which he could legally go to the pub, seemed to offer his younger brothers a great deal of promise when he had staggered home a little earlier, grinning widely and pointing to the ill-concealed half bottle in the pocket of his coat.

'Come here, gadges,'[38] he signalled to his youngest brothers with an exaggerated gesture of bonhomie. 'I've got a barrie joke tae tell you! There was this auld wifie that kept a pig in her bedroom and they were baith awfa' bothered wi' the win'!'

The boy's ears pricked up in expectation and Mary visibly reddened, but Lizzie had heard enough. 'That's enough o' that kind o' spik, Doddie. There wis nivver ony filth in this hoose when your faither was alive and we're no stertin' noo.' Robbie and Angus groaned inwardly as Doddie was stopped in his tracks and looked momentarily abashed, but as Lizzie averted her gaze his smile immediately reappeared. He patted his half-hidden

---

37 'The bells' is an expression used then and now to describe the arrival of the New Year, whether or not the ringing of bells actually occurs.

38 An expression still commonly used in Haddington, especially in the Nungate, as an affectionate term for a young man. From the Romany language.

whisky bottle, graphically mimed his need to urinate and with a huge wink of the eye steered himself unsteadily in the direction of the garden outside.

However, there was still one couple yet to arrive. Agnes Cranston and John McDowall sauntered slowly along the High Street dropping behind their friends, the Morrisons, with whom they had spent the evening. They were in no great hurry to join the family gathering, even though it was one that would hold special significance for them. By this time tomorrow they would be man and wife and while their union was a source of delight to the entire family, any hope of a private moment together would disappear as soon as they crossed the Cranston threshold. And for Agnes it was not just the chance of a stolen moment's intimacy that caused her to tarry.

'We have tae tell her tonight,' she pleaded without too much conviction. 'We're leavin' in six weeks' time, John. Efter whit she's been through this year, she deserves tae ken.' The frown on John McDowall's face was an unaccustomed one.

'Maybe, lass, maybe you're right,' he said, fingering the brown envelope in his pocket which had arrived from Australia House earlier in the week, 'but let's get this wedding by wi' first.'

They had arrived at the Cranston front door and the opportunity for further discussion on the subject was pushed to one side with the appearance of Doddie from the rear of the building, his good humour completely restored.

'Weel, weel, if its nae the young lovers!' he beamed with obvious affection for his older sister and prospective brother-in-law.

'It's bad luck tae wish you a happy New Year afore the bells, but och, I think it's gaun tae be a great one. Here, have a quick skoof[39] oot o' my bottle, they've a' signed the pledge in there – at least till midnight!'

---

39 swig

But Doddie's luck was about to desert him. As the well-sampled bottle was being passed from Doddie to John it somehow slipped from their grasp and crashed to the pavement. With a dismissive shrug of his shoulders, Doddie threw his arms around the engaged couple and escorted them into the house. He knew there were brothers who had brought more alcohol. If he was his usual cheeky and cheerful self, he'd skoof aplenty from his siblings.

Much had happened during Doddie's sojourn in the garden and as the three entered the flat, they had clearly walked into a party. Willie was back from his paid performance at the Foresters' Hall, his face flushed with the whisky of appreciative dancers and his fiddle elbow in fine fettle. James, with his wife Annie and their two infants close by his side, had produced his penny whistle, and from some corner of the room, a mouth organ could clearly be heard. Adam turned an upturned biscuit tin into a passable drum and from many such prior experiences the sound the brothers made was pleasant, lively and melodic.

The soon-to-be-wed couple were greeted by a great roar of general approval and above the noise someone could be heard shouting to John, 'Come on Johnnie lad, let's hear it frae your fellow Ayrshire man, Rabbie Burns. It's your last chance to recite him as a free man!' Beneath the table, from where they could enjoy a worm's eye view of the whole proceedings, 10-year-old Angus grimaced at his brother Robbie.

'Stand by for the timorous beastie,' he chuckled. John knew many of the poems of Scotland's national poet, Robert Burns, off by heart and would recite great screeds of them to anyone who would listen. This, coupled with his soft, mellifluous Ayrshire accent, meant that he was often called upon to officially perform at Burns night celebrations. But on this particular night John had other ideas.

With a flourish, he produced a sheet of paper from his breast pocket and said, 'Tonight, I give you ...', he paused as if to accommodate a fanfare on the drums but Adam and his biscuit tin failed to oblige, '.... *The Legend of Traprain Law*!'[40] Beneath the table, Robbie and Angus pricked up their ears.

'Traprain Law. Surely that's the odd-shaped hill just outside Haddington?' exclaimed Robbie in surprise. But before Angus could respond, future brother-in-law John began:

> King Loth, the Grim sat on his throne,
> Owre a' the Lothians, King was he;
> Nor friend nor kin loved he but ane,
> Ismolde, his ae fair daughter, she.
> To castled Hailes, his warriors beat,
> Thanes and wise men frae far and near.
> In troops, on horse, or sandled feet,
> With flowing locks and warlike gear.

This was indeed different and the boys' attention was held while the first four of five verses tripped off John McDowall's tongue. But noises from the kitchen diverted their attention to the status of the clootie dumpling, which at this very moment was being fussed over by their sister Mary. But all was not well in the ancient kingdom of the Lothians!

> By right and birth this seat were thine,
> By deadly sin now lost ere won!
> Alack the day, that child of mine,
> So base could stoop to born thrall's son!

Ismolde, the princess was pregnant to the unsuitable Ralph and

---

40 James Lumsden (editor), *The Battles of Dunbar and Prestopans and other selected Poems*, William Sinclair publishers, Haddington, 1896, pp 29–36.

must pay with her life. Agnes, enraptured by her fiancé's recitation, allowed herself the semblance of a smile in the knowledge that tomorrow she would marry John McDowall in a quite definitely unpregnant state. It was an achievement that had apparently been beyond many of her ancestors!

Her sister Mary still seemed uncertain about her clootie dumpling and quite missed hearing of the fate of the unfortunate Ismolde, thrown from the cliff tops while her lover fled to the safety of the Kingdom of Fife.

In the corner, a heavily pregnant Annie kept a watchful eye on her slightly tipsy husband James and nursed their two sleepy infant children. While she surveyed the assembled Cranston folk, her thoughts turned to the likely identity of the family's 'first foot', the all-important first person to cross the threshold after the arrival of the New Year. Ideally, the 'first foot' should be a tall, dark and handsome male bearing a gift, commonly a lump of coal. Such a visitor would supposedly ensure the family's good fortune for the next 12 months.

With two notable exceptions, the entire family was present. The eldest son Sandy had moved to Musselburgh a dozen years ago and had family of his own and Ian was currently working as a forester at the Bangour Village Asylum in West Lothian.

Meanwhile, all was not lost for the unfortunate Ismolde! Her fall broken by a birch tree, she had been rescued by her old nurse and spirited away to Fife in a fishing vessel. The same Fife to where her lover had fled; the same lover who was now on hand to rescue her from the sea:

This is the maid, for whom I said,
I'd flown her pagan father's ire!
Fair won, Ismolde, let me unfold,
A 'hooly prize,' indeed, my Sire!

Below the table Robert pulled a face. It was threatening to become too mushy for him.

Lizzie could not settle. Tonight would be her first Hogmanay without her husband and tomorrow her eldest daughter would marry without a father to give her away. She could be excused for being a bit on edge. Of John McDowall, however, she had no doubts.

'You've got a grand one there,' she confided to her daughter. 'A voice like that and a foreman as well.' Her tone changed slightly. 'Mind you he will still hae tae be oot o' this hoose by five tae twelve.'

Agnes groaned inwardly but she knew her mother was right. Much as she longed to kiss her fiancé into the New Year she knew it was out of the question. For a bride to see her husband on the morning of her wedding was most decidedly unlucky.

John was reaching the end of his performance and King Loth the Grim was about to get his comeuppance from Ralph and the King of Fife. Beneath the table, Robbie and Angus were enraptured.

When Oscar charged the tyrant Loth,
Their spears both in flinders flew;
Syne swacked they swords in deadly wroth,
But a churl behind King Oscar slew!
The sacred spot the hero fell
Tells to this day his Standing-Stanes;
Another, nearer to the hill
Where Loth by Ralph was fought and slain!

But for the table above his head, Robbie would have leapt to his feet. 'I ken thae stanes!' he exclaimed to nobody in particular. 'This must ha'e really happened!' He turned to Angus, 'The first fine Sunday o' the year we're gaun up there!'

As the well-deserved applause died down and the musicians got set to play something a bit more lively, Agnes was aware of her mother looking pointedly at John and then the cherished family clock on the mantelpiece; it was a few minutes before midnight and time for John to depart. It was not the time or place for declarations of undying love. Agnes caught John by the hand and their eyes briefly met.

'Sleep well', she whispered, 'see you the morn.' But before he could answer there were several hands on his shoulders and John McDowall was unceremoniously bundled out the door.

'I love you,' she mouthed silently to his back as he disappeared from the house.

When the town clock started to chime, glasses of whisky appeared on cue and Willie struck up 'A Guid New Year' on the fiddle he had inherited from his father. Mary and Robbie peered through the window: the all-important first foot would surely be arriving any minute and they were hoping he would prove suitable.

Down the poorly lit street they could see the vague silhouette of a man dimly appear. Slowly the figure came towards them in the darkness. He wore a large coat to ward off the intense cold and a cloth cap over his head, which meant that the watchers from the window could not make out who he was as the stranger grew ever nearer to the front door. Then a beam of light shone across his face when he drew closer to the house and Mary and her brother could make out his unmistakeable short, waxed moustache.

Young Robert was about to shout out a name, when Mary barked, 'Hush noo, Robbie! Dinnae tell anyone.' Suddenly the door burst open to reveal the Cranston's 'first foot'.

'A Guid New Year tae you a' and a' the best for 1912!' said Ian Cranston, who had travelled all the way from West Lothian to be present. As he handed his mother the customary lump of coal from his coat pocket there was a smile and a kiss from mother to son to thank him for respecting her secret request to attend. She was glad he could get some time off from the asylum, but until he walked through the door, Lizzie had not been certain he would be able to make it.

In any event, Ian would have attended his sister's wedding the following day. After all, he only had two sisters and he felt close to both, but he had made a special effort to get to Haddington for Hogmanay. It was a wish from Ma and a most pleasant surprise for all. All the females were flapping around Ian and they were delighted to plant a cordial New Year's kiss on his face.

But there was another reason why Lizzie had asked Ian to be present. Apart from it being the first New Year after the sad death of her husband whom she had married in 1878, it was also the last time, she suspected, that the whole family could be together. Weeks before she had overheard her daughter talking to John about leaving Scotland for Australia and even though Lizzie did not know when this would happen, she rightly anticipated it would be soon.

After the initial joyous reaction at Ian's arrival there was a slight lull in proceedings and Ian took the opportunity to address everyone. He began solemnly.

'This is the first time that this many family members have been together since Pa died on October. These past few years have been difficult for us all since Pa became ill, but none more so than for Ma.' He paused to nod in her direction. 'She has shouldered a burden that few of us know or appreciate, but on this nicht I want a' of us to acknowledge our love and support for the greatest Ma anyone could possibly have. Please fill up your glasses and toast good times, a better New Year and the best mother in the world! Tae Ma!'

Doddie, who for some time had been in a deep sleep on a makeshift wooden stool, leapt to his feet. 'Tae Ma!' he echoed with unbridled sincerity as he caught his first glimpse of the New

Year, the coming of which he had so clearly celebrated in advance. There was a roar of approval as everyone in the room clambered to their feet, turned to Lizzie and shouted, 'Tae Ma!'

If the Cranstons showed emotion, Ian would have given his mother a warm embrace at this point, but the Cranstons were a reserved lot, as were most families in Scotland. The best Ian could do was to raise the half bottle of whisky he produced from his coat pocket in his mother's direction. She would have to be satisfied with that.

Around the room a few tears were shed by the women, and handshakes between some of the men were a little more robust than usual. Everyone present indeed hoped that a new era was dawning. People grew closer together and with Lizzie leading, but others quickly joining in, the Cranston family of Haddington started singing 'Auld lang Syne'.

Down the street a little and out of sight from the house hovered John McDowall. He had dawdled intentionally to hear how his future in-laws were seeing in the New Year. As he heard Robert Burns' famous New Year greeting being sung, he started mouthing the words to himself. He then moved off to his own flat a short distance away and remembered another Burns quote that seemed to sum up how he felt about Scotland in general and the Cranston family in particular.

O Scotia! my dear, my native soil!
For whom my warmest wish to heaven is sent;
Long may thy hardy sons of rustic toil
Be blest with health, and peace, and sweet content.[41]

---

41 From a much longer poem *A Cotter's Saturday Night*, written by Robert Burns c.1785.

AGNES'S FAREWELL
(1912)

Agnes stood on the deck of the passenger liner with one arm holding onto the railing to steady herself in the slight swell. With the other arm looped through that of her husband, she nestled into the side of his strong body. There were many other people on the deck of the SS *Osterley* and they were all looking at the landmass of Britain slowly receding from view.

Agnes reflected on the whirlwind events of the past two years and how her life had changed so dramatically in such a short time. It had all started in 1910 when her brother James introduced her to the man she would subsequently marry. James, who just as easily answered to Jimmy or Jim, was working as a stonemason with Richard Baillie & Co, a local building company in Haddington, when he suggested she might like to meet his new foreman, John McDowall from Ayrshire.

Agnes felt comfortable with John from the instant they met. It was like being in the company of her brother, Ian. John and he shared many admirable characteristics, including the same name although this Ayrshire man insisted on being called John.

He was handsome, hard-working and of sober habits. And like

67

Ian, he also had a kind, generous nature. In a relatively short time, her feelings for John began to develop into love. They started going out as a couple and many onlookers remarked that they were so well suited to each other it would be only a matter of time before they married. Effie Fairgrieve appeared to sum up the sentiments of others when she stopped John in the street one day in June 1911 and embarrassingly announced, 'You've been winchin'[42] for months noo, it's high time you made an honest woman o' the lass, afore the bairns start coming in the go!'[43] John had been thinking of proposing, so Effie had jumped the gun by only a matter of weeks. Nevertheless, any time the subject arose she insisted that the marriage between Agnes Cranston and John McDowall had been entirely her own doing.

As the day of the wedding grew closer, John had one more important matter to discuss with Agnes – leaving Scotland!

John and his only brother, James, had been left orphans at an early age with the unfortunate death of both parents.[44] In 1911 James left for Canada with his new bride and young child. With no family ties left in Scotland, John felt free to relocate anywhere, even overseas. But he realised that Agnes might be horrified at the prospect of leaving her homeland and large family.

However, circumstances changed somewhat when John found out, to his relief, that previous generations of Cranstons had already departed for overseas, mainly for Canada and America. Furthermore, there was still intermittent correspondence between these relatives and on more than one occasion the subject of emigration had been mentioned by the present generation of Cranstons in Scotland.

---

42 courting

43 appearing

44 Andrew McDowall, father, died of phthisis (tuberculosis) in 1888 and Elizabeth McDowall, mother, died of paraplegia (spinal cord injury) in 1898 (source Registry House, Edinburgh, through Scotlandspeople.com).

Sandy Cranston, six years John's senior, told him in confidence that he seriously contemplated taking his family overseas. It was during this conversation John found out that Sandy had already been to America. Sandy went on to say that some time in the future when he found sufficient courage, he would talk to his wife about moving the whole family there.

The last matter that influenced John's decision to move was the attitude of his best friend John Morrison, who was also a stonemason from Haddington. He had been a personal friend for years, and the two were distantly related. One day when John and Agnes were playing cards with John Morrison and his wife, Harriett, the subject of emigration arose. The engaged couple listened intently to the Morrisons' plans to move to Australia and the more they talked, the more Australia loomed as a possible destination in John's head.

Later that night while John was escorting Agnes home, she seemed to sense that he wanted to say something important, but could not. Their wedding was only a month away and at first Agnes thought John might be having second thoughts about the marriage. Then it dawned on her that his reticence was associated with the topic of conversation with the Morrisons earlier that evening. She remembered that she had seen John in deep conversation with Sandy recently and had overheard the words America repeated often. There was also the time recently when she saw he had circled advertisements in the local paper for assisted immigration to both Canada and Australia.

Her mind raced, trying to make sense of these fragments of information. It suddenly occurred to her what might be on his mind. For a moment a panic set in as she realised life with her future husband might mean leaving family and friends in Scotland. What would her brothers and sister say? Even more importantly, what would her mother say? Ma was still very fragile following the death of Pa only six weeks earlier in October.

But she had given herself in mind and body to this man and knew she would love no other. If John wanted to go overseas, she accepted she had no choice. She would follow him to the ends of the earth. But to which destination would it be?

She stopped him under a gas lamp and said, 'What's on your mind?' But John was silent. Agnes decided to press the issue and said, 'Look, we'll be man and wife in a month and if you want to go to bide[45] abroad, I will follow you, of course I will. But I dinnae ken whaur you want to bide.'

He kissed her fully on the lips with passion and gratitude. After a slight pause while he thought through what to do next, he pulled out a silver florin[46] from underneath his coat and showed it to Agnes.

'Heids it's Australia; tails it's Canada.'

The gaslight glinted off the faces of the coin as it spun. John allowed it to fall back into his outstretched hand and without looking, immediately transferred the coin onto the back of his other hand. Standing directly in front of Agnes he slowly removed his right hand to reveal which side of the coin was exposed.

Agnes waited with bated breath until finally she saw the face of King Edward VII staring up at them. With a mixture of nervousness and relief, John exhaled deeply and said, 'Australia it is then, lass.'[47]

One of the last jobs that John completed prior to the couple's emigration to Australia was also one of his proudest. Baillie and

---

45 live
46 Replaced by the ten-pence coin when decimal currency was introduced in Britain in 1971.
47 The Edwardian florin coin was still in the family's possession up to the early 1970s, but it has not been seen since the death of John McDowall in 1972.

Co had been given the task of erecting a wrought iron and stone fence along the front perimeter of St Mary's Parish Church, which faced the Sidegate. The contract also included a pair of heavy iron gates at the entrance to the church grounds from the street. The iron fence and gates were to be fixed to stone columns and a stone base. John and his stonemasons had to complete the stone laying first, before the local iron foundry could proceed.

A team of stonemasons under John's supervision lovingly constructed the four columns in record time, knowing their foreman was about to leave the company and country soon. The task took on a life of its own as the stonemasons – who included Agnes's brother Jimmy Cranston – and John Morrison took extra care to finish the job as quickly as they could.

Always in the background was Lizzie Cranston, who came regularly to the church to visit the grave of her recently departed husband. At no stage did she utter a negative comment, but all the men were mindful that in a sense she was judging her future son-in-law. She spent almost as much time observing their progress as she did at the gravesite. So they applied themselves even more earnestly to make the job something of which they could all be proud.

Winter was rapidly approaching when the beautifully sculptured columns and wall were completed. The project was then handed over to the iron foundry to hang the heavy iron gates and posts. The men from the foundry had also performed well – the heavy iron balusters were topped with masterfully crafted broad spear finials to form a beautiful fence.[48]

One day Lizzie came by when the workers were packing up and remarked, 'No too bad', which, considering she was still grieving the loss of Alec, was high praise indeed. With the job completed

---

48 These were later removed to help the Second World War effort and were replaced some 60 years later around 2005. (Source: www.scotland.gov.uk/Topics/Environment/SustainableDevelopment/funding/communityprojects)

on time and to everyone's delight, John packed away his tools for the last time in Scotland and bade his workmates a fond farewell. But the men of Baillie & Co that he had kept company with for the past several years were not going to let him leave without a proper send off.

A formal ceremony was arranged at the close of work at which the owner and fellow tradesmen presented John with a handsome timepiece and a silver-mounted walking stick.[49]

Agnes and John were married at the Foresters' Lodge in the Hardgate on the first day of January 1912. It was a simple wedding ceremony, as was normal for the Church of Scotland. For Agnes, the best part of the occasion was having all the Cranston family present to share in her joy. Counting nieces and nephews, there were more than 20 family members in attendance. However, it was a very different feeling for John. Being orphaned at 13 and having only one brother, meeting so many in-laws, some for the first time, was slightly intimidating. After the ceremony the bridal party walked across the road to the studios of John Paton, photographer, and had a number of wedding photographs taken.[50]

On the evening of 17 January 1912, it started to snow. When people awoke on the morning of the 18th, a thick blanket of snow was everywhere. It was one of the heaviest snowfalls in many years.[51] When John and Agnes took a stroll through the church grounds, they were greeted with the wondrous sight of John's handiwork covered in soft white flakes. John McDowall did not have a camera himself, but he knew where to find one. He hurried off to John Paton's studio, which was a few hundred metres away in the Hardgate.

When the two men returned a short time later, John Paton was

49 Reported in the *Haddingtonshire Courier* in March 1912, after the couple had departed for Australia.
50 This was the same studio and photographer where the family portrait was taken in 1908.
51 According to the meteorological records maintained by the UK's National Weather Service.

carrying a tripod and camera case. The experienced photographer inspected the scene and confirmed the view was indeed ideal for a postcard image. Working like the professional he was, John Paton set the camera on the tripod opposite the gates. He then checked for lighting and finally placed his photographic glass plate in the camera. He stood to attention beside the device with the long shutter-release cable in his hand and pressed the button.

John heard a slight mechanical whirring sound coming from the internal workings of the camera followed by a definite click signifying that the camera shutter had captured an image. Two weeks later, when John and Agnes collected their wedding photographs just prior to leaving Scotland for ever, there was an extra photograph to accompany them.

Back on the SS *Osterley*, the afternoon wind had picked up and a sudden gust of cold air off the English Channel jolted Agnes from her reverie. As the last vestige of the British coastline disappeared beyond the horizon, the mood on the ship became subdued. The past was being severed as the ship full of emigrants started its journey to a new land. Agnes suddenly realised the enormity of what she and John were doing and that it was unlikely either would ever return to Scotland. She squeezed John's arm a little harder for reassurance and wiped away a small tear. She had no idea what the future held, but deep down she hoped and prayed that it would be good.

Knowing that a letter would take more than six weeks to reach Scotland, Agnes penned off a reassuring note to her mother as soon as the couple arrived in Sydney. But then unexpectedly a week later the newspapers were full of news about the disastrous sinking of the RMS *Titanic* after striking an iceberg in the North

Atlantic.[52] Agnes fretted that her mother could be thinking she and John were still on the high seas. If the unsinkable *Titanic* could go to the bottom of the ocean taking 1,500 passengers with her, then any ship could suffer the same fate.

By the time Lizzie finally received the letter, Agnes had been gone more than three months. Lizzie had been concerned about her daughter's safety before she had even embarked on such a long ocean passage, so the terrible news about the *Titanic* heightened those concerns considerably. Thankfully, the note from her daughter was a steadying influence on Lizzie. But as a result of the scare, there was one thing she promised herself she would never do. Lizzie Cranston determined she would never take a sea voyage in her life.

---

52 Agnes and John arrived in Sydney on 8 April 1912. The RMS *Titanic* sank on 15 April 1912. People around the globe were shocked by the catastrophe and over time this tragedy has become one the greatest maritime disaster stories ever told.

PART TWO
(1914-20)

1914

The year that should have been remembered for being one of the best British summers in living memory turned sour with the sudden declaration of war. A web of complex alliances had turned the isolated assassination of the crown prince of the Austro-Hungarian Empire in Sarajevo into a major international conflict.

There was an outpouring of patriotism across Europe as millions of men mobilised for war. In Britain, with its all-volunteer army, hundreds of thousands rushed to enlist in a glorious war for God, King and Country that many believed would be over by Christmas.

The year 1914 had started badly for Lizzie Cranston. Winter was slowly coming to an end and Doctor William McIntosh MD stared down in silence at Andrew Cranston who was lying in his bed with his chest heaving up and down in a struggle to breathe. He had just turned 19, but there were no birthday celebrations. Instead the Cranston lad was fighting to stay alive. Drew, as everyone called him, had always had a weak chest and this current bout of bronchitis coupled with his underlying emphysema meant that any lung infection could be his last.

Dr McIntosh knew most of the families in the Nungate; after all, his surgery in the Hardgate was only metres from the Tyne River and as only one of three doctors in the burgh[53] with a population of 4,200, many of his patients came from 'ower the brig'. William McIntosh believed that he probably knew more about the people of the Nungate and their secrets than almost anyone else.

And this was certainly true of the Cranston family. He had treated each of the children through their childhood illnesses. Dr McIntosh was secretly pleased that between himself and the resolute care of their mother Elizabeth, not one of the children had died while he had been their family doctor. This was an enviable statistic in Scotland at the time; as the good doctor knew, close to one in three children never made it to adulthood. Yet this poor working-class family had managed to go against the trend. He put it down to his superior medical skills of course, but also conceded that the mother's scrupulous cleanliness and insistence on a hygienic house may have played a part too.

Dr McIntosh could remember 10 years earlier when older brother James had lain in a similar bed at their previous tenement flat on the other side of the river in the Hardgate. He too had been very ill with a chest infection and there were grave fears that the family would lose Jimmy to one of the many lung diseases that were common in the crowded, damp residences of the working poor. He was amazed at how Lizzie had managed to pull him through with folk remedies when he himself had virtually consigned the lad's care into the hands of God. It was summer and Lizzie had picked wild flowers from the fields and laneways around Haddington and purchased some freshly harvested heather honey, a product of the nearby Lammermuir Hills, from a beekeeper. She had taken the field scabious flower, known locally as ladies pin cushion, and rare wall rue stems and made an

53 Burgh: an administrative area in Scotland, the equivalent of a town. The legal term was abolished in 1973 under the Local Government (Scotland) Act.

infusion on the stove in a pot of boiling water. The mixture was then reduced and when cooled, a ladle of the special honey mixed into the liquid by Lizzie to turn it into a thick, sweet syrup.

Young Jimmy, who had just finished school at the time, was made to slowly sip the concoction until the enamel mug that contained the brew was empty. A short time later violent coughing wracked his weak and fevered body. Throughout the night he coughed up blood, sputum and wads of yellow fluid from his lungs. By first light the next day he had collapsed from exhaustion. Yet, a day later his breathing was significantly less laboured, his fever had broken and his lungs were not as congested with fluid.

Each day he improved a little more, until by the seventh day Dr McIntosh was grateful and astonished to declare that Jimmy had completely recovered from his bout of pleurisy. Yet there was scar tissue present that would remain with him for the rest of his life and as a result his lungs would always be weak. He advised the family that James should seek a future in outdoor employment where he could build up his strength and lung capacity. He was pleased that the family had taken his guidance when James sought an apprenticeship as a stonemason. Based on the evidence available at the time, he also advised Jimmy to take up smoking tobacco to settle his cough. Everyone knew that it had a mild, calming effect on the lungs.

In the years since, he had admired how the young teenager had grown so strong and fit from the physical labour of being a stonemason. However, there remained the nagging belief that Jimmy Cranston could succumb to another chest infection at any time in the future and he might not be so lucky to survive next time.

Dr McIntosh had observed folk remedies before. In fact, his own mother in Aberdeen had several favourite remedies specific to the North-East of Scotland. But he had never seen a preparation that had such an immediate curative affect as Lizzie's remedy. It was episodes like this that formed the basis of his respect and admiration for Lizzie and the entire Cranston family. His last visit was years before when the family lived in ramshackle premises in the Hardgate and he was treating Alec Cranston, the father, for the intestinal cancer that eventually killed him.

Dr McIntosh treated Alec Cranston for four years from 1907; he had watched the cancer slowly eat away his patient's insides and all he had been able to do for him was make his life as restful as possible by giving him increasing doses of morphine. And morphine it was, although prescribed for intractable pain, that slowed down and finally stopped his patient's breathing, as the gentle doctor knew it must. In the end, there was no more pain for Alexander Cranston and no more medical bills for a family that could not afford them.

He could never be indifferent to the suffering of his patients nor of their families and was only too aware of the difficulties the Cranstons faced, the very difficulties that caused one of the eldest sons, William, to give up a job with prospects in Glasgow and return home to take up his father's employment as a forester.

There was one more reason why Doctor McIntosh felt closer to the Cranston family than most of his other patients: he felt a special linguistic bond with Lizzie.

William McIntosh was born in Aberdeen and for all his formative years had spoken the native 'Doric' of his parents, a fish market porter and seasonal filleter. The Doric, although not a language in its own right, was considerably more than a regional dialect and to William at least, could capture emotions and imagery far beyond the English in which he had conversed almost entirely for the past 40 years. On that score he had no option, for the Doric was all but indecipherable to anyone who lived outside the north-eastern corner of Scotland. To his knowledge, no one else in Haddington spoke a word of Doric – except Elizabeth Cranston. Lizzie had been raised in Keith, some 50 kilometres from Aberdeen, and although there are some differences in the city and country versions of Doric, these were easily ignored by these two exiles in the south. William McIntosh welcomed every opportunity he had to insert a few words of his mother tongue during conversations with Elizabeth. His efforts, however, were never entirely reciprocated since force of habit meant that Lizzie tried to 'talk proper' when conversing with a professional.

As the cold wind whistled through the wide crack under the ill-fitting door, Dr McIntosh adjusted his overcoat for warmth and wondered as to the motives of a God who condemned this worthy family to live in such poor conditions. It was cold, cramped and on freezing days in winter like this one in January 1914, it was a death trap.

In Drew's case this was a distinct possibility, for this was the second winter in succession that he had been seriously ill with bronchitis. Dr McIntosh was convinced another episode the following winter would probably finish him off. The doctor returned his stethoscope to his well-worn black Gladstone bag and turned to face Lizzie.

'He's nae weel at a',' Elizabeth. In fact if he wisnae sae healthy he wid be deid lang ago.' The apparent illogicality of the doctor's remarks was lost on Lizzie, but his message was clear. 'Fit am saying Elizabeth, is this. He's nae gan ti survive anither winter o' this.' He solemnly nodded in the direction of St Mary's graveyard. 'The wye things are gan he'll be ower that dyke wi' his al' man afore anither Christmas.' Lizzie understood clearly the import of the last words: one more cold winter would probably kill her son.

Dr McIntosh continued, 'Foo's thon quine[54] o' yours gettin' on? Her that got merrit and took aff ti Australia? That's the only thing I can prescribe, and of coorse, the Foresters' winna pye for it. Bit if she could gi'e him a corner o' her fleer[55] ti lie his heid on, he

---

54 girl
55 floor

micht hae a fightin' chunce.' Lizzie's eyes lit up, but the doctor had not finished with her yet.

'Lizzie, here's the hard part. It wid hae ti be foriver. Andra' could nivver come back, ever!' He looked down at the still heaving chest of Andrew and expressively shook his head.

Weeks later, when Drew had recovered sufficiently to return to his trade as a butcher, Elizabeth Cranston and son had a quiet, yet serious chat around the old, tired dining-room table. The rest of the household had gone to bed. There was no electricity or gas connected to the old house and under the weak glow of a flickering paraffin light, Lizzie started off the discussion.

'Drew, we're a' concerned aboot your health. You've been through the mangle again lately and every year you get worse.' Andrew did not interrupt. He listened quietly, for he knew it was true.

'The doctor has strongly recommended that you leave Scotland tae bide in a warmer climate.' Before Andrew could protest his mother ploughed on, 'So we've taen a whip roond frae every family member whae's working and we've managed to buy you a ticket tae Sydney, Australia in steerage class.'

Andrew was stunned. Two years ago his sister Agnes and her new husband had emigrated to Australia, so he knew the cost of an unassisted passage to that far-off land was at least 20 guineas. It was the equivalent of half a year's pay for the average man, way too much for the family to afford.

'I dinnae want to go to some god-forsaken country on the ither side o' the world,' he argued determinedly. 'If I wanted tae go abroad it would be tae Canada or America whaur ither Cranstons have already gone and made a name for themsels.'

As a young teenager he had listened to the stories his older brother Sandy had told about the wonder and adventure of his trip to the United States of America seven years before and how it was possibly Sandy's intention of returning there one day. But just as he was forming more words in opposition he noticed something missing from the mantelpiece above the hearth. He tried to recall what had once been there and then it dawned on him. The black marble mantelpiece clock that his parents treasured had been removed. His Ma and Pa had been given this by Alec's parents as a wedding present. The timepiece was exquisite and Andrew remembered being told it was worth many pounds when his grandparents had originally purchased it in the 1860s. Financially and sentimentally it was his mother's most treasured possession.

It was then he realised that individual family members had not collectively put money into the price of his passage at all. His mother had paid for the entire trip herself out of the sale of her beloved mantel clock. He now understood how sick he must be if his mother was prepared to go to these extremes to give him a better life. At a deeper level he also began to comprehend how much his mother loved him. Suddenly all the objections he was summonsing melted away. If his mother was going to sacrifice her last penny on him, then he had no choice. He had to accept this mother's unconditional love for him and graciously embrace her offer. In the flicker of an eyelid he had gone from rejection to acceptance.

He looked into the face of his anxious mother across the badly worn dining room table and said as meekly and as lovingly as he could, 'When do I leave?'

A few days later Lizzie wrote a letter to her daughter in Australia explaining the reasons why Andrew must leave Scotland and asking for the young married couple in Sydney to look after him when he arrived. Knowing that there would be no time for a reply, she added the details of the ship and the date of departure from London. She hoped that Agnes and her husband John would be at the docks in Sydney to welcome him on shore and provide temporary accommodation until her son could make his own arrangements.

Drew left on the morning train for London after a night where friends and family gathered at the Foresters' Hall in the Hardgate for a very enjoyable farewell. There were tears from his mother and Mary and some of the lasses in town he had courted, but the evening was not morbid or sad. Everyone knew Drew's condition and there was widespread relief that he was going to a better location for his health.

Drew had never seen such a city as London in his life. It was huge, crowded, busy and putrid. But it also emanated a feeling of enterprise, prosperity and fortune from every building he passed. As he presented his boarding pass to the purser at the gangplank and stepped aboard the SS *Otway* he was stunned at the size of the passenger ship. He settled into his cabin, exchanged pleasantries with his fellow passengers and took a stroll around the ship's decks to acclimatise. In the afternoon the ship slipped its moorings and was pulled away from the wharf on the Thames River by steam tugboats. There was an announcement broadcast throughout the ship that final mail would be collected by Royal Mail packet as the SS *Otway* passed Plymouth the following day. Andrew hastily obtained some ship's writing paper and wrote a rushed thank you to his mother, pointing out that the ship was like a huge hotel and carried over 1,000 passengers. Andrew could not contain his excitement when he wrote that his comfortable cabin in third class contained four beds only, leaving his mother to wonder how it was possible that so many of her boys had slept at one time in a tiny room in Haddington.

The 45-day journey to Australia via the Suez Canal was as invigorating as it was relaxing. Every day the temperature became milder as the ship steamed south. A highlight was the stop in Colombo, Ceylon, where the passengers were allowed to disembark for the day as the ship was refuelled with coal. It was hot, humid, vibrant and the most exotic location he had ever seen. Two weeks later, having crossed the Indian Ocean, Andrew was faced with the enormity of his changed circumstances.

An announcement was made that the vessel was approaching Australian landfall and Drew hurried to his cabin and hastily packed his possessions. The next day he was puzzled that the ship was not in Sydney but had berthed in a place called Perth, Western Australia instead. As the ship subsequently steamed its way around the coastline of his new homeland, stopping next at Adelaide and then Melbourne, Drew was convinced every stop must be his.

Finally, after waiting two further weeks since the initial sighting of the Australian continent, the SS *Otway* sailed through the Heads of Sydney Harbour and came to rest at one of the passenger wharves in Balmain, Sydney. He could hardly believe that one country could be so large that it took two weeks to steam around it.

As Andrew strode down the gangplank with all his worldly possessions rolled up in a canvas bag he looked like a fit, tanned and healthy 19-year-old. His wheeze was barely audible. There on the wharf he saw his dear sister Agnes and her husband John waiting to collect him. She was 10 years older than Drew and looked radiant in the seventh month of pregnancy. Hanging on John's hip was a 16-month-old boy who was introduced as Alec. The young married couple had done well for themselves since he had seen them last, over two years ago in Scotland. As they embraced, Andrew thought to himself, if his sister could make it in Australia, then so could he.

The first few months in Sydney were uneventful as Drew easily found a job as a butcher and stayed with his sister in Balmain. Yet the small cottage was a bit of a squeeze for everyone, especially now with the addition of another baby in the McDowall family. Andrew was thrilled when his sister named the newborn, Andrew, after him and asked him to be the unofficial godfather of the baby. Agnes and John told Drew of their dream to buy land and build their own house, which he took to be a polite way of saying that eventually he would have to find a place of his own.

When first told of their plans to buy land, Drew had thought the whole proposal audacious and unrealistic. His sister had only been in Australia barely two years, yet they had already accumulated enough capital to seriously consider the prospect. This would have been unheard of in Scotland and gave Drew the heart to believe that in the future he might be able to do the same.

Young Robbie Cranston bravely hid his disappointment as his hero and big brother Ian slipped him a dirty looking coin-like object with a conspiratorial wink. They were standing on the platform of Haddington Station, waiting for an overdue train. Instead of some useless old coin, Robbie had been hoping to be surreptitiously passed a few Woodbine cigarettes. As if aware of Robbie's lack of gratitude, Ian smiled broadly.

'Hing on tae it for the rest o' your life, young man. Twae very clivver blokes in the George told me it's got the Roman Goddess o' fortune on it and its hunners o' years auld.'

Ian thought of the exertions of the previous night that had won him the Roman coin and smiled. The last couple of years had been the very best time of his adventure-filled life. Ian's many years as a regular soldier with the Queen's Own Cameron Highlanders had taken him to such exotic places as Gibraltar, Malta, South Africa and even to northern China.

It was the stuff of which heroes were made and he always had a ready audience in Robbie and Angus when he made his all too infrequent visits to Haddington. His newfound domesticity and employment as an asylum attendant in Dechmont, West Lothian, left him little time for keeping up with his original family. But in July, Ian, together with his wife Agnes, had been pleased to come to Haddington to introduce their second child, a son named Alexander.

It was a glorious summer in Scotland and the birth of a new child should have been a joyful occasion, but Ian was pensive. He was predicting that events in Europe would lead to war. To settle his brooding feelings, Ian had visited the George Hotel, located prominently in the centre of town, the night before and walked into a scene he had witnessed in many army mess halls around the world – an arm-wrestling contest.

The activity had captured the attention of all the occupants in the bar and seemed to be orchestrated by two young men whose slightly better cut of clothing and refined speech identified them as strangers. The larger of the two was stripped to his waistcoat with his shirt neck open. He sat at the bar with his shirt sleeves rolled up, a row of drinks in front of him and an unmistakable look of triumph on his face. At least he had the courtesy to sweat profusely.

'Roll up gentlemen,' beamed the younger and smaller of the two strangers, his face slightly flushed from helping to consume his friend's winnings. 'Are we to assume George Watson's reign supreme?[56] Surely one of you country chaps can give us a run for our money. After all we're just poor and humble archaeologists you know, not prize fighters!'

Most of the likely opponents had already tried and failed to beat the stranger and were reluctant to give any more drink away to some toff who seemed to have the better of them. Ian was aware of being nudged slightly in the back and turned to see a face he remembered vaguely from his schooldays at what was known locally as the Knox Institute.[57]

'Archae bloody oligists, whitever that's supposed to mean,' the old school pal whispered. 'Apparently they're pairt o' whit they

---

56 George Watson College in central Edinburgh prided itself as being the 'nursery' of Scottish rugby champions. Many went on to play for the old boys team, known as the Watsonians, and were selected to represent Scotland directly from this club.

57 The school's official name was Haddington Public School when it opened in 1879. (Reference: Gray and Jamieson, page 137.)

ca' a "dig" up at Traprain Law. Bit God kens how much diggin' they'll dae dressed like that!' Suddenly his tone became altogether less hostile. 'Mind you they say that biggest yin is on the verge o' playing for Scotland at the rugby and if a' gangs weel he micht be playing for the Lions afore the year's oot!'

Ian conceded that the stranger certainly had the build of a rugby player but the loud and boastful attitude of the two young men convinced him that they had already consumed a large quantity of alcohol. Ian was short and sinewy and gave the impression that he lacked physical strength, but eight years in the army and many more of forestry work had given him muscles of steel. The man from Edinburgh was certainly bigger and stronger than himself, but Ian was convinced the alcohol had made him vulnerable. For Ian, an arm wrestle in the pub would be a welcome diversion, as well as a way to make a quick shilling or two. He met the stranger's eye from across the room and defiantly exclaimed, 'I'm up for the challenge, I'll gi'e you a go.'

'Oh my,' said the rugby player sarcastically, 'is there no one younger left to fight me? Come forward grandfather (Ian was only 10 years older). I've got sixpence here that says you'll be no match for me.' A voice from the corner shouted back boldly, 'I've got a tanner[58] here tae back the workin' man! Come on, son. Let's see what you're made o'!'

Ian needed no second invitation and in a trice was sat in the stool facing the stranger. Their eyes met yet again and their right hands came together in a firm grip. The pub had gone quiet and all eyes were focused on the adversaries. Ian's identity was becoming known to a number of drinkers. 'He's Willie Cranston's aulder brither,' they whispered to each other and soon everyone was on his side as first Ian and then the stranger seemed to gain the upper hand.

---

58 Slang for sixpence.

But just as the arm wrestle looked like being an even contest with the crowd in the pub becoming more vocal, the stranger exerted a well-practised surge of strength and Ian's hand crashed to the surface of the bar. The locals groaned and the stranger triumphantly scooped the sixpence into his pocket. Ian Cranston was emotionless. He stared the triumphal rugby player in the eye with steely determination.

'Again,' he half whispered and their hands locked once more.

In common with many drinking establishments in Scotland, the George did not always stick rigidly to the licensing hours. The local 'bobby' was known to enjoy the occasional pint outside trading hours as he made his way home from an evening shift and besides was rumoured to have an eye for one of the pretty barmaids. He was therefore very understanding when he arrived to find the arm-wrestling contest in full swing.

Thus, the contest went on, round after round, well into the night. It was fiercely fought, but finally Ian gained the upper hand and what had become a considerable pile of sixpences were now at his end of the bar. Yet still the stranger was not beaten, although now he had no more money to play with. He exchanged glances with his friend and produced an ugly coin from his handkerchief.

'Damn it man,' he retorted, 'this was meant for my pension pot but I'm buggered if I am going to let you beat me! You should know that this one coin is worth more than that pile of sixpences you've accumulated at your end of the bar. In fact,' he whispered as if sharing a secret, 'this little coin I dug up on Traprain Law is probably worth more than the average man would earn in six months!'

Everyone in the hotel was now totally engrossed in the conversation as the handsome stranger briefly talked about Romans, an ancient tribe of Britons called the Votadini and their hill fort on Traprain Law. But all that Ian could remember was that the coin was valuable and the symbols on it would bring luck to the possessor. They eagerly clasped hands one last time and to the roar of the crowd started to push the other's arm with all the strength they had left.

Twenty minutes later, Ian gave Agnes a handful of sixpences that both knew would come in handy with household expenses, but he kept one old coin in his pocket. There was a young brother just starting his apprenticeship in a world that faced an uncertain future. He could do with a little luck.[59]

Doddie Cranston did not have a care in the world. The previous year, at 21, he had successfully completed his butcher's apprenticeship and was officially designated a 'journeyman', meaning a fully qualified tradesman without the need of a master. He and his friend Klaus who had finished his apprenticeship a year earlier were both working at George Pringle 'Flesher' (Butcher) located at No. 17 Market Street, Haddington. Doddie worked long hours – 6am to 6pm, six days a week – but he liked the work and the company. He also enjoyed the banter with the customers for which butchers were universally renowned, especially if a pretty young woman walked into the shop. He had an easy manner about him, which the customers appreciated, and his boss, Mr Pringle, relied upon. Doddie was always quick to point out how a customer's health would be markedly improved with the consumption of some red meat, a ploy that often resulted in increased sales.

'Och, Mrs Gray, I was doing deliveries on Saturday when I saw your son playing fitba' and I must say he looked like he could do

---

59 Later that year, the entire First XV of the Watsonian Rugby Football Club volunteered for service with the British army *en masse*. The fate of this individual is unknown, but statistically 605 old boys from George Watson College died out of approximately 3,100 who served in the Great War – an appalling death rate of 19.5 per cent. (Reference: www.gwc.org.uk/cms/our-school/history-of-george-watsons-college/watsons-war-records/)

with some iron in his diet. Have you thought about the wonders a nice beef sausage would do for the boy?' Klaus produced the best sausages in the district. It came from his exposure to advanced processing methods back in Germany where he was born. Everyone accepted that the Germans made the best processed meats in Europe and George Pringle was lucky that Klaus settled in Haddington to become a butcher when he emigrated from Bavaria as a teenager.

Klaus and Doddie made a good team. Klaus made superior sausages and Doddie used his banter to charm the customers into buying more products than perhaps they really intended. The two young men liked each other and got on well. It did not matter at all to Doddie that Klaus was originally from Germany, or that he spoke broken English with a strong German accent. They were both young men, good at their jobs and both in love with life. Furthermore, thought Doddie, of all the major countries in Europe, Germany and Britain had most in common with each other.

But there were one or two activities Doddie involved himself in that were not shared with his friend. On Sundays Doddie intermittently attended St Mary's Parish Church in Haddington with the rest of his family, while Klaus went to the German Evangelical Church of Edinburgh-Leith in the Scottish capital. The other activity that Klaus did not participate in was the Territorial Army. The Cranston family had a long-standing involvement with the Royal Scots Territorial Army unit based in Haddington, with their father serving when he was alive and several sons still serving.

Klaus was not a naturalised British subject and was therefore ineligible to join, which actually suited him because he was not in favour of the military. In a highly martial country such as Germany in the early 20th century it was hard to avoid the uniforms, the parades and the flag waving. It was one of the reasons why Klaus had decided to leave Germany in the first place.

Every Tuesday evening Doddie would attend the drill hall of

the 8th Royal Scots Battalion in the Nungate and participate in lectures, drill practice and a final evening parade. It was easy work and enjoyable too. It seemed that the Cranstons were born to wear uniform as most of the sons up to now had served in one British regiment or another, either full time, such as Ian, or part time, like Sandy and Doddie.

Undoubtedly the best part of being in the part-time army was the two-week camp held every year during summer. It seemed as if every soldier looked forward to the paid time off from work and the chance to live under the stars in summer, marching, drilling and firing live rounds of ammunition. Rifle shooting was where Doddie excelled and he proudly wore the crossed rifle badge of a marksman on his uniform to prove it.

Leading up to the annual camp in August 1914, Doddie was disturbed by two conversations. The first was with his brother Ian who, when over in Haddington from Dechmont, had expressed his concerns about the possibilities of war. The second was an address by a colonel at the last week's drill before the camp. The Haddington contingent of the 8th Royal Scots was assembled in the Nungate drill hall to listen to a visitor from Brigade Headquarters in Edinburgh. The small elderly gentleman was almost as wide as he was tall, but had the bearing of an aristocrat. He was introduced as an intelligence officer and the red flashes on his collar as well as the silver-tipped cane he held signified that he was of senior rank. The visitor heaved himself onto a dais thoughtfully provided to allow the soldiers to see him more clearly and in a crisp upper-crust accent addressed the troops.

'Men, I hope you're all looking forward to a jolly good annual camp, but I regret to inform you that matters may shortly get very much worse.' There was a distinct softness to his voice which took the men by surprise and the soldier next to Doddie whispered, 'Heriot's?'

'No', replied a second soldier quietly, 'he's too much o' a queer tae come from there.' After a pause, this man responded in a low voice, 'Fettes,[60] I bet'.

'Aye,' said the first soldier, 'Fettes, it would have tae be.' The Colonel did not hear the slanderous discussion about which school he must have attended based on his effeminate manner of speaking.

'Many of you probably won't know but the Crown Prince of Austria was assassinated a few weeks ago in the Balkans.'[61]

'Eh?' the first soldier again whispered, 'did he say the balls?'

'No,' replied the other man, 'he said he was assassinated in the Balkans.'

'Where's that?' Doddie could not restrain himself and chimed in quickly, 'It's lower doon.'

The Colonel pressed on: 'Since then, matters have escalated considerably and now Germany has declared its support for the Austro-Hungarian Empire in any armed conflict.' At the mention of Germany the room suddenly became quiet. Matters were indeed serious if Britain's European rival was involved in what was up to now an isolated diplomatic incident.

'I'm sorry to have to inform you that according to the very latest military intelligence, war involving France, Germany, Russia and Austria-Hungary seems imminent.' No one was sniggering at his accent now.

'The British Empire has treaties with both France and Russia and even though we will do our best to avoid war, all of you should quietly prepare for it.' The Colonel realised he had shocked his audience into stunned silence. Now was the time to deliver some good news.

---

60 Fettes College and George Heriot's School were and still are two elite, independent schools in Edinburgh, with boarding facilities.
61 Franz Ferdinand, the Crown Prince of the Austro-Hungarian Empire, was assassinated on 28 June 1914 in Sarajevo, Bosnia and Herzegovina (then part of Austria-Hungary).

'However, even if there is war between our great empires, I can assure you that you won't have to fight overseas. It is our opinion that this war will be over within a few months of starting and therefore if you are called up, it will be to perform coastal defence duties in this area of Scotland only.' There was an audible murmur of relief, even approval from the men in the hall.

'I promise', finished the Staff Officer, 'none of you will ever see fighting in Europe.'

Doddie went home that night more contemplative than he had been in a long time. Would there really be a war between the great powers of Europe? It seemed hard to believe, especially when there was not much reporting about the events in the papers. It was not the topic of conversation with customers in the butcher's shop either. It was then that Doddie realised for the first time that war with Germany might affect his friendship with Klaus. Doddie vowed he would not discuss the officer's prediction with Klaus. After all, there was a chance armed conflict with Germany might never happen.

How wrong he was.

A week later, just as Doddie was about to leave for annual camp, postmen started delivering official notices from the Ministry of War throughout Great Britain. In Haddington the following notification was dropped through the Cranston's letterbox.

Territorial Force – Embodiment

To 1090 Lance-Corporal George Cranston 8th Royal Scots. The Army Council in pursuance of His Majesty's proclamation have directed that the 8th Royal Scots be embodied on the 4th August 1914 at Haddington. You are directed to bring rations, fuel and light to last 24 hours.

On the same day church bells rang out across Haddington

summonsing people to the town hall, where the Provost[62] solemnly announced that the British Empire had indeed declared war against the Empires of the Central European powers.

Doddie scrambled to finish getting his partially prepared uniform and equipment together and raced off to the drill hall. He was certain that the same urgent activity was happening in Ian's house too. He stopped at the doorway to give Ma a kiss and tell her he had been mobilised for war. But Lizzie insisted he was just going off to annual camp and at this stage would not listen to anything else Doddie had to say.

From Haddington, Doddie made his way to Edinburgh where the rest of his battalion rested overnight, convinced they were all heading overseas the next day. During the night the orders must have changed, because the entire battalion was sent back to Haddington where they would spend the next three months 'toughening up' with route marches, drill instruction and training. During this time Doddie and the other soldiers were allowed several 24-hour and 48-hour leave passes. In Doddie's case, he was home within minutes and helping out wherever he could.

Only two weeks into his training Doddie was on leave when he met Klaus coming out of the butcher's shop looking very glum. He said to Doddie, 'Police come last night to my place and give me papers. He zay I must fill out or go to prison. Can you help?' He then produced a two-page document headed, 'National Registration'.[63] Before Doddie returned to his campsite in Amisfield Park, on the outskirts of town, the two sat down to fill in the form together. Doddie felt uneasy about the task as it was obvious the information supplied was designed to make it easier

---

62 Civic head, similar to a mayor.
63 The Aliens Registration Act 1914 – passed within 24 hours of war being declared made it mandatory for all enemy aliens (foreign nationals of enemy countries residing in Britain) over the age of 16 to register with the police.

for the police to check on people like Klaus. The term that was being used repeatedly in the form was 'enemy alien' and Doddie did not care for the connotations.

Another two weeks passed and Doddie heard that several customers in the shop were now suspicious of Klaus still working diligently in the back room processing the meat. One person had even muttered 'bloody spy' as he left the shop and the sale of sausages dropped markedly. Mr Pringle was becoming nervous and Doddie was becoming concerned for Klaus's welfare.

The papers were full of reports about German nationals seen recording the names and numbers of British warships at anchor nearby in the Firth of Forth. Doddie recognised that people were whipping themselves up into an anti-German hysteria, but still Klaus and he remained friends.

Then in September, the entire east coast of Scotland, from Aberdeen to the English border at Berwick-upon-Tweed, was declared a 'restricted area' for all enemy aliens. This prohibition included all of Haddingtonshire and meant that all those so defined were not allowed to reside there.[64] On the same day police officers suddenly appeared at the doorstep of Klaus's flat in the Hardgate and arrested him. He was marched to the police station and detained overnight pending his transfer to a detention camp the following day.

The next day Doddie was granted permission by his commanding officer to see what he could do for his friend. He raced across the fields from Amisfield Park to the police station, only to find he was not alone. Word had spread across town that the police had arrested an enemy alien and a large, angry crowd had gathered

---

64 Much of the background research for this section comes from Stefan Manz, 'Civilian Internment in Scotland during the First World War', appearing in Richard Dove (ed), *Totally Un-English: Britain's Internment of Enemy Aliens in two World Wars*, The Yearbook of the Research Centre for German and Austrian Exile Studies, The Netherlands, Vol., 7, 2005.

outside the station waiting for this person to appear. Doddie was surprised to see his younger brother Angus present and already in a state of agitation. A constable informed Doddie that Klaus was being transported to a detention camp being built at Stobs, near Hawick in the Scottish Borders, but before Doddie could obtain any further details the crowd erupted with a roar as the prisoner appeared at the front door of the station.

Doddie could see that the whole affair was carefully arranged. Reporters were present from the local papers. Klaus, surrounded by four policemen, was marched unceremoniously along the street to the nearby train station. This was the moment the sullen crowd had been waiting for. There was a huge release of pent-up anger as the unfortunate Klaus was suddenly held responsible for every atrocity, real or imagined, carried out by his fellow countrymen.[65] Doddie could see expressions of genuine hatred on many faces and right in the middle of the mob he saw Angus, all of 13, yelling and screaming invectives.

Doddie grabbed his younger brother by the collar and pulled him out of the crowd. One withering look of disgust from Doddie to the younger brother was all it took for Angus to start calming down. Unfortunately, dealing with Angus meant that an opportunity to talk to Klaus had been lost, for the prisoner was hastily bundled up the stairs to the platform of Haddington railway station and into a waiting train. The only items he was allowed to carry were in a tiny bundle tucked under his arm.

Doddie was saddened by the whole episode of Klaus's detention. He did not like the way the event had been stage-managed by the authorities and he was particularly upset by the way fellow townsfolk had turned on Klaus with such loathing. Some of the

---

65 Even at this early stage of the war, Allied propaganda was reporting German atrocities being committed in Belgium, including executions of defenceless citizens, the rape of nuns and the bayoneting of babies.

crowd had purchased sausages from him only days earlier. But one of the most disturbing aspects was Angus's reaction. Doddie was shocked at how Angus had delighted in the ill-treatment of Klaus, even though he knew Doddie and Klaus were good friends. But there was little Doddie could do about Angus, or Klaus for that matter, because training back at the army camp had reached a new level of urgency.

The situation in France was going poorly for the Allied troops and the 8th Royal Scots were informed they were desperately needed to stabilise the front. They had to be ready to move at any moment. On Sunday 1 November 1914, the battalion was ordered to leave for France the following day. The time for departure was fixed for the evening, so farewells had to be quickly made. Men criss-crossed the town saying goodbye to their girlfriends or wives, family and friends. There was great excitement too. Many people were convinced that after a short, sharp war the boys would return home victorious in a matter of weeks.

'We'll be back hame by Christmas' were the reassuring words soldiers repeated often and sincerely during the afternoon.

At 17:50 hours the 1,000 men were assembled on the cobblestones of Market Street in full uniform and with all their equipment to march off to war. As light rain started to fall, they were addressed by the local MP, Mr Arthur James Balfour,[66] who wished them 'God speed in the name of friends and neighbours'. Accompanying the statesman were the Provost, George Young, and the Town Council; likewise Major Alexander Brook, the commanding officer of the 8th Royal Scots.

At the close of the address by Mr Balfour, the men, preceded by the pipe band, marched to the railway station, where they

---

66 Arthur James Balfour (1848–1930) was a British Conservative politician and statesman. He served as Prime Minister (1902–1905). At one point or another he was also Leader of the Opposition, Foreign Secretary and First Lord of the Admiralty.

embarked in two detachments an hour and a half apart.[67] Four days later, the 8th Royal Scots arrived on the continent at the port of Le Havre on the SS *Tintoretto*.

The battalion was attached to the 7th Division, which was rushed up to the line to join the rest of the British Expeditionary Force that was fighting desperately to repel a major German offensive, later known as the 1st Battle of Ypres (Nov–Dec 1914). The 100,000 men of Britain's regular volunteer army were facing up to a million German soldiers threatening to break through the British line at any moment. Under these critical circumstances even part-time soldiers were pushed to the front without delay. At least they could point a rifle and shoot!

As Doddie's battalion was rushed up to the firing line, he hastily wrote to his family, 'I feel great and probably will never feel this good again. I'm so fit I think I'll burst. Can't wait to teach the Hun a lesson.' The date on the letter was 11 November 1914.[68]

In the course of a month, the 8th Royal Scots fought three separate battles in quick succession. The combined French and British armies managed to achieve the apparently impossible and halt the previously unstoppable German advance. As Christmas 1914 approached, both sides in the conflict were badly mauled and seriously depleted in numbers. The 8th Royal Scots had lost 40 per cent of its number to death, wounding or capture. Both sides stopped, exhausted and started to dig in.[69] It was then that

---

67 The events of the departure of the 8th Royal Scots are corroborated in W. Forbes Gray & James H. Jamieson, *A Short History of Haddington*, (1986 edition, pp 78-79 by SPA Books, Stevenage, Hertfordshire UK, though originally printed by the East Lothian Antiquarian and Field Naturalist's Society in 1944).

68 The war would drag on four more years to the day, but of course young Doddie would not have known this at the time.

69 Of all the Cranston sons who served in uniform, the record of Doddie is the most difficult to clarify. His individual service record, which would have been crucial in understanding the details of his time in uniform, was destroyed in the Second World War (along with 60 per cent of all service records from the First World War) leaving only his Medal Card, which shows that he served in four separate units during his time in the Army.

Doddie and the 8th Royal Scots Battalion participated in one of the strangest episodes of the Great War, the Christmas Truce of 1914.

On Christmas Eve, British troops in some sectors were astonished to see many Christmas trees with candles and paper lanterns being placed on enemy parapets. Then the Germans began singing carols, which were well known to the British, such as 'O Tannenbaum' and 'Stille Nacht' and both sides started singing them together, but each in their own language. A gradual exchange of communication between some soldiers started, which included junior officers making arrangements for the collection and burial of bodies still lying in no man's land. At one or two points along the front, cautious meetings between enemies commenced. The activities involving the 8th Royal Scots were not as extensive as elsewhere, but one serviceman wrote home about the battalion's experience in a letter which was subsequently published in his local newspaper:

Lance-Corporal Felix Mcnamara, E Coy, 8th Royal Scots, writing from France to his brother in Dalkeith on December 30th, states that his Company were at the time resting at a farm. On Christmas Eve they went into the trenches, where they remained for four days. Their trenches were only 250 yards [230 metres] distant from the enemy and they could hear the Germans singing.

On Christmas Day, shouts of 'A Merry Christmas' could be heard coming from the German lines.

The Royal Scots returned the greeting, and some of them went out and met a party of Germans halfway between the trenches, and shook hands with them. As soon as they returned to their respective lines the fighting went on as usual.[70]

---

70 *Dalkeith Advertiser*, Monday 4 January 1915, with the kind permission of John Duncan, 'Newbattle at War.' (Source: www.freewebs.com/eltoro1960/boysoldier.htm)

On Boxing Day, senior officers on both sides gradually reasserted their authority over the troops and normal trench activities were resumed, which included snipers killing enemy soldiers they had fraternised with only the day before.

In 1914, Ian was still on the reserve list when the newspaper articles reporting on international affairs began to fill him with alarm. In August, just as he feared, diplomacy broke down between nations over the assassination in the Balkans and suddenly Britain was at war with the German Empire and her allies. He had received his call-up notice within 24 hours of war being declared and now he was back in uniform, ready to fight in yet another conflict.

Although Ian lived and worked as a civilian, he was still technically a professional soldier. After joining the colours in 1900 as an 18-year-old, Ian had served with the Queen's Own Cameron Highlanders (Cameron Highlanders) in a number of outposts of the British Empire. When he finally returned home eight years later, he was placed on the 'reserve list', with an obligation to return immediately to the regular army if ever called up.[71]

It had been one of the best summers in living memory and as Ian sat on a train bound for Inverness and the headquarters of the Cameron Highlanders, he was still shocked at how rapidly circumstances had deteriorated.

He had seen active service many times and it had never troubled him before, but this time, he sensed, was different. He had more to leave behind. As the train rumbled north he smiled inwardly as

---

71 After an initial period of service (usually seven years), soldiers of good standing were offered a further seven years on the 'reserve list'. They would be paid well to attend a two-week camp every year as well as the occasional training course.

he recalled how life had progressed over the past few years. He closed his eyes and was back at the asylum gates and it was 1912 once again...

There! That was the noise he had been waiting to hear all afternoon. It was a sound he had heard several times before and had committed to memory. It was the sound of a bicycle chain scraping against the metal guard of a woman's bike. It was quite noticeable and distinct to someone like Ian Cranston whose entire adult life had been devoted to understanding and interpreting the noises and scenes around him. He had been waiting for this particular sound for hours and its arrival signalled the start of an activity he had been planning all day.

Ian had been observing the comings and goings of a young woman employed as a domestic servant at Bangour Asylum in Dechmont, West Lothian, ever since he had secured employment there as a forester in early 1911. There was something about this woman that attracted him.

At 30 years of age, Ian was no stranger to women. He had enjoyed their company in many different parts of the world, but this particular lass struck him as somehow different; not as a casual sexual encounter, but possibly for a more long-term relationship.

Was it because she was fit and healthy, proven by the fact that she peddled 30 minutes or so every day to and from work from the neighbouring town of Bathgate? Was it the strength of character she had shown when caught in a sudden thunderstorm she had arrived bedraggled yet undeterred at the asylum? Was it possibly the fact that when he made some enquiries about her with fellow asylum staff, he was told she not only looked after the residents all day, but then peddled home to look after several family members who were also in desperate need of her care? The consistent message that Ian received about this woman, Agnes Thomson, was that she had a loving, caring character. From his observations, Ian would add a resolute and determined nature to this list. Ian found her physically attractive, her perseverance unflinching and her ever-present cheerful personality charming. As far as Ian was concerned, Agnes shared many of the same traits as his own dear mother Lizzie and this alone made her a serious matrimonial prospect.

She never travelled the main road that most vehicles took to enter the sprawling asylum complex. Instead, Agnes travelled along dirt roads past farms and fields between work and her family's home, entering the asylum through the rear gate. It was here that Ian would spring his trap.

He had been given instructions to plant pines along the back fence of the asylum[72] and each day he tried to finish off near the back gate so he could speak to her. Almost a week passed without Ian catching her, but finally, as he was planting the last few trees for the day, the object of his attention came peddling out of the complex.

'Excuse me miss,' he said as she slowed to exit the asylum, 'but you've got a bad squeak there.' Agnes appeared to have misunderstood him and thought he was pointing to her and not the bicycle.

'I beg your pardon!' she replied indignantly, 'How dare you make personal comments like that.' She angrily started to cycle off.

Ian took a step forward to block her exit and said, 'No, no, nae you lass. I'm talking aboot the bike. It's got a nasty screech and I'd like to fix it.' Agnes blushed, stopped her bike and looked a little shame-faced.

'Oh, sorry aboot the mix up. Aye, certainly you can help me if you like.'

It was only a short step from this clumsy introduction to the two exchanging particulars and then going out with each other. After

---

72 These pine trees planted by Ian Cranston in 1912 still stand today along the side of the now defunct Bangour Asylum.

some months, Agnes took Ian home to meet her parents with whom she lived. Robert Thomson was a railway guard working with North British Railway at the Bathgate station. He was also a man of some military experience and when he was informed of Ian's martial background, he encouraged his daughter to get to know him better.

In February 1913, in front of family and friends at the Thomson home at Sunnybank Cottage, Ian and Agnes were married. Ian's brother Willie came across from Haddington to be best man.

Soon after, Ian arranged for them to move into their own flat at the asylum, where he had now accepted a job indoors as an asylum attendant. It came with a residence. Unfortunately, Agnes had to leave her employment as a domestic as was the custom then when women got married, but it was balanced by the news that she was soon pregnant with their first child. Ian was happy with how matters had developed. He was pleased to be married; thrilled at the prospect of being a father and glad he had secured a relatively well-paid position.

One day, when Ian was relaxing in the living room of their flat, Agnes innocently asked, 'Do you mind the day you stopped me to fix the squeal on my bike?'

'The best move I ever made,' he answered, quite pleased with how well his tactics had worked.

'Well', she said, 'you should know that I had been waiting weeks for you to get up the courage to ask me oot. I even bent the guard on the bike to get you tae notice me.'

Life progressed more or less normally for the new branch of the Cranston family. Agnes gave birth to a baby girl, named Greta, and then to a boy called Alexander just over a year later. Greta mispronounced her brother's name as 'Sauny' instead of 'Sandy'. Both parents thought this was so endearing so 'Sonny' became his nickname.

At the baptism of Greta, Willie came through from Haddington, bringing his violin with him. When much younger, both boys had been taught to play the fiddle, although Ian was never as proficient as Willie. They set themselves up in the front room of their flat in the asylum and played jigs, reels and airs for hours. It was a grand day indeed, especially for the two brothers. They had not played together like this since they were teenagers and although much had happened in the intervening 15 years, both remembered how deep the bond was between them and how much they enjoyed each other's company.

Willie Cranston signed his name on the enlistment form with a flourish. He was determined to be part of any military action the future might bring. In fact, at the age of 30, Willie was looking forward to any change in his life. What he needed most of all was a new direction, because even though he was surrounded by family and friends, at this point in his life he felt utterly alone.

To Willie, it seemed that his childhood had been a confusing memory of a succession of new addresses and Ma giving birth to new babies. He reckoned that the Cranstons must have moved at least eight times during his formative years, never moving far and criss-crossing the river Tyne for reasons which, to his young mind at least, seemed unfathomable.

Now war had been declared and Willie raced off to enlist. A soldier's pay was more constant and much higher than an estate forester, which he had been employed as for the previous three years. On offer was the 'King's Shilling',[73] bed, board, a full stomach and a chance to make a name for himself on the

---

73 By accepting money for the recruit's signature on a document, a legally binding contract had been struck between recruit and government to serve in the army for a specific length of time and obey all lawful commands.

battlefield. How that would impress the Haddington belles! When Willie enlisted he was directed to join the Seaforth Highlanders, which was based at Fort George, Inverness, the unofficial capital of the Scottish Highlands. He found himself in the 7th Battalion of the Seaforth Highlanders and the newly created unit was sent to Aldershot in Surrey, England, to complete basic training. It had been hard, the marching and drilling rigorous, but the atmosphere had been truly exhilarating. Everyone was still excited at the prospect of fighting and confident of an easy victory.

The battalion was billeted among the local inhabitants of nearby Alton and its surroundings for several months. To keep the troops occupied, there were a number of activities organised by the locals, including musical concerts. The English seemed to speak a foreign language and some of their customs were quaint to Willie, but some languages are universal: music and love. As an accomplished violinist, Willie was an expert in the first and experienced in the second.

During one of these concerts, Willie met Martha (Pat) Arnold – a diminutive, slim-waisted 24-year-old farmer's daughter from the neighbouring hamlet of Binsted. What set her apart from the many other local lasses was that Pat was also a very good violinist. William was 30, handsome, cheeky and in the peak of physical health. He had no right to be so happy again, he would chide himself.[74] Imagine his surprise, therefore, when he realised he had strong feelings for Pat. As they played wonderful music together, their all too brief relationship started to grow closer.

Young Angus appeared unchastened following events at the

---

74 William's first wife, Christina Herbertson from Glasgow, had died in 1907 in childbirth; her baby, was stillborn.

police station, his appetite for all things war-related well and truly whetted. Immediately after war was declared, up to 3,000 soldiers from all over Scotland and beyond were quartered around Haddington. They occupied such places as the Corn Exchange, various malting houses, public houses and finally were billeted among the citizens in their private homes.

Early in the war, Amisfield Park, an extensive country estate just to the east of Haddington, was requisitioned by the Army as a training camp for recruits. Wooden huts, which provided accommodation for the Lothians and Border Horse Yeomanry, the Royal Scots and afterwards several other regiments in quick succession, occupied practically the whole of Amisfield Park. The wonderful old mansion nestling in the middle of the estate was converted into lodgings for British Army officers and the old church in Newton Port was transformed into a military hospital.

Military trucks and wagons ferried men and equipment in and out of Haddington every day. There were uniforms, patients, nurses and officers everywhere. It was as if Haddington had become a military garrison and Angus loved every minute of it. He drank in the sights of kilts and khaki uniforms, learning what every stripe and every shoulder insignia meant. He began collecting cap badges and shoulder flashes that he obtained through badgering visiting soldiers, but pride of place were the cap badges of his brothers. He laid them out on the windowsill beside his bed and every time he caught a glance of them they would instantly bring back a flood of memories about each of his brave, heroic brothers.

Whenever possible, Angus would sneak out of the house past the ruins of the 12th-century St Martin's Kirk and across an open field to Amisfield Park. For hours he would sit on the high stone boundary wall hidden behind a tree hoping for a glimpse of his brother Doddie as well as watching raw recruits being turned into soldiers through endless drill exercises. Soon, Angus was able to slope arms, right dress and stand to attention with the same precision as the soldiers he was observing. Occasionally, as he marched home back across the wheat field with a tree limb for a rifle sloped across his left shoulder, the 13-year-old imagined he was already marching along a dusty French road towards the trenches and the fighting.

In the meantime, while he impatiently waited to be old enough to enlist, he had to be satisfied with experiencing life in the army vicariously through his brothers, Ian, Doddie and Willie. As they went off to war one by one in different regiments and different uniforms, Angus had romantic notions of brave Scottish soldiers going off to save civilisation from the barbarous Germans.

Willie was still living at home and when he enlisted in the first days of the war, the family got to say farewell respectfully and quietly in the Cranston flat over breakfast while he finished packing his bag. When it was time to leave, Angus walked proudly alongside his older brother all the way across town to the railway station. But this reserved, understated form of goodbye did not suit Angus's view of how departing soldiers should be treated. He wanted military bands, speeches, parades and cheering crowds of well-wishers lining the street.

In early November, he finally got his wish to see a full military send-off when Doddie and his battalion were issued orders for the front. It was a grand farewell indeed and Angus was overjoyed. The battalion's pipe band was playing marching music; there was bunting, colourful flags, speeches and full-throated 'hurrahs' from the crowd. Angus marched beside his brother again all the way to the station and imagined that he too was in uniform and going off to war. The very thought of being waved off to the battlefield by an adoring public caused Angus to shiver with anticipation.

'If only I was older,' he said to himself. 'If only I was older.'

Within days of his call-up, Ian was shipped over to France along with almost 100,000 British soldiers hastily assembled and named the British Expeditionary Force (BEF). Shortly afterwards, Lance-Corporal John Cranston felt the full might of the German army at Mons in Belgium where the armies of Belgium, France and Britain were forced to continue their retreat. He wrote in his diary:

> And such smells. Horses lying at the side of the road with straw being placed over them and saturated with petroleum, were set alight. Partly skinned sheep lay unburied. No doubt where the Germans were going to have a feed.
>
> Wounded horses moving about, quite close to the roadside. Some of them hardly able to move and still bleeding freely, till some of our veterinary men came up and put an end to their miserable lives. And still our own soldiers lay on the roadsides with a waterproof sheet over them, dead. And I could see fatigue parties digging their graves and paying their last respects to their fallen comrades.[75]

The Battle of the Marne followed, in which the Allied armies somehow managed to halt the German advance against all the odds. A miracle is what the people called it. Then came the lead-up to the largest battle of the war so far, at Ypres in Belgium.[76]

By this time, Ian's battalion had become part of the 1st Division BEF and their task was to hold the ground around the major

75 Extract for the personal war diary of John Buchan Cranston, originals of which are in the possession of Cranston descendants. A transcribed and typed copy has been given to the Highlanders' Museum at Fort George, Inverness, Scotland – the home of the Queen's Own Cameron Highlanders.
76 This was the same battle that Ian's brother Doddie was engaged in, though the two were in different divisions and separated by several kilometres.

railway junction of Ypres at all costs. As their Colonel told them during the briefing before the battle, 'If Ypres falls into German hands, then the war is lost.' Ian wrote the following account of his actions during the battle in his diary:

The following day brought the 22nd October and about 10am the battle started. They seemed to come right through like bees. After letting them have it from a range of 800 yards with difficulty, but could catch glimpses of them through the trees. They came to about 50 yards of us before we retired, as the number we were up against we had no chance and therefore that was the only plan. I fired my last round, having sent 170 rounds into them in half an hour and I just got out of my trench and turned to retire, when I felt my hand struck and two or three holes drilled through my coat on the left side. I got a dressing and bandaged it ...

We lay down at short intervals and poured lead into them but no sooner had you shot the ranks thin, a little while would elapse and again they were coming at you as thick as bees till reinforcements came and we held them there.

Gods [sic] inhumanity to man makes countless thousands mourn.[77] Never were truer words spoken by our national poet and bard Robert Burns, to say that Christians and civilised nations shoot one another down like rabbits. I hope and trust in God that I may never see the same again but to live in peace and goodwill to all men.

The First Battle of Ypres, as it came to be known, cost Ian's battalion more than 500 killed, wounded or missing, out of a complement of less than 1,000 officers and men.[78] With so few

---

77 Correct quote is 'Man's inhumanity to man ...' from *Man was made to mourn: A Dirge*, Robert Burns, 1784.
78 Ian's brother Doddie's 8th Royal Scots battalion also suffered terrible losses in the same battle.

experienced soldiers left, Ian was promoted to full Corporal prior to being shipped back to Britain. It took Ian five months in a London hospital to recover from the gunshot wound to his hand; a wound he insisted was only minor, yet, in truth, was so severe that for a while doctors considered amputation.

Caught up in the fervour and patriotism which gripped Australia after the declaration of war and knowing that his brothers would be enlisting into the British Army back in Scotland, Andrew stood in line outside Victoria Barracks in Sydney's eastern suburb of Paddington waiting to join up. But having made it almost through the entire recruiting process, a doctor checked and rechecked his lungs with a stethoscope and finally declared he had emphysema. His papers were unceremoniously stamped: 'Rejected, Medically Unfit'.

Not knowing what to do next, Andrew was reading through the afternoon Sydney paper when he saw an advertisement for butchers needed at Silvester Brothers located at 71 Regent Street, Redfern.[79] Before 1914, Silvester Bros. was a modest yet growing speciality meat manufacturer concentrating on traditional British and European cold meats such as salami, German sausage and bratwurst. The brothers even employed four butchers from Germany to prepare the more exotic products that the Australian and British butchers did not seem to know how to make, such as the more intricate rolls of salami and wurst. But all that changed in August 1914 when Britain declared war.

The Silvester Brothers, under the War Precautions Act of 1914, dismissed their German workers and were happy to replace them with butchers of 'good British stock' as they described Andrew

79 State Archives of New South Wales.

as soon as they heard his strong Scottish accent. This act of patriotism was for purely economic reasons, as it helped the owners secure some very lucrative contracts with the Department of Defence. Silvester Brothers even stopped calling one of their products the 'German sausage' and renamed it 'Devon' to sound more acceptable to a growing anti-German public.

Back in Scotland, Lizzie's attitude was beginning to change. Was it only a couple of months ago that she had felt something akin to sympathy for that Klaus chap who had been interned in Stobs? Or to be more accurate, had felt sorry for Doddie, whom she knew had taken the arrest of his workmate badly? She could barely describe the mixed emotions with which she had viewed Ian, Doddie and Willie's deployment in the first months of the conflict. Like the rest of the family she had been concerned for the welfare of her boys but was not unduly upset. Cranston men looked good in uniform and never flinched from their duty. If only her Alec had still been alive. Too old to fight surely, but he would have known exactly how to react to the rapidly changing circumstances.

Ian, they told her, was now a corporal (how proud his wife must be), but he was somewhere in England nursing an injury to his hand. 'Slight,' he had reassured everyone who asked, but Lizzie did not like the sound of it. If it was only a minor wound why was he in hospital so long and why could he not come home for a visit? And now, her Doddie was also in France. Perhaps she had been too relaxed in her attitude to these Germanic warmongers.

Lizzie Cranston lifted the large family Bible from the shelf and allowed it to fall open at one of her carefully marked favourite passages. Christmas had come and gone and her boys had not returned home.

1915

The War had become a truly global conflict with fighting occurring in most corners of the world. In Europe, Germany had given up hope of a quick victory in France and instead concentrated her men and material on an offensive campaign to defeat the Russians in the east first. The Germans therefore focused on a defensive strategy along the Western Front, strengthening their trench lines, while the Allies mounted several costly and ultimately futile attempts to break through the German lines. While the War was still one of movement and countermovement elsewhere, all along the Western Front it had already turned into a stalemate.

Lizzie Cranston was perplexed and unhappy. The victory over the villainous Germans that had been promised before Christmas had not materialised. The boys of the Cranston family who had been so close were now scattered God knows where and the official censors seemed to make it their business to keep the likes of her uninformed.

Some things she did understand only too well, however: three of her sons were in the thick of the fighting somewhere on the continent and others seemed set to join the colours some time soon. Those left at home had to grow up fast and assume an ever increasing responsibility. Sometimes she felt the family only told her what they wanted her to know while at other times she seemed to forget what they had said. There was more than one set of censors at work in the life of Lizzie Cranston.

Of one thing, however, she was certain. The British Empire was the most magnificent that had ever existed, industrially, militarily and morally; and for that they had to thank the old Queen. Victoria had been the Empress of India and ruler over most of the civilised world, the bits that mattered anyway, and any notion of defeat at the hand of the barbarous Huns was unthinkable. But why was it taking so long?

Thoughts of the Empire made her think somewhat guiltily of that branch of the family now in Australia. Her daughter Agnes wrote faithfully to several members of the family, including of course her mother. Mary usually read these letters to Lizzie, whose eyesight was not up to the task. Lizzie knew that she should reply, but the effort was getting beyond her. She was comforted by reports that Agnes, husband John and her brother Andrew were flourishing.

Things were happening to the Cranstons wherever they lived and Angus, who knew he was the last Cranston male in line to serve, was also experiencing significant life changes. In 1915, he left school when he turned 14, as was normal in the family. He took a big step towards becoming a grown-up, spending the next year working as a shop boy, after which he signed up to become a plumber's apprentice. It was the war and more precisely the exploits of his older brothers that most exercised his mind, however.

When the older brothers returned to Scotland on infrequent home leave, Angus was eager to hear what life was like at the front. He greedily devoured every piece of information he could extract from his soldier brothers. Once, when Ian finally visited home after spending months recovering from his gunshot wound to his hand, he told his younger brothers, 'The first time I was in the line, waiting for the call to go o'wer the bags[80], I was so scared I thought my bowels would turn to water. Then a piper started playing doon the line and suddenly I wanted tae get at the enemy right away. When they played the bagpipes, I felt invincible.'

Angus easily imagined he was in the trench instead of his brother and it was he, not Ian, who heard the piper as he crossed no man's land to kill as many Germans as he could.

Progress on the Western Front may have been indecisive, but for one more member of the Cranston family, it was time to act. It was 1 March 1915 and this was the day that James Cranston was leaving home to join the army.[81] Jimmy had been born in Newton Port, Haddington 28 years previously and although he had moved with the family many times as a child and young man, home was now in Court Street some 200 metres from where it had all began.

He stood at the front door of his flat two flights of steps above the busy street below. He turned and gave each of his four children a kiss and then a hug. Elizabeth (usually called Mae) was seven and named after her grandmother, Lizzie. Next was Alexander, followed by Agnes. She was only three and although too young to know, was named after Jim's sister who had left for Australia the same year she was born. Finally, there was little Jimmy, barely one

---

80 While the expression 'over the top' was used commonly throughout the British army, soldiers in Scottish regiments preferred to say 'o'wer the bags'.

81 Much of the background material for this section is derived from James Cranston's Service Record, obtained from the National Archives, Kew.

year old. When the father had finished giving the baby a kiss, he handed the child back to his mother, Annie, whom he had married in 1908.

With four children under seven years of age and living in a flat overlooking busy Court Street in the market town of Haddington, there was constant noise and hectic activity in the household. And yet everyone thrived on it. More importantly there was genuine love between James and Annie that had grown over the preceding eight years. They had met in Musselburgh in 1907, shortly before James had finished his stonemason's apprenticeship and just over a year later they were married with a child.

In 1911, the young family had returned to Haddington and by the next year had moved into the flat in Court Street. When war was declared in August 1914, Jimmy held off joining as he had a young family to take care of, but he could not resist the patriotic urge for long.

As he stood on the landing outside the front door to his flat he kissed Annie once again and gave her a long embrace.

'I still dinnae ken why you're doing this. You don't have tae go. I wish you'd stay at hame wi' me tae help bring up the bairns,' she pleaded.

Jimmy looked at her sympathetically and replied, 'Annie lass, we've had this talk before. I couldna look my brithers in the e'e if I didnae jine up. It's my duty to go and fight and I'll no' be hidin' behind my wife's apron.'

Ever since his brother Ian had been shot in November the previous year, Jimmy had been wrestling with his conscience. It was one thing to wave able-bodied brothers off to war, but it was another matter altogether to see them come home wounded and still stand idly by.

He kept reminding himself that after years of working with stone he was the fittest and strongest of all the Cranston sons.

He was tall, had a chiselled chin, luxurious moustache, powerful biceps and a barrel chest. If anyone should be fighting for God, King and Country, it should be him. Barely 100 metres from his tenement he entered a doorway at the town hall with a sign saying 'Recruiting Office' above it. Fifteen minutes later after a medical examination and the acceptance of the 'Kings Shilling', he was no longer a civilian; he was a soldier in the British Army.

By this stage of the war, engineers to assist with trench construction and battlefield infrastructure were crucial. Jimmy may have wanted to join an infantry regiment like the majority of his brothers before him, but the army had other ideas. He was sworn in as a Royal Engineer, given the service number 69417, and sent immediately by rail to the headquarters of the Royal Engineers in Chatham, Kent.

Because of interrupted train timetables, it took Jim two days to appear at Chatham. When he presented his papers to the duty officer at the front gate, he was admonished for his tardiness and then directed to report to the main office to await further orders.

When Jimmy walked into the main office, it was a hive of activity.[82] On one side of a long counter stood new recruits like him, jostling to be served by a smaller number of army orderlies on the other side of the counter. After what seemed an eternity, Jimmy finally managed to get to the front of the somewhat disorderly queue and handed over his papers to a clerk, who took a short time to inspect the documents with his practised eye. He then checked Jimmy's papers against another list of names he was holding on a clipboard in his left hand.

'You're late,' he barked at James, 'you should have reported here yesterday.'

'I'm sorry,' Jimmy replied, 'the trains from Scotland were

---

82 At this stage of the war, new recruits into the Royal Engineers were arriving at Chatham at the rate of almost 1,000 a week.

delayed. We had to wait at Gretna Green for half a day.'[83] The official had long since lost interest. He flicked through the sheets of papers on his clipboard one more time and said, 'It seems like the 127th is still below quota in stonemasons.[84] They're already part way through their training prior to going over to France in a few months. Have you had any military experience?' he asked.

'No,' replied Jimmy, 'but many of my brothers have taken the colours, as did my late father.' The clerk did not care about the answer; he had already made up his mind. The orderly made a handwritten annotation on his papers and then stamped the papers with the official seal of the Royal Engineers Corps. He gave Jim some last words of advice, 'Right it is then, the 127th Field Company. They're training near Seaford, south of here in Sussex. Here are your travel papers, but I wouldn't dawdle on your way there like you did on your way here from Scotland.'

'But I didn't—' Jimmy started to protest. However, the clerk was not interested. He cut him off by saying, 'No excuses. Get your arse over to the Quartermaster's store immediately and get kitted out without delay. You're due on the afternoon train to Seaford tomorrow where you'll have to shake a leg to catch up with the rest of the unit.'

At the Quartermaster's stores it was the same thing: hurry up and wait. There were dozens of other men dressed in civilian attire also waiting to be issued with their uniforms. Jimmy joined the queue and was eventually issued with as much of his uniform as was available at the time. It included underwear, shaving kit,

---

83 Two months later, on 22 May 1915, a troop train carrying over 500 soldiers from the Royal Scots heading for Gallipoli collided with a local passenger train, which was then struck by an express train less than a minute later. A fire started that engulfed the three trains in the original crash, plus two goods trains standing on nearby sidings. Over 230 passengers (mainly soldiers) were killed and another 250 injured. It remains to this day the worst rail disaster in the United Kingdom in terms of loss of life.

84 127th Field Company, Royal Engineers.

army boots, socks, toothbrush, jacket, braces, puttees,[85] trousers, cap, kit bag, complete web equipment, entrenching tool and handle, water bottle, cup, mess tin, greatcoat, buttons, badges and finally one shirt. All had to be signed for. James was assured that he would receive his full complement of gear, which included his all-important rifle, before he saw any real fighting. He quickly changed into as much of his uniform as he could and stuffed everything else into the kit bag provided.

He spent a quiet evening staying in barracks and writing a letter of reassurance home to Annie. After an uneventful morning walking around the headquarters of the Royal Engineers and familiarising himself with the history of this illustrious corps, he boarded the scheduled train in the afternoon bound for the seaside town of Seaford.

Three hours later he and other new recruits were standing on the railway platform at their destination. Jimmy could smell the salt air, but could not see the ocean from where he stood. Finally, a corporal arrived at the station and ordered everyone into line. They were then marched two by two out of the unpretentious seaside town and into the hills behind to a small village called Alfriston. As they crested a low rise in the gravel road, Jimmy could see a huge and hastily constructed army camp laid out before him.

The camp was designed to accommodate thousands and when they entered the front gates at Alfriston, Jim saw a sign stating '22 Div HQ'.[86] As he marched towards the grassed central parade ground, Jim saw that there were many bell tents and a few wooden huts stretching out as far as the eye could see. The Corporal told

---

85 From Hindi, long, narrow strips of cloth wound tightly round each lower leg from ankle to knee.

86 174th Field Company, Royal Engineers was attached, along with 5 other companies of Royal Engineers, to 22nd Division. The division consisted of 15 infantry battalions, with supporting units of artillery, transport, medical corps and engineers. At full strength, there would have been approximately 20,000 soldiers in this division.

the group to wait on the parade ground for a representative from their respective units to collect them.

Sergeant Harry Hack, Royal Engineer, took one look at Jimmy standing on the parade ground with other late replacements and instantly liked what he saw. Here was a man the same age as himself who was tall, confident and looked as fit as a prize-fighter. The Sergeant approached Jimmy and introduced himself. The handshake from the replacement he had been sent to collect was firm and his hands were rough from hard work, both attributes the Sergeant admired. What Harry Hack liked best about this man was that he looked Harry directly in the eye like a man who had earned the respect of all around him. The more he saw, the more impressed he was. As he escorted James Cranston across the immense tent city to the encampment of the 127th Field Company of Royal Engineers, Sergeant Hack explained how he would be his drill instructor from tomorrow. 'With your arrival, we're almost at full complement now.'[87] Pointing to a small bell tent, one of thousands erected in neat rows, he continued, 'You'll stay here for the moment.'

When James pulled back the flap of the tent, six other faces looked up and moaned. One person spoke for the group when he looked past Jimmy's shoulder and said, 'Does he have to sleep here, Sergeant?' The answer was curt. 'Yes, it's only temporary; now make some space, lads.'

For the next week, James Cranston and the few other late replacements with him learnt how to slope arms, march, left wheel, salute and right dress. Jimmy quickly fell into the routine of training which was pinned to the Company's noticeboard for all to see, and obey. The printed instructions read:

---

87 At full strength a Field Company of Royal Engineers consisted of 5 Officers, 23 Non-Commissioned Officers and 186 other ranks. Most soldiers were selected because of their specialised trade or qualification, including carpenters, surveyors, masons, welders, painters, bricklayers, veterinarians, wheelwrights and blacksmiths.

06:30 hrs	Reveille. After rising, soldiers will fold their beds; clean their tents, wash, and hang up accoutrements.
07:45 hrs	Bugle call; 15 minutes to dress before breakfast.
08:00 hrs	Breakfast in the Barracks. After breakfast, prepare for morning inspection.
010:00 hrs	Morning Parade. After parade, soldiers will be assigned duties such as fatigues, punishment parade or training and drill.
11:45 hrs	Bugle call; 15 minutes to Lunch.
12:00 hrs	Lunch. After lunch, soldiers to continue with more drill or fatigues.
16:45 hrs	Bugle call; 15 minutes to Dinner.
17:00 hrs	Dinner. After the meal, more training, lectures and sometimes free time for letter writing and repair of personal equipment.
19:00 hrs	Roll Call
19:30 hrs	Back to sleeping accommodation.
20:00 hrs	Tattoo

For Jimmy, this timetable was similar to the daily work schedule he was used to as a tradesman back in Scotland, though the work was not as arduous as that of a stonemason. Sergeant Hack was impressed by how seamlessly Sapper[88] James Cranston had fallen

---

88 Soldiers without rank are called Sappers in the Royal Engineers.

in line with army routine, as well as how quickly he had picked up military drill.

The food was generally acceptable, but one incident Jim witnessed caused him some concern. One day when he and the rest of his training unit were lining up for a meal at the mess hall after a hard day's fatigues, a sergeant from one of the other regiments saw that the cook was serving the meal dressed only in his vest[89] and khaki trousers. Appalled at the gross breach of standing orders for dress, the Sergeant stormed up to the cook and said, 'Put your shirt on man, you're a disgrace!' To which the cook said in a heavy cockney accent, 'I don't 'ave it at the moment Sarg'.

'Why not man?' insisted the Sergeant. The cook replied, ''cause I'm using it to boil this 'ere pudding!' At which point he lifted the lid on a large pot to reveal his shirt wrapped around a large lump of something mysterious boiling away in the steaming water. Needless to say, Jimmy and quite a few other soldiers chose not to have any pudding that night. The next phase of training was route marches in full kit up and over nearby hills. It was back-breaking work and several of the new recruits needed to rest regularly in order to get their breath back.

But not Sapper Cranston. He was strong and fit and looked comfortable marching over hill and dale, even with the heavy weight of equipment and rifle, which had now been issued to him. There was only one time he ever stopped and that was at the top of a steep hill behind Alfriston. But he had not halted to catch his breath. He had chosen this place to allow the stragglers to catch up because it offered the most scenic view overlooking the whole valley.

In a few months' time, when the division would have finished training and be relocating to the trenches in France, Sgt Hack

89 Vest is the term used in the United Kingdom for what is known as a singlet in Australia and Asia.

was determined that Sapper Cranston should receive the first of what would hopefully be many promotions. As far as Hack was concerned, James Cranston was a natural soldier and promotion to Lance Corporal would confirm his assessment.

Jimmy wrote a letter home to Annie, which she shared with her mother-in-law Lizzie. When she read that there were too many soldiers crowded into a poorly ventilated tent, Lizzie was concerned.

'I should go doon there and clean the place for them,' she said. 'Cleanliness is next to godliness, you ken, and if he's living in unhealthy surroundings, he could catch all sorts o' terrible things.'

How right she was. Over the next few days, some of the soldiers complained about the cramped accommodation in the bell tent where Jimmy and the six other soldiers slept. There was one soldier in particular who had been coughing and spluttering every night for weeks, keeping everyone awake. Soon, several soldiers felt run down, even fatigued, but James in particular felt even worse. He showed signs of having developed a chest infection, evidenced by a hacking cough.

The following week, Jimmy and the other late replacements started entrenchment training in the hills behind the camp. It was hard work digging a trench down to the regulation depth and reinforcing the sides with wooden planks to prevent collapse. It was while the soldiers had been conducting these training exercises for several days that Sapper James Cranston's health took a sudden turn for the worse. His persistent cough turned into gasps for air and he appeared to have developed a fever. Sergeant Hack ordered him to report immediately to the company's medical officer. Jim had been in the army for only four weeks when the medical orderly diagnosed what he thought was a bout of bronchitis and transferred him to a nearby hospital in Seaford to recover. However, after another three weeks, his condition had not improved. The doctors decided to conduct further tests, including taking sputum samples for culture analysis. A month later and still in hospital, Jimmy's life fell apart.

'Pulmonary tuberculosis,' announced a rather brusque doctor whom he was seeing for the first time. 'That's TB,' he explained, a little more kindly. 'We're working hard on it, but to date there's no known cure. You'll have to stay here meantime, but I'm recommending that you be discharged from the army as medically unfit.' Jim was completely devastated. How could he go from being a healthy recruit to a terminally ill invalid in such a short time? he asked.

The doctor responded, 'There are aggressive strains of tuberculosis you know. Some people can succumb within two weeks! From what I've been told you were lucky to last as long as you did in the confines of an overcrowded tent, with the fellow next to you already infected.' By the time Jimmy had digested the news, the doctor was already talking to his next patient.

Matters moved swiftly from then on. Within weeks he had to hand back most of his equipment and his documentation was stamped 'Discharged under Kings Regulation 392 (xvi)'.[90] Jim was allowed to keep his uniform and given a travel pass for the train journey home to Scotland.

Out of four months in the British Army, Sapper James Cranston had spent only one month on active duty. The rest of his service had been spent in a military hospital succumbing to a terminal illness.

On the night before Jimmy was due to depart Sussex and his Royal Engineer battalion for good, Sergeant Hack came to see him in hospital. It was a sad time for both men. Harry Hack had grown fond of Jimmy and was sorry to see a promising career in the army cut short by disease. They shook hands and wished each

---

90 Medically unfit for further service.

other well, even though both knew it was only a matter of time before one of them would be dead.[91]

While James was discharged from the army with an incurable disease, his brothers in France had already suffered many close shaves with death. It had been a hellish winter in the trenches and spring was offering no respite from ever-present danger. The surreal experience of the 'Christmas Truce' was soon forgotten and for Doddie the real war resumed a short time later when he and the rest of his battalion went into battle again. This time at Neuve Chapelle, between March and April 1915, then the Battle of Aubers in early May 1915, and finally the Battle of Festubert in late May 1915.

The Battle of Festubert, near the French supply centre of Béthune, resulted in 4,123 casualties[92] in the 7th Division in a futile attempt to break through German lines. But it was what happened to Doddie's 8th Royal Scots that many people found shocking.

During the battle, the battalion managed to take the front line of the German trenches, but then found themselves pinned down by accurate, heavy and deadly retaliatory German shellfire. The British soldiers could neither advance nor retreat. The troops had to stay put and hope that the enemy bombardment would abate, but for two days it did not. At one point the artillery barrage

---

91 What neither party knew was that Harry Hack would also die prematurely. Sergeant Harry J. Hack, service number 65571, 127th Field Company, Royal Engineers, went to France with the 22nd Division in September 1915. The division was then drafted to Salonika, Greece in December 1915, where Sgt Hack died on Monday, 23 October 1916. He left a widow, Emily, and two small children in Clevedon, Somerset. His name is commemorated on the Doiran Memorial, Greece. Both Harry Hack and James Cranston were 29 years of age when they died. (Source: Commonwealth War Graves Commission: www.cwgc.org and Clevedon Civic Society: www.clevedon-civic-society.org.uk/Content/Records/Military/WW1Casualtiesf.html)
92 Missing, wounded, taken prisoner or dead.

was coming in at the rate of one shell every 10 seconds. Then on the morning of the second day, the rains came to turn an already terrible situation into a catastrophe.

As the trenches were shattered by high-explosive shells, the walls collapsed, turning walkways and dugouts into choking, drowning mud. With the incessant sounds of fury all around, shrapnel and body parts flying about and men screaming in agony, many soldiers went temporarily insane.

When the Germans finally ceased their artillery bombardment and the British troops could be relieved overnight, the senior officers were appalled by the number of soldiers who they discovered were suffering from a newly recognised phenomenon called 'trench hardships'.[93] Lance-Corporal George Cranston was among them.

While Doddie was sent to the rear to recuperate, his oldest brother was just about to enter the fray. Sandy was not surprised when he was finally mobilised in June of 1915. As a Reservist in the Royal Scots he had expected a much earlier call. His brothers Ian and Doddie had been mobilised at the very onset of war and both had already received serious setbacks. However, some Reservists had been held back in the mistaken belief that the conflict would be short-lived. That was about to change. Sandy had fully expected to continue as an infantryman in the Royal Scots, but instead was reassigned to the Royal Engineers, who at the time badly needed skilled workers.

Sandy was specifically involved in maintaining the horse-drawn transport of the division, which, despite increased mechanisation still carried most of the equipment and supplies for the soldiers. Wagons and carriages needed wheels and he was an expert at making and repairing wooden spoke wheels.

---

93 The description 'trench hardships' used to describe soldiers suffering from nervous collapse was itself replaced a short time later by the expression 'shell shock'.

Roseanna (Annie) was understandably reticent about her husband going to war and was only too aware of the possible dangers but Sandy tried to allay her fears.

'I'm telling you, lass, dinnae worry your head aboot something that will never happen. I'm daeing the same job as I hae done in Musselburgh for years, only wi' a uniform on.' And so he left for the front.

While recuperating in England, Ian reflected on the events that had taken place since war had begun and especially about his impending return to the front. The last entry in his diary summed up his thoughts at the time.

> Now that you have got my story, you ask me if I'd like to go back to the front again. I say <u>No</u>. I will certainly go back if ordered to, but I will never volunteer. But being with the regular army, I will go where I am sent.[94]

When he was finally ready to rejoin his unit Ian was surprised to learn he had been reassigned to the newly formed and inexperienced 7th Battalion Queen's Own Cameron Highlanders. He could hardly have looked forward to this turn of events but accepted it with professional equanimity.

At least he would be reunited with his old company commander Major Sandilands who had been promoted to Lieutenant-Colonel and given command of the raw battalion. It was he who had personally requested Ian's transfer to help him get the men into shape. Ian must have been a welcome addition to the battalion's

94 Ian Cranston stopped writing his personal diary at this point in the war.

ranks as he was a battle-hardened veteran. In July 1915, the 7th Battalion, now attached to the 51st (Highland) Division, finished its training in England and was hurriedly shipped off to France where, just over a month later, it was thrown into the Battle of Loos.[95]

Tens of thousands of men went 'ower the bags' as the mainly Scottish battalions in this offence attacked enemy fortifications in and around the German-occupied town of Loos.[96] The 7th Cameron Highlanders and three other regiments were given the task of attacking and securing a strategically important elevated location beyond the town of Loos, known as Hill 70. It was the regiment's first engagement with the enemy in the war, but Ian's sixth.

By early morning the British troops had managed to capture their objective, but so many men had already lost their lives in achieving this asset, their grip on the hill was tenuous. For the rest of the day, these battered battalions managed to fight off wave after wave of ferocious German counterattacks. The conflict descended into hand-to-hand struggles, where men fought each other at such close quarters that their rifles were useless. The soldiers used bayonets, pistols, clubs and even rocks against each other.

In Corporal Cranston's regiment, a sergeant by the name of Lamb planted the Battalion flag and stood his ground to defend the position. Lamb put down his rifle and picked up the flag to wave it around his head, deliberately drawing fire to himself. With complete disregard for his own safety he screamed out, 'Rally to me boys!'[97]

---

95 Loos is a small French town near the Belgium border in northern France.

96 The incidents and actions involving the 7th QOCH in France are derived from the official history of the 7th Queen's Own Cameron Highlanders, written by Colonel J.W. Sandilands CB., CMG., DSO., Eneas Mackay, Stirling, Scotland, 1922 (accessed at http://archive.org/deta ils/7thbattcameron00sanduoft).

97 The flag, which consisted of a yellow background representing the 51st Division with a patch of Cameron tartan taken from an old kilt sewn on it, now hangs in pride of place in the Highlanders' Museum at Fort George, Inverness.

Cranston brought many young and frightened raw recruits to Sgt Lamb's side and placed them under his command while waiting for the arrival of the battalion's commanding officer. In those first desperate hours, Sgt Lamb, Corporal Cranston and a few dozen soldiers from various units managed to withstand several overwhelming enemy charges.

When Lieutenant-Colonel Sandilands and other troops finally managed to get through the mayhem to stand under the banner, the only weapon he had was a Browning pistol, but he had run out of ammunition. While men screamed, fought valiantly and died around him he stood calmly pointing his officer's cane at the enemy as they emerged through the gun smoke. Corporal Cranston positioned himself close to his Colonel and became his shield against the enemy.

Days later, when the battered battalion was finally withdrawn from the lines, the pitifully under-strength unit straggled into a small French town, broken and bedraggled. The town happened to be occupied by one of the Cameron Highlander's sister battalions. The men billeted in the town had already heard of the incredible bravery of these men and spontaneously arranged to have them piped through the town as heroes.

The highlight of the episode, which Ian would never forget, was when the Colonel in charge of the other Scottish battalion came out from his headquarters and stood on the porch beside the road. He straightened his back and saluted every man from the depleted battalion as they passed him. All along the town road, Scottish soldiers came out of their billets, their cafés and their sleeping quarters and stood in silence. Not a word was said. There was no clapping or cheering from the men, just soldiers silently paying their respects to members of a fellow battalion. The soldiers may have been silent, but there was one sound that filled the air that day as the men of the 7th Cameron Highlanders marched through the town: it was the sound of bagpipes. By the time the battered battalion passed out of town they had regained their spirit and a spring in their step.

For his actions in the battle, Sgt Lamb was awarded the Distinguished Conduct Medal (DCM), then the second-highest award for bravery in the British Army. Lieutenant-Colonel Sandilands was also decorated. Corporal Cranston's gallant action was recognised by way of a promotion that came with a much higher rate of pay.

Willie and the Seaforth Highlanders were anxious to see action after training on the Surrey plains for almost six months, even though reports from the front indicated the fighting would be much tougher than anticipated.

The 7th Seaforth Highlanders, along with another dozen mainly Scottish battalions were assembled into the 20,000-man 9th Division of the British Army. The soldiers were given their own distinctive divisional shoulder badge in the form of a stylised Scottish thistle and proudly became known as 9th (Scottish) Division. Willie thought it was strange though, when he learnt that a Scottish division included a few thousand South African troops as well.

In mid-May the division had landed in the northern French port of Boulogne, where train after train took Willie and all the other soldiers of his division from the port to Béthune, the railway station nearest the British front. It was all very exciting for Willie. This is what he had signed up for. It was hot and dusty when the 7th Seaforth Highlanders finally assembled outside Béthune station for the long march in full kit and uniform the 30 kilometres or so up the dirt roads to the front. The Colonel was determined to impress the civilians and other military units with how well turned out they were.

At this point in the war, the French citizens had seen many Scottish soldiers, so the image of men wearing kilts was no longer exotic. Yet it was still a very colourful sight and crowds gathered whenever they passed through a village. There was something magnetically appealing about the sight of 1,000 men with their Mackenzie tartan kilts rhythmically swaying in unison to the sound of Scottish pipes as they marched along. The Scottish soldiers had not seen French mademoiselles before and these were indeed exotic! William Cranston felt good about life.

While it may have been novel for a time to be part of an infantry unit that included no other local lads from Haddington, Willie did start to miss his daily contact with friends from his home town. He was thus delighted when suddenly a few metres ahead of him one morning he spotted Davie Moran from the Cockles, a small collection of houses a couple of kilometres beyond the town's boundary. Amidst the backslapping and squeals of delight Willie had been able to ignore the fact that Davie had never been much of a pal of his during their school years at the Knox Institute. In fact the only memories he had of him in those far-off days was Davie's unfortunate facial tic, which caused him to squint involuntarily and frequently. The cruel school children had called him 'Blinky' and the name had stuck with him into adulthood.

Davie had been different, in that he came from the country and was considered 'thick' by the boys from the town. He was therefore fair game for a bit of teasing and more. Now, years later, he was thankfully blessed with a generous nature and past differences were rapidly forgotten. From out of nowhere, this country bumpkin had also developed a more than passable singing voice. In short, he had become the perfect companion.

And in this engagement, companionship would be a necessity.

As they waited their turn to participate in what they were assured would be a glorious slaughtering of the enemy at the Battle of Loos, the friends laughed, sang and talked of good times back in Haddington.

While he was listening to Davie, Willie found his thoughts occasionally returning to the young violinist, Pat, he had fallen for so heavily during basic training. He wrote to her regularly and was amazed to receive a reply every month or so when his name was called out during mail call. He realised his strong feelings were turning into love. Willie made plans to visit Pat again when next on home leave, along with a quick trip north to Scotland to say hello to Ma and the family, but in the meantime, Willie and Davie waited to take part in yet another great offensive of the war – the Battle of Loos.

From September into October 1915, over 200,000 British soldiers threw themselves at well-prepared German trenches manned by well-trained German soldiers. The 9th Division was given the task of securing a very well-defended fortification, known as the Hohenzollern Redoubt.[98]

Against great odds and after sustaining high casualties, the division captured the redoubt briefly on the morning of the 25 September 1915, but could only hold it for a few days. The battalion was badly depleted of men who were needed elsewhere and a German counter-offensive swept it out of the Hohenzollern Redoubt and back to the division's original starting positions.[99]

Another large-scale attack against the same feature was launched a week later with even greater losses, but thankfully by

---

98 Hohenzollern was the name of the German royal family at the time of the Great War. Uncannily, this was the same location that William's brother, Ian, and his battalion of Cameron Highlanders, would be assigned to a few months later.

99 While Willie was taking part in the struggle for Hohenzollern Redoubt, less than 5km away Ian Cranston and his fellow soldiers from the 15th Scottish Division were fighting for their lives, and creating a legend, on Hill 70.

then the 7th Seaforth Highlanders had been withdrawn from the line. The Germans would not allow this strongpoint to fall into British hands again for another three years.

And the result of the Battle of Loos? No gains whatsoever. The cost? Sixty thousand British casualties, of which almost 8,000 lost their lives. One of those was Davie 'Blinky' Moran who was struck down by a bullet in the throat as he crouched by Willie's side.

As blood spurted from Davie's carotid artery in thick crimson sprays, Willie knew his friend was dying. Quickly the flow lost its strength and turned into a trickle, at which time his friend quietly died. Just before his pal passed away, Willie happened to notice that Davie's nervous tic had completely disappeared leaving his face round, symmetrical and totally at ease.

The Battle of Loos had been a shocking initiation for Willie and the rest of the British Army into the real horror of warfare. Willie's own commanding officer, Lieutenant-Colonel Gaisford, had been shot dead while crossing no man's land, the victim, it was said, of a stray German bullet. The previously happy-go-lucky Willie somehow survived that battle, even though 150 of his close comrades in the battalion had not.

Jimmy Cranston returned to Haddington after his discharge from hospital in Sussex a changed man, but the town that he had left a few months earlier had also changed in his absence. It had taken on the appearance of a busy garrison town with strangers, mostly in uniform, scurrying around the streets at all hours of the day and night. And bizarrely, right in front of his Court Street tenement, something reminiscent of a giant henhouse had sprung up in his absence: its mission was to act as a social centre for the transient troops.

A snatched conversation as he slowly passed the building on his way back to his flat proved a painful reminder to Jimmy of a life he would never experience again. Several soldiers were lounging around the construction which had been hastily erected earlier in the year. They seemed not to notice Jimmy. Instead, they were intent only on smoking cigarettes and discussing the evening's attractions, which were displayed on a noticeboard near the entrance. It seemed the comedy acts listed on the board were of little interest to the men. What they wanted was another opportunity to dance with the young women who were operating the hut.

'I'd love to wrap my arms around one of them women again,' said the first soldier, 'I miss my wife so much.'

'Aye,' said the second man in uniform, 'pity we can only dance with them.'

'That's not what "Slippery" Stevenson says back at the camp,' said the third soldier.

'Och, don't believe a damn word that liar says. He's more likely to be shaggin' sheep than having his way with these lovelies.' At which point there was general agreement between the three men.

Jimmy walked slowly, painfully, achingly up the stairs to the landing in front of his flat. He unlocked the door and found Annie standing inside staring strangely at him. 'I'm sorry lass, I've let you a' doon,' said Jimmy, still struggling to find both his words and his breath. Annie did not say a word. She was in shock. The man in front of her was nothing like the fit, strong husband she had said goodbye to only four months earlier.

Inside the flat, in the absence of their children, the couple were alone. Having rested on the couch, Jimmy continued, 'If only the army had given me anither three months, I could ha'e jined up wi' them in France.' It was clear that neither he nor Annie believed a word of it. 'Unfit for active service. Or ony kind o' service at a" – a hint of a tear welled up in the once strong man's eyes. Annie felt she could not have coped with him crying. 'It says it right here!' Jimmy waved the official looking papers in the direction of his wife. 'Nae bloody use to man or beast.' It was the day after his 28th birthday.

Annie thought of the difficult conversation she had had with the chaplain some 10 days earlier. The army had accepted that the disease had been contracted while on active service and he was to be discharged on 2 July. The chaplain was an old man and clearly not up to the task of consoling a grieving wife. Not that King George himself could have made her feel any better as she slowly digested the implication of his message.

'It's the air,' she announced firmly. 'The chaplain says that everybody kens that East Lothian air is the best cure gaun for...' – she hesitated, uncertain how much her husband had been told – '...for your complaint,' she finished lamely.

The now ex-Sapper Cranston could barely look at his wife. 'There's quite a few gravestones owerby,' he said, nodding in the direction of the churchyard, 'that wid say different.'

Jimmy Cranston's time in the army was over, four months and a day after it had begun and without having fired a shot in anger. But his real battle had only just begun. Despite their lack of medical knowledge and the euphemisms with which they chose to communicate with each other, Jimmy and Annie both knew the score. James Buchan Cranston had been sent home to die.

To change the subject, Jimmy asked about the rather flimsy construction he had passed outside on his way from the railway station.

'They ca' it the Guild Hut,' she explained. 'It belongs to the Kirk's Young Men's Guild, but as you can imagine there's very few o' them aboot these days and the women folk hae the rinnin o' it. Your ma and that Fairgrieve woman are up here twa or three days a week, dishing oot teas and things. I sometimes gie them a bit o' a hand mysel' when the bairns are settled doon.'

The mention of his mother's name allowed Jimmy to ask, 'How is Ma copin' wi' a' this?' Annie was vaguely aware of how easy it was becoming to tell her husband half-truths. 'Ma's just fine, revelling in a' the company, I think she would miss a' the excitement if things ever die doon.'

In fact it was very hard to decide how Lizzie was actually doing. Nobody could get her to sit still long enough to find out. Many people around the town, residents and strangers alike, were delighted to have Lizzie on their side and Annie herself was grateful for the help she received from her mother-in-law. Yet, behind Lizzie's carefully constructed mask, Annie knew her mother-in-law was devastated by Jimmy's complaint. It was the first proof that the Cranston family would not go through the war unscathed. And Lizzie knew exactly who to blame. The Germans were as responsible for her son's condition just as surely as if one of them had stuck a bayonet into his innards.

'She must be really disappointed, in me,' Jimmy remarked as Annie helped him, exhausted after the long train journey home, into bed, 'me barely fit to wipe my erse while my brithers are oot there in France makin' their mark.'

Annie seized the opportunity to lighten the conversation. 'We a' ken you were the first Cranston tae mak' your mark,' she grinned impishly...

The year 1908 had been, until this year, the most important in Jimmy's young life. Everything had promised so much and started so well, perhaps too well, with the youthful Jimmy madly in love with an older woman. Annie was two years older and equally smitten, so it was no surprise when daughter Elizabeth (as she was to become) started to make her tiny presence felt.

Having a child out of wedlock was considered to be the most unpardonable of offences if the older generation was to be believed and yet it was hardly a new phenomenon. Both sets of parents raged a little when Annie announced that she was with child, but the biggest disaster seemed to be that the young couple's naivety and embarrassment meant that they had left off sharing their news until it was too late to arrange a wedding. Baby Elizabeth was born at the home of her grandparents as healthy as one could have hoped for. Thankfully, Annie's parents were totally won over by their first grandchild. A wedding was then hastily arranged to coincide with Jimmy's 21st birthday and his emergence as a journeyman stonemason at the end of his apprenticeship. It had been heady times.

As the wedding day neared, Annie readily agreed to go for a walk along the banks of the Tyne with her husband-to-be and their newborn daughter. Jimmy's destination was the rugged and ancient Abbey Bridge approximately one mile from the elder Cranstons' home. They had almost reached the ancient arch, which showed some signs of recent repair, and Jimmy was clearly in the highest of spirits. 'Noo gi'e me the bairn, close yir eyes and come an' see this.' Annie complied as best she could.

'I've been working here for the last twae weeks as you maybe ken,' he chirped, 'and though I say it mysel' it's the best job I've ever done.'

And there it was, above their heads on the underside of the archway and expertly chiselled, 'J B Cranston 1908'. 'It took me a' denner time to mak'. Aye, and a wee bit mair besides. Standin' on the hand cairt wi' others lookin' oot for the gaffer.'[100]

---

100 Gaffer: A colloquial term for foreman.

'What a shame,' chided the cheerful Annie, who was suitably impressed by the repairs to the bridge, 'it will be near 20 years afore she will be tall enough tae read this. And here's me imagining that we would be coming along here wi' a' oor brood every summer tae show them whit a maister o' his trade their faither is. You should have done it much nearer the grun'!'

Jim's smile was almost immediate and Annie would never know that she had mildly deflated him. But as the sun rose on the morning of their wedding a few days later, the name 'J B Cranston' carved in identical lettering had appeared once again on the bridge. This time it was close to the earth on a foundation stone and could clearly be seen by everyone.[101]

For just a moment back in the Court Street flat, Jimmy's eyes seemed to light up as he clearly got Annie's meaning. She was delighted that he remembered the incident and hoped that perhaps the smile was for some of the tender moments they had frequently shared in the vicinity of that old bridge as they returned from time to time to admire his handiwork.

Jimmy recalled the anger of his father, several days later when word had got out about his folly at the bridge that landmark weekend. His unthinking behaviour could so easily have cost him his job at the very time when he was about to establish his own little family. But father more importantly thought his son's actions might tarnish the Cranston's reputation that he and the rest of his tight knit family had always strived to maintain.

Annie jolted him back to the present. 'Come on,' she scolded gently, slipping easily and unconsciously into a mothering role, 'Off tae sleep noo. Wi' a bit o' luck we can maybe manage along tae see your Ma the morn.'

---

101 The name 'J B Cranston', chiselled twice into the stonework by a mason's tool, can still be seen underneath Abbey Bridge today. They are located under the northernmost arch.

A photograph of the Cranston family in 1908. Lizzie and Alec are seated, second and fourth from left. They had twelve children, one of whom, Margaret, died in infancy. Back row, left to right: William (born 1884); Mary (1891); James (1887); Agnes (1885) and Adam (1889). Second row, left to right: John (1882); father Alexander (1854); Angus (1901); mother Elizabeth (1855) and Alexander (1879). Centre: Robert (1899). Front: Andrew (1895; left) and George (1892).

Above: The sixteenth-century Nungate Bridge and the 'Steamie' (at left), Haddington, *c.* 1890s – when Lizzie and Alec lived in the town. A postcard sent to Mary Weir (née Cranston) by her son in 1943.

Below: Haddington in about 1900, some years after the Cranstons had moved there.

(*Reprinted with the permission of East Lothian Council*)

Top: Alec Cranston, forester (second from right), on the Lennoxlove estate in 1907.

Above: Agnes, *c.* 1910 – a picture-postcard she sent from Musselburgh to her brother Ian in Bathgate.

Left: A postcard sent to John (Ian) Cranston, serving with the 2nd Battalion, Cameron Highlanders in Pretoria, South Africa, by his two sisters, Mary (left) and Agnes, in 1907.

Above: Builders from Baillie & Co., *c*. 1910.
John McDowall supervising at right with his
best friend John Morrison at extreme left rear.
Future brother-in-law James (Jimmy) Cranston
rear centre (in white shirt).

Centre: Agnes Cranston with niece Agnes and
brothers George (Doddie) and Alexander
(Sandy) with John McDowall (seated), *c*. 1911.

Below: The gates of St Mary's Kirk, Haddington,
winter 1911–12.

Above: Ian (left) and William (Willie) Cranston, *c.* 1913. Like their father, both were fine fiddle players, especially Willie.

Below: The Guild Hut in front of the Plough Tavern in Court Street, Haddington, erected for the duration of the war. After his death in 1916, Jimmy's widow, Annie, worked in the Plough as a barmaid.   (*Reprinted with the permission of East Lothian Council*)

Above: Royal Scots marching off to war down Haddington's main street behind their pipe band, 1914.

Below: The 12th Australian Light Horse parading in Sydney in 1915, before being shipped overseas – 'The sight and sound of the ... Regiment proudly parading down Macquarie Street affected Agnes [McDowall] and almost every other person present.'

Top: A British officer in a bombed-out strongpoint during the battle for Longueval, part of the Somme offensive, in July 1916. Willie Cranston was wounded during the action.

Above: Graffiti written by Paul Hubschman, a young German observer, at his underground listening post near Serre, on the Somme front, at Christmas 1916.
(*By kind permission of the Durand Group of military researchers*)

Left: James (Jim) Weir and his wife Mary (née Cranston) in 1918. After the war they farmed in rural Ontario, in Jim's native Canada.

Left: Four of the five surviving Cranston brothers in Sydney, 1921. Left to right, rear: Andrew and George; front: Robert and Angus. Andrew died from TB in a sanatorium at Waterfall, south of Sydney, in 1923; his widow, Elsie, was pregnant at the time.

Below: Elizabeth (Lizzie) Cranston and two of her sons, Angus (left) and Robert, aboard the SS *Euripides* during the family's voyage to Australia, March–April 1920.

In Australia, John McDowall had accumulated enough money by 1915 to purchase a property, a feat he said that would have been beyond him back in Scotland. A workmate had referred them to a block of land he knew was available on Sydney's upper North Shore. It was certainly affordable. They took a ferry across the harbour and then a steam train to Gordon where they walked down a hill and through bush towards a property on Ryde road. As they stood on the sloping block, Agnes remarked how much the surrounding countryside reminded her of the rolling hills of the Lammermuirs to the south of Haddington, which can be clearly seen from the town.

Those hills had been too far away to walk in normal circumstances, but they were within cycling distance once Agnes had purchased her bicycle. Significantly, even though they were always there overlooking Haddington, they were rarely visited by the busy townsfolk.

Agnes spoke first: 'We have to buy it. This place reminds me o' that wonderful day we spent in the Lammermuirs.' How could John forget?

Back in Scotland, John and Agnes had had only one day a week to themselves. For the rest of the time, John was supervising work all over Haddingtonshire and Agnes worked in Musselburgh, where she was employed as a housekeeper to the Bank of Scotland's branch manager.[102] On Saturday afternoons, she travelled back to Haddington to help Ma with the dozens of household chores that never seemed to stop in a bustling household of men and boys.

---

102 One of John's favourite jokes was to say that Agnes was the only person he knew who had 'cleaned out the Bank of Scotland'.

Sunday was different, though: after church in the morning Agnes and John were free to be alone. John would often borrow a bicycle and the two would ride through the countryside for the afternoon. The Lammermuirs became their favourite destination, especially to be by themselves. Agnes would pack some sandwiches and fill John's newly acquired thermos flask[103] with boiling water from the kettle for the inevitable picnic they would have when they reached their destination. Hopes Reservoir was a particular favourite location for the couple. Nestled among low-lying hills and surrounded by woodlands, it had an unexpected beauty, which Agnes felt again while she was standing on the rough bush block on Sydney's North Shore.[104] But there was one day in particular the couple would never forget; the day John proposed.

That Sunday's outing started off as many others with a picnic being packed, but Agnes soon noticed that John was unusually nervous. Perhaps it was the particularly difficult work contract on which he was currently employed. Whatever was bothering him, she was sure the glorious June day in 1911 would provide the necessary tonic to lift him out of his condition.

As they rode up a gravel path near the top of a rise, John unexpectedly stopped peddling and walked over to a bush of Scots Rose[105] in magnificent bloom that was growing wild beside the road. He picked the largest and brightest rose bloom that was on the bush and presented it to Agnes. To her astonishment he started quoting poetry.

---

103 Invented in 1892 by Sir James Dewar, a scientist at Oxford University, the 'vacuum flask' was first manufactured for commercial use in 1904. Initially pioneered by mountaineers and explorers, the device quickly proved widely popular and by 1909 had become embraced by the general public. (Taken from the 'History of Thermos' accessed at www.thermos.com/history. aspx)

104 Initially created by an earthen embankment, the reservoir wall was rebuilt out of concrete and masonry in the 1930s to significantly increase the storage capacity.

105 Botanical name *Rosa pimpinellifolia*.

O my Luve's like a red, red rose
That's newly sprung in June;
O my Luve's like the melodie
That's sweetly play'd in tune.
As fair art thou, my bonnie lass,
So deep in luve am I:
And I will luve thee still, my dear,
Till a' the seas gang dry.[106]

'What are you saying, John?' Agnes asked hesitantly, realising her man was struggling to say something important. Then it suddenly dawned on her what John was trying to ask and Agnes wisely decided to help him get to the point.

'Are you asking to marry me?' she said coyly. John coughed in relief and a little embarrassment that his girlfriend had anticipated his motives and said, 'Aye lass, I was wonderin' if you would like tae be my wife?'

Agnes threw her arms around John, kissed him passionately and answered his question in the affirmative. She could not wait to get home and show Ma the rose that nestled protectively in the handlebar basket of the bicycle and tell her the great news that soon she would be known as Mrs McDowall.

The afternoon excursions to the Lammermuirs had always been enjoyable for Agnes, but that particular day made it one to remember for ever. She hoped that the block of land in Australia, which displayed many similar features, would deepen the love they already had for each other, and in an instant, they agreed to purchase it.

Agnes and husband John were both extremely hard working and industrious. Every weekend, the couple took the time-

---

106 This poem was written by Scotland's most loved poet Robert Burns in 1794.

consuming journey from the inner suburbs out to their block of land and start clearing it. From rock hewn from the site itself, John first constructed a rough stone building that would serve as a temporary roof over their heads. It was hard work, clearing the block of its eucalyptus trees and then breaking up the steep land to form a series of gently sloping terraces. From the exposed rock John then produced more blocks of sandstone and with the help of John Morrison, they set about building a substantial stone cottage for the family. It was back-breaking toil, but Agnes and John threw themselves into the task enthusiastically.

One day in April 1915, John came home with some big news. One of the Morrisons' neighbours who had joined the 12th Australian Light Horse months earlier had completed his training and he and his regiment were about to be shipped overseas. The Premier of New South Wales had decided their farewell should be celebrated with a major parade down Macquarie Street in the city and all citizens were invited to join in the festivities.[107]

When the McDowalls and Morrisons arrived on the appointed day, they were surprised to see that many thousands of Sydneysiders were already present. The crowds on each side of the street were several people deep and police and soldiers were lining the road to prevent the huge crowd from spilling onto the thoroughfare. A short time after they had settled into their positions standing on the footpath, they heard the sound of a military band coming down the street towards them.

Soon the crowds were cheering wildly as the band of the Royal Australian Navy, escorted by a large and impressively turned out detachment of sailors, marched by. Next, the sound of horses' hooves could be heard on the hard road surface, scarcely audible at first, but growing louder by the second. Before long, the sound

---

107 *The Sydney Mail* newspaper, 28 April 1915, page 6, sourced at the State Library of New South Wales.

rose to a thunderous noise as hundreds of soldiers on horseback rode by at a walk. Agnes was awe-struck by the athleticism and suntanned skin of the fit young riders. They looked magnificent she thought silently to herself, mindful that her husband and his best pal were standing beside her. They were holding their horse's reins in one hand and casually supporting their .303 rifles upright in the other with the butt resting on the horse's shoulder. The horses were all chestnut in colour and uniformly tall, standing at least 16 hands high said a knowledgeable man in the crowd just behind the McDowalls. The horses looked strong and eager to gallop. The same onlooker pointed out that the horses were called 'Walers', because they had been originally bred for stockmen in the colony of New South Wales. The army preferred them because of their strength and endurance.

The sight and sound of the 12th Australian Light Horse Regiment proudly parading down Macquarie Street affected Agnes and almost every other person present. The soldiers looked invincible, like romantic heroes from the past. Men in the crowd roared themselves hoarse. Women screamed and one or two young ladies swooned with excitement. About halfway through the parade, John Morrison excitedly pointed to one of the horsemen and said, 'There, there's Richard' and the four followed his finger to a young 20-something riding in the parade. Even though the Morrisons had only been neighbours to Richard's family for a short time, the Scottish couples felt it was their patriotic duty to wish him well. They waved and yelled furiously and Richard acknowledged their presence with a slight nod of his head.

As Richard rode by, Agnes was full of thoughts of her brothers on the other side of the world. She hoped they looked as handsome and brave as Richard and his fellow troopers. She was overcome by how much she missed her family and in the middle of all the cheering, she felt profoundly homesick. She held onto John's arm and shed a few tears, which he interpreted as an emotional reaction to the occasion.

When the McDowalls returned home later in the day, Agnes wanted to make something that would remind her of home, so she chose one of her favourite dishes – rumbledethumps.[108]

This is a traditional dish from the Scottish Borders that was taught to her by Lizzie. Ma told her it was a favourite of father's, but being from the Scottish North-East, she had to give the dish a regional twist to 'improve' it. Into a large frying pan, Agnes lightly sautéed shredded onion and cabbage in butter until the onion was transparent and the cabbage wilted. Then she added some mashed potatoes, but here was the regional twist. Potatoes were traditionally mashed in butter with a little salt and pepper added for seasoning, but Lizzie used cream instead. This gave the dish a much richer flavour than normal. All the ingredients were heated through and thoroughly mixed after which they were placed in a dish with shredded cheese on top and baked until golden brown.

But Agnes had not finished. Insisting on giving the dish yet another twist to celebrate their new lives in Australia, she had meanwhile cooked a dozen fat sausages that her brother Drew had supplied from his work and she served them up with the evening's meal.

Relaxing after eating their fill, everyone agreed it had been a grand day indeed with the riders, the pageantry and ceremony, but John insisted that the best part of the day had been the rumbledethumps and sausages!

Agnes was receiving regular updates from Scotland by post and occasionally a newspaper clipping would be included in the letters. She mainly corresponded with her sister and sisters-in-law and it seemed natural to her that the women were holding the family together. Occasionally, Agnes received a rare postcard from

---

108 Similar to 'Bubble and squeak' (England), 'Bauernfrühstück' (Germany), 'Stamppot' (the Netherlands) and 'Hash' (United States).

one of her brothers and it was a red-letter day in the McDowall household when that happened.

Before the war, the letters had contained cheerful news about weddings and the arrival of new nieces and nephews. Even when war started the news was still uplifting, informing Agnes about the enlistment of her handsome, much-loved brothers as they went off to the army one after the other. But lately the tone of the letters had ominously changed to something much more disturbing. The war was treating the Cranstons badly.

Still smarting from his rejection by the Australian Army on medical grounds, Drew Cranston decided to work for the cause of his Motherland. He would do his best to ensure the Allied troops were supplied with as much meat as possible.

By 1915 the Silvester Brothers' business had expanded into a state-of-the-art meat processing plant on an industrial scale. Every day it was the same routine. In the early morning, dozens of beef carcasses would arrive by refrigerated cold-storage rail carriage from the State abattoir at Homebush, then on the outskirts of Sydney. The meat would be unloaded by hand and brought directly across the road by trolley to be hung on meat hooks in the cool room. Each butcher employed by Silvester Brothers would select a carcass from the cool room and start breaking it down on one of the butchering tables.

The best cuts were set aside and re-sold to butcher shops and restaurants around Sydney for a handsome profit. The rest of the meat would end up as processed meat, of which 'Bully Beef', or corned beef, was the most in demand. The current defence contract with the Department of War had come as a godsend for Henry Silvester and his brother William. The meat that Drew was butchering was now being shipped throughout Australia and overseas to not only the Australian and New Zealand Army Corps (ANZAC), but also to feed the British Army.

Andrew and the other butchers would venture in and out of the cool room dozens of times a day. After stripping down each carcass, the off-cuts would be taken to the brining bins. There they would be pickled in a saltwater and potassium nitrate solution overnight. The next morning the pickled meat along with some of the brining liquid would be scooped out of their huge tanks and transferred to large stainless steel vats which had gas heaters underneath. The meat and brine had fresh water added to it and the whole mixture was boiled for two hours. After cooking, the meat would be turned out on to flat cutting tables, allowed to cool and finally cut up into smaller pieces ready for canning, which took place at another factory.

This was Drew's routine, day in, day out. He and the other butchers would be chilled to the core in the cool room and minutes later be soaked in a lather of sweat working next to huge vats of steaming, hot meat.

The longer he worked at Silvester's the worse Drew's persistent cough became, but he ignored the warning signs. He and the other butchers were earning so much overtime trying to keep up with the army's insatiable demand for 'Bully Beef' that he was rapidly becoming a wealthy man. In Scotland his average wage had been just £1 per week, but in Australia he was now earning the staggering sum of £5 per week.

One of the other butchers that had started at Silvester's on the same day as Andrew was Edwin 'Ted' Ball. It was Ted's father James, already working at Silvester Brothers, who brought his son into the company and introduced the two to each other. Within months Drew and Ted had struck up a strong friendship and by the middle of 1915 they had decided to rent a family-sized home together in Stanmore, an inner western suburb of Sydney.

One day on his way to Central Railway Station after finishing work at Silvester Brothers, Drew was approached by a matronly old woman. 'Excuse me, young man,' she said, as Drew was about to descend the steps into the station. Having been unexpectedly shaken from his private thoughts, Andrew was not prepared with an answer. The lady forged on. 'The Anzacs are fighting at Gallipoli. Why aren't you in uniform and fighting with your mates at the front?' She then moved forward and pressed something into his hand. Andrew looked down and saw that it was a white feather.[109] Andrew's blood started to boil. He blinked a few times in disbelief as he marshalled his thoughts and then turned towards the self-appointed guardian of morality and opened his mouth.

'I did try to enlist. You dinnae ken anything, you old hag.' He threw the feather to the ground as if it was a poisonous object. Never the most educated or articulate of the Cranstons, all Drew could do was to wave his arms around and become agitated. His voice rose in anger and a number of travellers moving in and out of the railway station began to form a crowd around the two. The elderly woman was so convinced of the righteousness of her cause that she always ignored any protests, including those this day from Drew.

'My husband is fighting you know, and so is my son. They would gladly give their lives to protect us women from the beastly advances of the Turk and the Hun. Shame on you!' Several voices shouted out from the bystanders, 'Yes, shame on you!'

The greater noise that was being made attracted even more people to see what all the fuss was about and soon there was a fairly large and vocal crowd surrounding the two antagonists.

'I've got five brithers serving already,' shouted Drew.

---

109 The white feather was universally recognised as a symbol for cowardice. In Britain during the Great War, there was even an organisation, called the Order of the White Feather, aimed at shaming men into enlisting.

'So why aren't you, mate,' shouted back a young, fit man in uniform whose threatening voice convinced Drew this confrontation was not going well. The crowd was quickly turning against him.

Drew thought that discretion was probably the wisest course of action and stormed down to the station's concourse, still fuming at the insult to him and his family but also a little embarrassed by the truth that men on poor wages were dying in uniform while he was making a fortune in safety.

The next day Andrew obtained a badge from the Paddington barracks showing that he had volunteered for service with the Australian Imperial Forces but had been rejected on medical grounds. That took care of any overzealous patriotic women and for the remainder of the war he wore the badge on the lapels of his civilian clothing. Over the next three years he avoided the public as best as he could by working excessively long hours at the factory. As a result he grew wealthier while his cough grew worse.

One of the tasks he enjoyed most was spending the occasional weekend with Agnes and John on their block of land at Gordon. At first he tried to assist them with the strenuous work, such as land clearing or helping John with stonemasonry, but the physical exertion caused him to become short of breath. However, it did not take long to find alternate ways to help and Drew ended up taking on the less arduous tasks of dressing timber, plastering and preparing mortar.

But the best part of the weekends he spent with the McDowalls was the luxury of bringing them fresh meat and sausages, which were cooked on a primitive outdoor hotplate to the delight of everyone.

On Saturday nights the adults, who sometimes included the Morrisons, would quietly sit around an open fire under the bright stars of a southern sky, surrounded by the Australian bush. The men would share the occasional bottle of beer or two and smoke their pipes while everyone reminisced about Scotland. Lying at their feet, the young children would listen intently as they tried desperately to stay awake. Afterwards the adults would put them to bed and then fall asleep themselves, exhausted but content.

Back home in Scotland, in the absence of older brothers, 26 year old Adam had become the man of the Cranston household. Employed as a baker, he was busy enough sharing his life between work and his wife and infant child. Now he had willingly accepted the burden of looking after the families of his brothers as well as mother, sister and younger brothers.

He shuffled uncomfortably on the large sofa and looked almost shyly at his younger sister Mary. There was only two years between them and they had always been close, but by the quality of the standard lamp and floral wallpaper in the room where they sat, it seems that she had surely come up in the world.

Mary had returned to Haddington to be nearer her mother, after years of working in Edinburgh. She had settled employment in service to Dr Wallace-James and his wife in the 14-roomed Tyne House close to the river. Mary fitted in well with the childless couple's busy routine in an arrangement that suited all parties, and the live-in requirement of her job meant that it provided her with somewhere to live in Haddington other than the overcrowded two-bedroom flat in St Martin's Gate.

Her mother and those of her brothers still at home had moved there in early 1915. It was slightly better accommodation than some of the places they had lived in recently, though it was still cold, damp and far from the centre of town. But mother was overjoyed with one aspect of the new flat: it had gas lighting installed and the paraffin lamps she had used for decades could finally be put away.

'It's awfa fancy, Mary,' Adam exclaimed of the room he was sitting in. 'Imagine the good Doctor and his wife bidin' in a place like this, it must cost them an absolute fortune!'

Disconcertingly, Mary burst out laughing. 'Dinnae be sae daft, oor Adam, Dr Wallace-James widnae bide in a dump like this. This is the servants' quarters. Molly Divine and me hae this bit to oorsel's. Then we have oor bedrooms through there of course,' she indicated. Adam felt this explanation did not make his task any easier as he had seldom seen such splendour and felt this gave his sister the upper hand, almost by association. And yet his status within the family had changed dramatically in the year that was coming to a close. Good riddance to it, too, he thought..

This change of status could be traced back to his promotion in the Co-op's bakery from the headquarters in Tranent to Haddington in June 1912. It was a move that had been the catalyst for his declaration of love for Margaret (Maggie) Hoggan who had been working in the town as a domestic and the couple becoming engaged. They were married the following year and moved into a small company-owned flat in Haddington's High Street.

As part of the Cranston tradition, Maggie presented Adam with a baby son named Alexander and in rapid succession he had watched his brothers Ian, Willie, Jimmy and Sandy go off to fight with the British Army. With Jimmy subsequently being invalided out of the army with what was looking increasingly like a terminal illness, Adam was keeping a fraternal eye on him and his family also. In short he had become the man of the house and acting head of the extended family. Yet here he stood in the splendid surrounds of Tyne House almost afraid to speak to his younger sister. Mary had no such reservations.

'You'll be here about Hogmanay, I suppose, well I'm sorry,

Adam, I'm afraid I cannae help you.' Adam was astounded. New Year's Eve was a good five weeks away and the subject had never been mentioned. How could she possibly know that he was about to ask her to look after Ma and his wee bairn, while he took Maggie out to see in the New Year?

Then it was that he recalled the curse of the Cranston menfolk: their womenfolk seemed to possess a sixth sense. Over the years he had come to accept that the females in his family were blessed with an innate skill of being able to foretell the future. It all started when Adam must have been about 10 years old when he overheard Ma's friend Effie Fairgrieve once describe her as 'fey'. Adam was intrigued by this strange sounding word and decided to find out what it meant. So he did something he had never done before – he went to the library.

He made his way to High Street in the main part of town and into the grand town hall building which housed the Haddington Library. Adam hesitatingly approached a bespectacled woman who was working behind the counter. In his most proper voice he inquired if he could possibly look up the meaning of a word. When the lady heard the word in question, she let out a stifled laugh and said, 'Och, you dear sweet lad. It's quite a common word. I could tell you right noo, what the word means, but I need to show you something very important.'

She ushered him down a corridor of shelving filled with books to his left and right until she came to a section marked, 'References'. There, she took down a beautifully leather-bound book embossed with the words *Jamieson's Dictionary of the Scottish Language*.[110] She quickly flicked her way through the large tome until she found what she wanted and said with an air of satisfaction, 'Here it is, "Fey", a noun from the Old Norse meaning possessed of

110 *Jamieson's Dictionary of the Scottish Language* (four volumes), John Jamieson, published by William Tait, Edinburgh, 1846 (abridged 1867).

supernatural abilities, such as prophecy.' She showed Adam the entry so that he could confirm for himself the truth of what she had just said. With a flourish, she then slammed the book shut. As the librarian returned the book to its place in the shelves, Adam noticed that the book she was still holding was only one of a massive four-volume set. The librarian watched the young 10-year-old scanning the books in awe and she seemed to read his mind: 'Aye lad, we need this many volumes to capture the number of words we use.'

Adam quickly thanked the lady for her help and was making haste towards the outside door when she said, 'There's one more thing you should know, many Scottish women are fey. It could be a family member or someone working in a shop.' Then she paused slightly and with a twinkle in her eye continued, 'or even a librarian!'

Back in Mary's sitting room, Adam realised his sister was waiting to make an explanation. 'It's Molly,' she said, 'her mither's got a growth o' the ...' She nodded her head to indicate a part of the body below the waist and continued quickly, 'ye ken. She winnae see the month o' January oot and Molly has got tae be wi' her on Auld Year's nicht. The Doctor widnae hae it ony ither wye, and neither would I. But he's got a party o' folk comin' for denner and I'll be workin' till thon time. I'm sure that Ma would like to look efter your bairn.'

Adam walked slowly along the Sidegate in the direction of home. He was in no great hurry to get there as the flat was small and the atmosphere could be fraught. He smiled at the thought of his enigmatic younger sister. Adam mused at how strange it was that he had always thought of Mary as somehow being vulnerable, yet she was in steady employment to one of the town's respected doctors. And then he remembered that it was she alone out of all the children who had never had a single day's absence from school.

1916

By January 1916, the Western Front was still locked in stalemate. Hundreds of thousands of soldiers on each side cowering in their trenches faced each other across no man's land. Artillery bombardments, trench raids and violent battles were continuing to cause thousands of casualties each week, but little or no territory changed hands. Both sides needed a breakthrough. The Germans would launch a massive assault on Verdun, the symbolic heart of France, in an effort to bleed the French army white. For the British, it would be an all-out attack on the German lines at a previously quiet sector of the front called the Somme.

The ringing of the wretched clock's hour chime woke Lizzie with a start. How she hated that clock and silently bemoaned yet again the selling of her pride and joy, the family heirloom that had belonged to her in-laws and had been a wedding gift all those years ago. Yet Andrew seemed to be thriving in Australia, so the sacrifice had been worth it. What was she doing here, sleeping on the chair, with the fire no longer lit and only half cleaned? Why was she all alone?

Slowly the truth began to sink in. It was January the 1st and the year 1916 was upon them. Things could only get better, she hoped. And she was not entirely alone. Adam and Maggie's 18-month-old child had long since fallen asleep in Lizzie's bed as she was in charge of the infant.

It was strange how uneasy that made her feel, although her whole life it seemed had been spent looking after children. She had seen her daughter-in-law's look of concern before she had agreed to accompany Adam to the Lodge in Hardgate to while away the last couple of hours of 1915. But that was typical Maggie.

The war had lasted a whole year longer than had been promised and her boys were beginning to pay the price, and all for the greed of that Kaiser Bill. What a disappointment he would have been to his granny if Queen Victoria had still been alive; but she had been dead for three, maybe four years, she couldn't quite remember. They said Kaiser Bill had been her favourite grandson.

Favourites? Lizzie had tried hard never to have favourites with her children, but in truth she had. Ian and William were out there, God knows where and in what kind of danger? It was better not to know. And there was James, just a short distance away in Court Street. She had to wonder if he would see another New Year.

Was it only four years ago that the whole family had gathered on New Year's Day, except her Alec of course, for the wedding of Agnes and John? Where had they all gone? Mary was at work tonight and even her best friend Effie was indisposed. She had spared no details when she described her diarrhoea and vomiting attack to Lizzie during a flying visit that afternoon. It was New Year's morning and Lizzie had no other adult to talk to.

The Cranstons had always been a popular port of call at Hogmanay. The fiddles, the whisky, the tin whistles and the comb and paper. Lizzie smiled and for one moment thought of singing a favourite song just as she had that night four years ago. Then she remembered.

She remembered quite clearly one of the revellers on that most special of nights. It was that Klaus from the butcher's, large as life and if she remembered rightly even Sandy Pow had been taken in by him. The cheek of it – dancing and singing in her house while his countrymen were plotting to kill her family. If he came through that door again tonight she would despatch him single-handed. They were a murderous tribe.

Where were Robbie and Angus? They should not still be out after midnight. Robbie, who was 16 years old, was probably with his football pals. If she was perfectly honest few of the Cranstons would have been sober on New Year's morning when they were 16. But where was Angus? He was younger and what was it her granny used to say about people like him? 'A nickum o' a loon'. Aye, he was that all right, a real handful.

She had to wait up for them. She had to make sure they were both all right and she would have to welcome in the first foot, whoever that may be. It was half past twelve. The Cranstons had never had to wait until this time for a first foot before. Lizzie took the family photograph off the mantelpiece, shivered a little at the lack of fire and settled down to wait for Robbie and Angus. Slowly she ran her finger over the reflections of each of her dear children, and soon, once more, she was asleep on the chair.

Lizzie woke with a start as the clock struck two. There was still no sign of Robbie or Angus. They would be out there somewhere, making merry. She dragged herself off to bed. Her boys were not coming home.

The youngest two Cranston boys had been uncertain as to what to expect of the New Year. Every month that passed with no end to the conflict in sight meant that one or both of them might be called upon to take up arms. Robbie viewed the prospect with a good deal of equanimity. He feared for his brothers already at the front although he had complete confidence in their ability as soldiers. His main concerns were Jimmy and his family in Court Street and nearer to home, his mother. Jimmy's war was over but Robbie knew that his main battle was still raging and the longer it went on the less convinced he was that his brother would be the victor. Ma was, well, she was taking it hard.

Yet life was not all bad for Robbie. His apprenticeship was going well and joiners would always be in demand, whether here, or God forbid, nearer to the battle-front; and the war had helped him in another way. The advent of war had meant that promising young footballers, as he undoubtedly was, who would have normally expected to slowly work their way through the ranks of Haddington's Amateur Football Club, suddenly found themselves promoted to the first 11.

For Robbie this had happened almost two years earlier at the tender age of 15 and from then on he had found himself playing alongside top-quality players who, when not at the front, would frequently 'guest' for the Haddington team or for their opponents from other East of Scotland sides. One time, he scored a goal against a vastly superior team from Musselburgh, something which gave him much to gloat about when he next wrote to his older brother Sandy at the front.

He told nobody, but he felt quite certain that his good fortune was at least partly due to the 'lucky coin' that had been given to him by his brother Ian and which Robbie kept with him at all times.

Around town Robbie was gaining an enviable reputation for being an athletic, competent young man. Some may say even handsome. It certainly seemed that he had no shortage of young women wanting to be asked to the many dances that were being held in the town to raise funds for the boys at the front. Angus, however, was another matter.

Winter had changed to spring and it was 10pm on 2 April 1916 when Angus was woken by the sound of a neighbour's dog barking. At first he could not hear anything and was about to open the window to tell the animal to be quiet, but then he heard the faint throbbing of powerful engines far off in the distance coming from the east. They were unlike anything he had ever heard before. As the sound grew louder, it seemed to become more threatening. Angus woke his brother Robbie with a violent shove and opened the window so that both could crane their ears in the direction of the growing sound.

'I can hear mair than one engine,' said Robbie.

'Aye,' replied Angus, 'at least two maybe mair. What on earth do you think it is?' he added, slightly apprehensive. Robert made an educated guess, 'I think it's an airship.'

By now other dogs had joined in the barking and the lights had come on in a few windows in the street. They were not the only ones to be disturbed. The sound was now loud enough for it to be heard clearly. The throbbing of four powerful engines formed an ominously pulsating vibration, which quickly reached a deafening roar. Suddenly through a break in the clouds, the boys could see the silhouette of a long cigar-shaped object slowly coming towards the town.

'Zeppelin!' shouted Robert, who had more of an idea about aircraft than his brother.[111] Angus immediately leapt out of bed

---

111 According to Trevor Royle, *The Flowers of the Forest* (pages 164–65), Zeppelin L-14 crossed the North Sea from Germany and made landfall on the Scottish coast at St Abbs Head, near Eyemouth. From there it flew in a direct line to Edinburgh and the naval base at Rosyth on the Firth of Forth, a route which would have taken it directly over the township of Haddington.

and ran from the room. He returned a few seconds later with a .303 rifle in his hands. The Cranstons had always kept firearms. As a forester, his father Alec had needed rifles of different calibre to shoot the occasional animal on the estates of his employer. The first weapon he used to teach his sons how to shoot was a .22 single-shot rifle. With that weapon, the occasional rabbit that was shot and brought home was always a welcome addition to the family's modest diet. And a rifle was not only for work purposes, but also a requirement for those in the military reserve. While serving in the Territorial Army, he was required to maintain a fully operational military rifle at home. At one time, when Alec was alive and most of the sons were still living at home, the front cupboard contained up to half a dozen rifles of different calibre, but by 1916 only Pa's old .303 and .22 remained.

Angus raced over to the open window and placed the .303 Lee-Enfield rifle against the wall. With his right hand he quickly pushed a number of individual bullets into a magazine he was holding in his left. He loaded the magazine into the action so that it locked in place with a loud click. He then slid the bolt forward and back in one well-drilled movement. The rifle was now cocked with a live round in the breach. With the precision of an experienced marksman, Angus released the safety catch on the left of the action first and then quickly brought the rifle up to his shoulder. He aimed it out of the open window towards the dark object that was about to fly over the town and squeezed the trigger. The first round went off with a load bang, much louder than expected in the confines of the small bedroom. There was a sharp yelp from a neighbour's dog and one or two people in the street started yelling in alarm.

With the proficiency of someone much older, Angus quickly fired off two more rounds before the Zeppelin passed overhead and out of range behind the house. Clutching his rifle, he raced downstairs onto the dirt road of St Martin's Gate, but the Zeppelin had moved off and Angus knew any more shooting would be useless.

Everyone in the neighbourhood was now awake and many had spilled out onto the street. Lizzie had woken up with a start when she heard rifle fire close by. What she did not know was that the shots were coming from the bedroom next to hers in the same flat. It took several minutes and a lot of soothing from the rest of her family to calm her down.

In almost every street in Haddington people were now awake. Everywhere you looked there was confusion and alarm, but it was only Angus who had acted decisively. No one else in the town had fired a weapon. As the sound of the menacing Zeppelin droned off towards the capital of Edinburgh, Angus stood in his bare feet and nightclothes surrounded by admiring family and neighbours in St Martin's Gate.

Meanwhile a policeman on duty a short distance away had the presence of mind to alert his superiors in Edinburgh of the impending arrival of an airship and this gave authorities in the Scottish capital half an hour or so to react.

Next morning the town was abuzz with the news of the Zeppelin and the young Cranston boy's decisive actions, yet sadly no one outside the town would ever hear the details of the incident. Government censors deemed the episode too dangerous to print anything other than a sanitised version of events. A few days later, after the censors had finally given their approval, Scottish papers reported the Zeppelin raid in the following terms:

The invader, flying at a great height, approached the town [of Edinburgh][112] from an inland direction, and dropped bombs in rapid succession in a line. The visit had been

112 The censored newspaper articles were not allowed to mention the name of the bombed city.

anticipated and trams had been stopped and the electric lights were extinguished. The loud detonations awakened the inhabitants, many of whom went into the streets. An empty tramcar was blown to fragments, and a tramway inspector was killed. Close by a hotel was much damaged. Many small shops and other buildings suffered, and considerable damage was done to working class dwellings, several of which were completely wrecked. One house collapsed, but the inmates escaped injury. In another case a bomb fell in a bed, but did not explode. A well-known Magistrate, the leader of the local Labour party, was killed in the street. The Zeppelin went off to sea, the visit lasting only a few minutes.

It is reported that sixteen persons were killed and thirty injured. The victims include a baby and several little children. There were three small fires which were speedily extinguished, No panic occurred; and yesterday crowds thronged the streets inspecting the damaged buildings[113]

Within days, Angus was telling people he was certain he had in fact hit the Zeppelin. Later still his version included the news that he had caused considerable damage to the airship, which probably resulted in it crashing into the sea as it attempted to return to Germany.

The family and the townsfolk may have been pleased with Angus's quick-thinking without necessarily believing everything that he would later say about it, but Angus himself was deeply unhappy. In his opinion government censors had prevented him from receiving the recognition he believed he richly deserved. As he allowed his anger and frustration to grow, he discovered that the occasional drink of alcohol seemed to soothe his distress.

---

113 *The Scotsman*, 4 April 1916, and a similar article appeared in the weekly *Haddingtonshire Courier* on Friday 7 April 1916.

Angus was barely 15 and supposedly too young to purchase alcohol legally, but for years the older Cranston sons had been sending their younger brother to the Black Bull to buy the occasional bottle. So the continued visits after the older brothers had gone to war were barely noticed. Little did anyone realise that he was hiding the whisky from the prying eyes of his family and consuming it himself.

In Court Street, spring held no promise of new beginnings for Jimmy, Annie and their young family. The die had already been cast. Christmas had come and gone. The couple knew it would be their last together. The usually boisterous children sensed something foreboding and grew quiet.

New Year had been worse and word got back to them that Lizzie was taking it hard. They heard how she had welcomed it in all by herself and was beginning to fear for the future of her boys. And well she might. But whatever fortunes might befall his brothers, Jimmy was resigned to his fate and the fact that the rest of his short life was likely to be spent in bed.

Bed for Jimmy comprised of a stretcher-type piece of equipment and two small benches on which it could be placed, all individually designed and manufactured by members of the Haddington construction industry. The reason for two benches was simple. Since returning to Haddington, Jimmy spent most of his time being nursed in either his cramped living quarters or the semi-secluded courtyard behind the flat and adjacent to the Plough Tavern.

At first there had been no shortage of visitors to the Court Street tenement. Brother Adam, who had adopted the role of head of the family in the absence of his older brothers fighting overseas, had come regularly. He invariably brought some much appreciated bakery products with him, as food was scarce and getting scarcer. But Adam was becoming preoccupied. For him, the prospect of conscription was always a theoretical possibility and although until now the government had shown no inclination to call up bakers like him, things were constantly changing.

Young Angus had been at the head of the queue to visit when Jimmy first came home and had been desperate to digest every last detail about training and the art of killing, but his interest waned as soon as he discovered that Jimmy had neither made it to the battlefield, nor had he actually killed anyone.

Robert was always on hand to help carry Jimmy and his home-made stretcher-cum-bed outside into the 'healthy East Lothian air', which in summer had been reasonably pleasant. But as autumn turned to winter and no change to the regime was suggested, Jimmy's spirits had begun to fall. His children were finding it increasingly hard to keep quiet and well behaved around their father and Annie was rapidly losing any faith that she may have had in the medical profession and their methods.

Yet a couple of paces away in the Guild Hut, life went on regardless. From his bed Jimmy could hear the music of the afternoon and evening performances. He became used to the shrieks of pleasure and enjoyment emanating from the scores of young people who congregated there to snatch whatever respite they could as an uncertain future beckoned. When lying outside he would sometimes catch quick glimpses of couples disappearing up the side of the pub for a quick kiss, fumble or goodness knows what. Jim knew exactly what, but he had more serious things to worry about: he was beginning to develop bedsores.

Lizzie's activities, if anything, expanded as she crossed and recrossed the town in a frenzy of good works, but she found visiting the tenement in Court Street increasingly distressing.

One day Robbie came to the house in high spirits. He was

delighted to see that his older brother, Adam, was already at Jimmy's bedside when he called in unexpectedly at the Court Street flat. Perhaps the sombre tone by the bedside failed to register with him. They were now into the month of May.

'Have you heard aboot the big match?' he asked excitedly, waving what looked like a hand-made poster in the general direction of his brothers. 'Early next month, right here in the Neilson Park, no' 50 yards frae this bed. The Highland Light Infantry versus The Argyll and Sutherland Highlanders. It will be a sell oot. Nae doot they may baith ha'e some professionals in their ranks! We'll a' go and see it,' he said confidently. Fired up with enthusiasm for his favourite sport, Robbie went on, 'You've been lying there ower lang, Jimmy, you've got a month tae get on your feet, or at least intae a bath chair. I'm sure Ma must ken somebody that could lend us one for a couple of hours!'

Such was his excitement he barely noted his brothers' response. Adam managed a vague and incredulous half-smile while Jim's gaze seemed fixed on a distant spot on the ceiling. The same spot he had been gazing at for the last three hours. Robbie was unabashed, 'That's a date then! I think I'll tak' my boots, just in case they're a man short!'[114]

On 7 May 1916, Adam received a letter that suddenly and irrevocably changed his life for ever. It was an official notification delivered by post from the Ministry of War. The notice curtly 'warned' him to attend the Recruiting Office in Haddington on the 14th of the month at 09:00 hours where he would be 'required

---

114 The *Haddingtonshire Courier* later reported that Robbie's eagerly awaited football match duly went ahead as planned, with a capacity crowd in attendance and was won by the Highland Light Infantry. There was no mention of Robbie playing for either team.

to join for service with the Colours'. Adam Cranston, 28, married man, father of an infant son, fully qualified baker and the senior male of the Cranston family looking after his mother and younger siblings, had just been conscripted, the sixth Cranston son so far to serve in the Great War.

The evening before his attendance was required at the recruiting office had not gone well. The farewells between husband and wife had not started the way Adam had hoped. Ma and his younger brothers would not leave Adam and Maggie alone. There was much fussing and talk, especially from the brothers who wanted to know which regiment he would be joining. Where would he be fighting? How long would it be before he killed his first German? Adam had no answers for them; he would have to wait like everyone else to be told at the recruiting office which regiment he would be sent to. When Maggie and he did finally manage to be alone, their love-making was hurried, clumsy and ultimately unfulfilling for both of them.

When he woke the next day it was dawn, but Maggie had already left the bed and was packing some clothes and other items into the only bag they possessed, his battered canvas work bag. As he watched her work in silence, he saw a tear slowly run down her cheek and into the bag.

Adam climbed out of bed, embraced his wife and led her back to bed where they made love again, this time with a degree of tenderness and intimacy they had not enjoyed for a while. Later, Adam left the flat in St Martin's Gate and walked over Victoria Bridge to the town centre, but instead of going directly to the recruiting office, he proceeded along Market Street until he reached Court Street and knocked on the door of the flat at No. 9. When the door opened, a number of young children burst forth, yelling and smiling at the arrival of Uncle Adam. His sister-in-law Annie greeted him warmly, though it was obvious she had been crying and he was ushered through to the main bedroom.

There, on the crudely constructed sickbed was his brother Jimmy, whose laboured breathing and pale skin showed he was in the final stage of succumbing to tuberculosis. He was barely conscious. Adam tried to hold a conversation with him, but it was hopeless. Not knowing what else to do, Adam shook his brother's limp hand, kissed Annie tenderly on the cheek and left the building.

Outside the Haddington recruiting office stood a well-ordered line of men dressed in civilian clothes and holding bags of all description waiting to enter the building. Adam had seen queues like this outside recruiting offices in Haddington and Edinburgh every time he'd passed them during the past two years, but had not given it much thought. For some time now the daily line-up of people waiting outside such offices across Scotland had ceased to be a novelty to anyone.[115]

It was not long before he was directed inside to a grizzly old sergeant with a poorly shaven face who presented Adam with a one-page form with his left hand and told him to fill it out on a nearby table. It was only then Adam noticed the sergeant's right arm was missing as his jacket sleeve had been folded over and sewn closed. The document was headed 'Attestation' and required Adam to supply only the merest details such as name, age, address, occupation, next of kin and any prior military experience. When he returned the papers to the disabled sergeant he was taken to another room where his height, weight and chest measurements were taken and he was subjected to a cursory medical examination by an army doctor. The medical officer signed the Attestation form indicating he was medically approved for military service and Adam was back with the sergeant in what seemed like only minutes.

---

115 On average, over 430 Scots enlisted every working day of the week for the duration of the war (588,000 Scottish enlistments in the First World War in 1,340 working days, which is defined as Monday to Saturday inclusive).

The NCO (Non Commissioned Officer) handed him a worn edition of the Bible and said, 'Do you solemnly swear that the answers made by you to the above questions are true and correct and that you are willing to fulfil duties in the service of the King for as long as you are required. Say so help me God.' With the Bible firmly in his hand, Adam replied, 'So help me God'. He was then handed the Attestation form and told to read the next part of the document out aloud.

Adam cleared his throat and said, 'I, Adam Lindsay Cranston swear by Almighty God that I will be faithful and bear true Allegiance to His Majesty King George the Fifth, his Heirs and Successors and that I will, as in duty bound, honestly and faithfully defend His Majesty, His Heirs and Successors, in Person, Crown and dignity against all enemies and will observe and obey all orders of His Majesty, his Heirs and Successors, and the Generals and Officers set over me. So Help me God.'

To complete the contract, the recruiting sergeant pressed a silver coin into Adam's hand. By accepting the 'King's Shilling' Adam had now become a soldier in the British Army. The sergeant looked down at the clipboard he was carrying which listed the names of the regiments that were desperately waiting for new recruits to replenish their depleted ranks. He smiled to himself.

'You're in luck my lad,' he confirmed, 'you're going to one of the finest infantry regiments in Scotland. You'll report there today. Here are your papers, which you'll need to present at your destination, and a rail warrant to get you there. Good luck.'

Papers were thrust into Adam's hands and he was summarily shunted out the door as another conscript instantly took his place. As Adam stepped out on the street he could hear the sergeant's now faint voice back inside the building.

'Do you solemnly swear that the answers made by you to the above questions are true and correct ...'

Adam went directly to Haddington Railway Station to catch the afternoon train to Edinburgh. When the station assistant asked him where he wanted to go, Adam was flummoxed at first. He had completely forgotten to read his travel papers. Reaching inside his jacket pocket he pulled out the documentation that the sergeant had thrust into his hand only a half hour earlier at the recruiting office. It read, 'You are to report to the sentry on duty at Ayr Barracks, where you will be inducted into the Royal Scots Fusiliers.'

'Ah', said the station assistant, 'we usually only get recruits for the Royal Scots here, not the Fusiliers, but it appears that some of the other Lowland regiments must have had a bad time of it lately'.

'Why?' inquired Adam innocently.

'Because they've been getting large numbers of replacements like you through here.'

The first days at basic training were a bit of a shock for Adam, but as he looked around at the hundred or so other recruits, he realised it was a surprise for everyone. He had received his uniform and kit and was given an introduction to army discipline in the first days of the 12-week training course. Then as the weeks passed, training quickly settled into a seemingly endless rotation of musketry practice, drill, lectures, essential field craft, marching and physical training. Slowly, Adam grew accustomed to the routine, the food, the discipline and the accommodation – all of which were basic, yet somehow reassuring.

He also noticed how his body had changed. He had become fitter and stronger. Men who had been overweight lost their extra baggage gradually and safely; recruits like Adam who were a little on the thin side gained a healthy amount of weight and looked much better for it. Muscles became harder and endurance increased. By the final weeks, the group of recruits were taken on long route marches across the Ayrshire countryside. Adam thought to himself that it was a wonder what plain, wholesome food and plenty of exercise in the open air did for so many men going through basic training.

He also made a mental note to write to his sister Agnes in Australia and tell her he had marched through the beautiful countryside of her husband's birth. Adam had never been to Ayrshire before and thought that Agnes and her husband John would get some joy out of the correspondence.

At last, basic training was over and Adam was given 48 hours leave before being shipped over to France. He was required to wear full regimental dress and it was amazing how he had grown into the uniform in just 12 short weeks. As he stepped confidently off the train at Haddington he was aware of the sideways looks of admiration from a few young women he passed on the street. He was fit, good-looking and felt magnificent as he strode up St Martin's Gate. He was also eager to join his four brothers, Sandy, Ian, Willie and Doddie, at the front.

Four days after Adam's departure, an apparently comatose Jimmy Cranston suddenly sat bolt upright in bed and coughed up a large amount of blood. He died in the arms of his wife Annie with children Mae and Alec looking on. His younger children Agnes and James were being looked after by their Aunt Mary. Lizzie, who had arrived from the Guild Hut, was furiously scrubbing the communal stairs leading to their flat.

Jimmy was buried in the same grave as his father Alexander in the grounds of St Mary's Kirk. Although by this time he was well established as the head of his own household, Lizzie insisted that he should take 'her place' in the grave and on the gravestone. It would save the family a good deal of money that it could ill afford. Jimmy's funeral service was held at 3:30pm on Saturday 20 May. As tradition dictated, it began in their Court Street flat, next door to the Plough Tavern and the busy Corn Exchange and only yards from the Guild Hut.[116]

Some of Jimmy's closest female relatives and older children were indoors with the minister and the coffin, but the sizable crowd that spilled onto the street was entirely male. As was the custom of the day, women attending a funeral would have been unthinkable. Lizzie was grateful that Ian had been granted leave from the front to attend. He had a calming influence on her and was a formidable presence to everyone else. He was wearing the kilted uniform of his Highland regiment and the single brass crown on his sleeve, indicating his rank of Company Sergeant-Major, impressed the men around him.

The two youngest Cranstons had arrived at the funeral together. They had already seen the suffering of their sister-in-law, Annie, and the looks of confusion on the faces of their nephews and nieces. Robbie did not expect the next hour or two to be easy; he had never lost a brother before. As he strained to hear the words of the Reverend Wauchope-Stewart, he realised he had lost sight of Angus. He glanced around the crowd of fellow mourners – it was large but would have been larger had most of Jimmy's friends not been at war – but Angus was nowhere to be seen. Robbie muttered a semi-audible excuse to anyone who might have been listening and slipped away.

He did not have to go far. Angus had got no further than the side of the Guild Hut, where, watched by a three-legged dog and a dirt-ingrained schoolgirl, he swayed precariously in the slight breeze. Not for the first time, Robbie spotted the remains of a half bottle of whisky in Angus's right hand.

---

116 Information derived from funeral notice placed in *Haddingtonshire Courier* in May 1916.

'Nae, the day of all days,' groaned Robbie as he lunged for the bottle, but Angus was too quick and leapt out of reach. 'You're far too young tae be drinkin' that stuff, an' what would Ma say if she found oot?'

'She'll only find oot if you tell her,' Angus responded somewhat menacingly.

'I'll no dae that,' conceded Robbie, 'but just get rid o' it and come an' join the rest o' us.'

'When I'm good an' ready an' no afore,' muttered the younger brother.

A short time later the ceremony inside concluded and the funeral party took turns to carry the coffin shoulder-high on its final journey to St Mary's cemetery. Not everyone who had been to the house followed the cortege to the churchyard, but nevertheless a moderately large crowd converged around the freshly dug grave to hear the final liturgy.

'Dearly beloved,' began the Reverend Wauchope-Stewart, 'our brother James has gone to his rest in the peace of God. May the Lord take him and welcome him to Heaven. With faith and hope in eternal life, let us pray to the Lord together by saying the...'

Suddenly there was a crash of broken glass from behind the well-wishers and everyone turned around to see Angus sprawled across a grave. He had tripped over a headstone and smashed the almost empty half bottle of whisky he was holding. He staggered to his feet, his clothes dishevelled and with blood trickling from a cut on his hand. He reeked of alcohol and his speech was slurred. 'What dae you think you're starin' at?' he barked. 'Get shtuffed, the lot o' ye!'

His brother Ian, whom he worshipped, marched up to Angus, eyes wide with anger. Ian did not want to make a scene in front of the minister or the others attending the burial. He pressed his face up to the nose of Angus and whispered threateningly, 'Get home now, I'll deal with you later.'

There was something about Ian's voice that cowed Angus and he wisely decided to obey without question. Chastened, he staggered off in the direction of the Nungate Bridge and home. He felt ashamed that he had not only disgraced himself at the funeral of one brother but had angrily disappointed another.

Some two hours later, Lizzie stood by the now deserted graveside, to pay her last respects to her son. Beside her, half a pace back but close enough, was Effie Fairgrieve, silent, respectful and well scrubbed up.

Reports of Angus's shameful behaviour had rapidly swept through the town, although neither Effie or Lizzie were officially supposed to know anything about it. Not for the first time, various family members had colluded to save Angus the ignominy of having to address the effects of his outrageous behaviour. They justified it by convincing themselves that they were protecting their mother.

As Effie wrapped one of her huge arms around her friend to comfort her, Lizzie quietly mumbled, 'I wish my Alec was here to sort this oot. It's getting too much for me.' Effie gave her a squeeze, 'Aye, pet, it's gettin' too much for us a." Effie meant the war. Lizzie meant her son.

By the time Lizzie got back to the flat all was quiet. Mary had treated her brother's minor cut on his hand and left him alone to fall into a drunken slumber. Now was not the time for the admonition he so richly deserved. Instead Lizzie decided to address all of her brood who were present.

'We're a' gaun tae have tae keep an eye on oor Angus. He's a poor, wee sowel and unless he tak's a lang hard look at hissel he's gaun tae end up in a lot o' bother.'

Everyone knew that this was no idle caution. Lizzie was letting them know that Angus was going to be a long-term problem.

The news of Jimmy's death weighed heavily on Ian, though the opportunity of any home leave was most welcome particularly at the end of a very difficult time at the front. A month earlier, in April, the 7th Cameron Highlanders had once more been posted opposite the strongly defended German position called the Hohenzollern Redoubt, which was the same fortification that Ian's brother, Doddie and the 8th Royal Scots had unsuccessfully fought so valiantly to secure from the Germans the year previously. The enemy was still determined to keep it at all costs. To harass the enemy and wear down his resolve the British mounted frequent night raids to kill or capture as many of the enemy as possible.[117]

'Sir, Sir! Dae ye hear that?' said the corporal excitedly to Ian Cranston. He was referring to muffled sounds coming at them from across no man's land a short distance away. Of course recently promoted Company Sergeant-Major (CSM) Cranston had heard the noises. He had heard them long before anyone else in his small raiding party. His years of training in the British Army had provided him with an acute sense of awareness not matched by anyone else in his company. He knew what the muffled sounds were the instant he had heard them. They were the sounds of British soldiers fighting for their lives in the first trench of the German line.

Why his inexperienced lieutenant had taken half the raiding party off on his own was beyond Ian. Fresh out of officer's training school in England, this 25-year-old had not learnt the hard lessons of life at the front. For him, warfare was still a game and tonight he had been dismissive of his sergeant-major's cautionary advice when crossing over to the German trenches.

---

117 The passage that follows is drawn from the Unit Diary of the 7th QOCM, at the UK National Archives, Kew.

The young and untested officer was going to mount a reckless assault on the trenches in an attempt to win himself an award for bravery. Experience taught Ian Cranston that such a foolhardy action would probably result in his death, along with many of the soldiers who went with him.

Ian had asked and then pleaded with the officer to reconsider his reckless plan to attack the heavily defended trenches head on with just 12 men, but the lieutenant misread his CSM's caution as a sign of timidity.

In disgust the officer decided to split the raiding party in half, taking six men with him over no man's land and on to what he believed would be certain glory. The lieutenant had no intention of sharing any medals he confidently expected to receive from this courageous action. So he ordered his overly cautious and, as far as he was concerned, possibly cowardly sergeant-major to wait in a bomb crater for his return.

The looks of the six men the lieutenant had selected to accompany him said it all. None wanted to go to their certain deaths. All wanted to stay with their company sergeant-major. Their eyes begged to be relieved of this order, but Ian Cranston remained impassive. After years of army life, he knew that an officer's order had to be obeyed.

'What are we gaunae do?' implored the corporal again, referring to the death struggle taking place not far away. CSM Cranston knew exactly what needed to be done, even before the words were said.

'Follow me,' he hissed authoritatively to the men around him in the bomb crater. He half crawled, half ran towards the German front trench 30 metres away. Ian did not need to look back to see if his small detachment of soldiers were with him. The men of 'D' company, 7th Battalion Queen's Own Cameron Highlanders, regarded their company sergeant major with a mixture of fear, respect and awe. To his men, Ian Cranston was a real old-fashioned type of soldier, a terror for discipline when on duty and a thorough gentleman when off duty. A man who would sing a song or dance with the best; who knew everything there was to know about soldiering and took the greatest pride in his regiment. His word was law in the battalion and he treated officers with the same forthrightness as he would privates. All ranks looked up to him as a man to be respected.

The young men on the raiding party across no man's land that night would have followed him into the very gates of hell had their CSM ordered them to do so. And it looked like that was exactly where he was about to lead them.

As Ian leapt over the parapet down into the German trench below, his keen observational skills allowed him to take in the unfolding scene in front of him in an instant. Below him was his lieutenant and four of the six soldiers struggling to extract themselves from a much larger number of Germans pressing in towards them from each direction of the trench. Two of the Scottish soldiers lay motionless on the duckboards at the bottom of the trench. Without needing another look, Ian knew they were dead. On each side of the fighting there were a number of German dead, thankfully creating obstacles for the incoming enemy to step over in the narrow trench. The fact that the Germans were having difficulty pressing in on the British soldiers was probably the reason why these Cameron Highlanders were still alive.

But from the corner of his eye Ian could see more enemy reinforcements coming down a communications trench towards them from the second line of German trenches. They were hurrying and the glint of moonlight from bayonets held high showed Ian they were carrying rifles. Ian realised that they had made a vital mistake. Rifles were an ineffective weapon in the trenches as they were too long to wield in the trench's tight confines. A rifle with a bayonet attached was even longer, almost two metres in length, and in a typically one metre-wide trench, next to useless.

The British raiders on the other hand did not come armed with pistols or rifles. Gunfire would only draw unwanted attention to them. Stealth was the key to any trench raid; noiselessly and suddenly attacking the enemy and then melting away before the Germans could mount a conventional counter-attack. This meant that the British soldiers armed themselves with clubs, maces, knives and other primitive devices that would kill and capture German soldiers swiftly and silently.

When Ian Cranston dropped down into the German trench he carried a Robbins & Dudley fighting trench knife in his right hand and a lead pipe in his left. He had purchased the knife privately from a sword dealer in London when he was last in Britain on leave. It was a vicious, lethal weapon but very effective in tight spaces. Ian had never shown either the knife or pipe, which he used as a club, to his wife or any members of his family. The sight of them would horrify his wife whereas his young brothers Robbie and Angus would be too drawn to them. The weapons would always stay in France. He could not fathom how brutal, inhuman hand-to-hand fighting with primitive weapons could remain part of such technologically advanced warfare. But not only had this type of fighting remained, in circumstances like tonight it was essential.

The Robbins & Dudley fighting trench knife was made of aluminium with a 15cm carbon blade. It incorporated a knuckle-duster as the handle and John gripped it in his right hand with the blade facing downwards. A vicious right hook to the head would knock the enemy senseless, thereby exposing his vulnerable neck. A simple follow through with the leading edge of his razor-sharp knife would slice flesh or cut an artery. The German would be dazed and bleeding at the least, or dead, within a minute.

The pipe in his left hand was a brutal device. There was no way to hide its deadly purpose, which was to bash in people's brains. Even if the weapon missed its mark and struck an arm, or a shoulder or a helmet, the impact would still break bones and dent metal.

Ian Cranston had developed a pattern of trench fighting that had up to now proved sickeningly effective. He would slowly progress down the trench swaying slightly from his right to his left. As he leaned right he would throw a swinging right punch at the nearest German and cut exposed flesh with the blade's follow through. Then he would seamlessly shift weight a little to his left and swing his lead pipe in a horizontal motion, smashing the head or some other body part of any German it connected with. It was an awkward, jerky movement, which took much practice to perfect, but in the desperate and brutal activity of trench warfare, grace and poise did not matter – only survival.

So it was on this night. In the German trenches of the Hohen-zollern Redoubt, a small group of Scottish soldiers frantically fought off a larger number of German soldiers pressing in on them from both directions of the trench. It was Company Sergeant-Major Cranston who was the focus of everyone's attention as he ferociously crept forward swaying from his right to his left, punching, slashing and smashing. As long as the Germans bunched up they could not level their rifles and engage the Scottish soldier. The more Ian pressed forward centimetre by centimetre with his deadly rhythm of punch, slash and smash, the more the Germans became crowded together, momentarily defenceless.

Punch, slash and smash – again and again. Blood started gushing out of some German soldiers and one spray caught Ian with a great arc of red, thick liquid. Punch, slash and smash – once more. Ian could hear the sound of men's bones being broken, flesh being cut and helmets being dented. Such was the crude nature of this fighting that more people were being injured or stunned rather than killed, but even if only temporarily incapacitated, it still meant one less enemy soldier was capable of retaliating.

However, Ian knew he could not keep up the savagery for much longer. It was so exhausting that he would shortly have no energy left. Even now the lead pipe in his left hand felt heavier and was becoming more difficult to swing.

Punch, slash and smash again and suddenly the German reinforcements hesitated in the face of this madman in a 'skirt'. This was the moment Ian had been praying for. A quick order was barked and the Scottish raiding party rapidly scrambled out of the German trenches leaving four of their comrades dead or dying behind them. It was a desperate scurry to reach the safety of a foxhole ahead of the Germans firing their rifles, but as the first shots started zipping overhead Ian managed to get his depleted group bunkered down in time.

Amid the heavy breathing, the sobbing of a few of the soldiers, the sheer exhaustion felt by all the men as the adrenalin drained away, Ian happened to look into the face of his lieutenant and saw a completely changed man. Gone was the bravado and superior attitude. In its place was the look of a man who knew how close his arrogance had come to costing the lives of his men and himself. He reached across the gap between himself and his sergeant, offered his outstretched hand and with as much gratitude as he could muster said a simple but heartfelt, 'Thank you.'

The raiding party was forced to lie low in the crater for hours until it was safe to return. As dawn broke, a humbler and wiser officer reported the truth about the part he played in the botched raid. He also included a strong recommendation for the bravery of his sergeant major to be recognised. The colonel of the battalion listened to the young lieutenant's report in full and then ordered his trusted company sergeant major to report.

Colonel Sandilands had known Ian Cranston for many years since Cranston had been a private and Sandilands only a junior lieutenant. They had seen action together for 10 of the past 16 years in the Mediterranean, China, South Africa and now France in what people were starting to call, 'The Great War'. The year previously Colonel Sandilands felt he owed Ian Cranston his life for protecting him during the Battle of Loos in 1915.

At the time he had chosen to reward Corporal Cranston with a promotion rather than a recommendation for bravery. The promotion was a more practical recognition, in that Ian would permanently receive a much-appreciated pay rise. Corporal Cranston was promoted overnight to the rank of company sergeant-major, in effect a rare and remarkable 'double jump' in rank. Another year on and Colonel Sandilands had the opportunity of completing the debt he felt he still owed Ian Cranston.

As CSM Cranston stood to attention and saluted, Colonel Sandilands said, 'It is my pleasure to inform you that your actions on the raiding party last night have not gone unnoticed. I will be recommending you for the Distinguished Conduct Medal for your bravery in rescuing the lieutenant and his trapped party.'

It was more than Ian could have hoped for. Only the Victoria Cross ranked higher. His head was still reeling from the remarkable compliment when Colonel Sandilands, disregarding military protocol, said, 'Ian, you've done more than anyone I know to faithfully serve this regiment. You deserve a rest. As well as the award, I'm also recommending that you be transferred back to Scotland as an instructor of recruits. There, you can serve out the remainder of this dreadful war out of harm's way.'

For once in his life, CSM Cranston did not know what to do or what to say, but after a brief pause military training reasserted itself. Sergeant-Major Cranston straightened his back and was about to throw a precise and smart salute at his commanding officer. But to his shock, Colonel Sandilands ordered him to stop. The colonel smiled at his CSM and respectfully said, 'Not today Ian. On this occasion I salute you.'

It was now July 1916, and apart from a few brief days in Scotland attending his brother's funeral, Ian's promised medal and transfer had still not materialised. But Ian was optimistic both would come to pass; he just had to be patient.

Meanwhile, the Cameron Highlanders were back in the same trenches they had occupied off and on for the past 12 months, facing the Germans at the Hohenzollern Redoubt yet again. The Germans and British had allocated their best troops to this sector, and both sides hated each other intensely. In some other areas along the front there had developed an unofficial 'live and let live' policy where aggressive actions were kept to a minimum. But at the Hohenzollern Redoubt the Germans reserved a special animosity for the Scottish soldiers facing them beyond no man's land. They called them, *Damen aus der Hölle*, 'Ladies from hell', because of their kilts. On the British side, the Scots had no time at all for the German elite units they were facing. They were regarded as cruel and barbaric sadists who enjoyed killing.

The sector was always alive with the crackle of gunfire and sporadic shelling. It had a reputation for being one of the most dangerous locations along the entire British front. The Germans would bomb the British trenches regularly with heavy artillery and mortars. In the meantime the Scottish soldiers would mount sudden and vicious raiding parties across no man's land at night – such as the one CSM Cranston had participated in a couple of months previously – to kill or capture as many Germans as they could. The area was always tense and would explode suddenly into violent madness at the least provocation. The weekly toll of casualties from snipers underscored the heavy penalty extracted from both sides for any casualness or the slightest loss of concentration.

Thankfully, a British soldier did not spend all his time in the front line. Life in the trenches quickly developed into a familiar pattern that both sides independently came to adhere to in a never-ending cycle of deployment. Every British infantry battalion would spend about two weeks at a time in the front line on high alert. This would be followed by about a week spent at a lesser state of readiness in support and then two more weeks in reserve. Finally, a week's rest would follow and then the whole cycle would repeat itself.

It was not just the enemy that soldiers had to remain vigilant against. Hygiene and the unsanitary conditions were never far from the minds of officers and senior NCOs like Ian. Rats, lice, nits, trench foot[118] and venereal disease could incapacitate a soldier just as easily as a German bullet.

While in the front line, Ian insisted his men of 'D' company shaved regularly and washed their underarms and groin at least twice a week. He was also a stickler for ensuring his men changed their socks regularly and applied grease made from whale oil to each other's feet. There was much grumbling from the men, but everyone knew the company sergeant-major's uncompromising attitude resulted in fewer casualties from illness and disease than suffered by many other infantry companies at the front.

However, Ian's insistence on proper hygiene resulted in at least one unusual episode, which he documented in a letter to Agnes: 'This afternoon was bathing parade at nearby coal mine. We were only given two tubs per Company. At the time D Company was

---

118 A fungal infection caused by prolonged exposure of the feet to the cold, wet and unsanitary conditions found in the trenches. If left untreated, trench foot could turn gangrenous and result in amputation.

up to strength – 203 Officers and men. Would take too long for Company to bath, so "In & Out two men in a tub" was the order. Still took 3 hours for Company to finish, because water needed constant changing.'

One night after the evening meal CSM Cranston set about performing his usual evening routine, making sure everyone was safe and accounted for before he would give his final report to his lieutenant for the day. As he moved along the trenches and dugouts occupied by the 200 or so men from his company, he passed small groups of soldiers playing Crown & Anchor and sentries peering out into the darkness of no man's land. Other soldiers were writing or reading letters and there were one or two solitary soldiers smoking pipes and wanting to be alone with their thoughts.

Ian was satisfied all was in order, but as he started to enter the NCOs' dugout he heard the distinctive sound that his acute sense of hearing knew only too well – across no man's land the unmistakable noise of a German heavy mortar[119] being discharged. The sound had registered with Ian before anyone else had even heard the characteristic whoosh of the shell leaving the short 25cm-wide barrel over 600 metres away. Then he heard the unique wobbling sound as the round tumbled end over end on its trajectory up from the German trenches. From experience born of decades as a hunter, forester and soldier, he knew instinctively where the shell was heading.

Right on top of him!

'Mortar!' Ian yelled at the top of his voice and turning to the NCOs inside the dugout screamed urgently, 'Get out now!'

The men knew they only had seconds before the shell would hit. They scrambled past Ian to safety around the nearest bend in

119 *Minenwerfer* (literally, mine launcher).

the line. Satisfied that his men were safe, Ian turned to join them when the 96kg shell smashed through the entrance and exploded.

CSM John Cranston was instantly obliterated.

In another part of the British sector Willie Cranston, survivor of the Battle of Loos the previous year, woke with a start. This was 14 July 1916 and the battle for Longueval was about to commence.[120]

All the troops were ready with bayonets secured to their rifles. Extra ammunition had been handed out as well as a cup of rum to each soldier on the orders of the Colonel. At precisely 03:25 hours a captain stepped up on a crate further along the trench from Willie, took one last look at his watch and blew his chrome officer's Kinglet brand whistle to signal the start of the offensive. Willie started to climb out of his trench and go 'o'wer the bags'.

Willie's division was now facing the German lines at what was once the little village of Longueval. It was now a heavily fortified enemy stronghold. All the attacking troops were carrying their full kit – all 20kg of it – 'to save bearers from having to bring it up later', the senior officers patronisingly explained.

Despite setbacks elsewhere else on the Somme, the British Generals were still optimistically forecasting that each successive engagement would be easier than the last. Perhaps the ultimate breakthrough they had been promising the soldiers for the last two weeks would occur today at Longueval. But in the past two years of war, Willie had been told many things by his officers that had never taken place. His promised promotion had never

120 The following events are based on the Unit diary of the 7th Battalion Seaforth Highlanders. Archive Reference No. WO95/1765 National Archives, Kew, London.

materialised and neither had his transfer to the Divisional Band, which, he had been assured, his extraordinary fiddle playing merited.

After the horrors of Loos the previous year he had looked forward to his removal from the front lines, but it had never happened. As he climbed out of his trench with the rest of the lads from his battalion, Willie wondered how much faith he should put in his superior's statements regarding how relatively easy the day would be.

The German officers blew their whistles too, signalling their men to emerge from the bunkers and cellars and take up defensive positions along the trenches and around the heavily fortified houses. If this was the so-called 'big push' that the Germans had heard so much about, then the men from the 153rd Infantry Regiment of Thuringia were determined to rob the British of their moment of glory.

Flares were fired into the night sky and no man's land was bathed in an eerie glow of phosphorescent light. The Germans had the advantage of a slightly elevated position and could see enemy soldiers emerging from their trenches right across their field of vision as far as they could see. There were thousands of them, marching in neat rows across open ground towards them. It was as if they were performing a drill on the parade ground.

Willie had only marched a dozen metres or so when he realised that the smooth grassed fields that once stood between the British and German trenches were now a quagmire of shell holes, and that the ground underfoot was so churned up that his fellow soldiers were beginning to break order. That was when Willie heard the first rounds of enemy fire whizz past him. Willie recognised the sound at once: the dreaded German machine guns. A feeling of helplessness overcame him as he realised he was so exposed in the open ground.

A German corporal from the Thuringia Forest also heard the loud chatter of the machine guns off to his left and right. He both admired and loathed them. They were effective and coldly clinical, whereas he prided himself on the more personal nature of his method of killing. Throwing grenades at the enemy when they were so close he could hear them breathing was more exhilarating than the indiscriminate slaughter of soldiers at a distance. The German soldier felt the immediacy and the intimacy of death after every engagement and it always made him feel more alive. In his opinion machine gunners felt nothing. They were merely killing machines on an industrial scale.

Willie picked up pace. He was not going to be caught out in the open and chopped down by any unseen machine gunner. He had to get across no man's land as quickly as possible, or die. Everyone else instinctively had the same thought. Fellow soldiers to his left and right started to run, but the going was tough and agonisingly slow. The ground was soft underfoot and they were weighed down with the useless equipment, such as rations, coats and tents, they certainly did not need at that moment.

Willie jettisoned his haversack containing his overcoat and personal effects, leaving just his ammunition belt and water bottle underneath. Suddenly lighter by some 20kg, he picked up speed as he slipped and stumbled across broken ground. Others followed his example and soon Willie found himself at the head of a small detachment of men trying to close the distance between them and the nearest German front line. He could see out the corner of his eye that men were beginning to fall around him. He could hear the heavy breathing of about half a dozen fellow soldiers who were with him. Willie started to run forward as fast as he had ever run in his life.

As the British soldiers came towards the front line, the German corporal calmly stood on the firing step and withdrew four stick grenades from his canvas bags.[121] He carefully unscrewed the base cap on the bottom of the wooden handle and smiled grimly as a weighted cord fell out. He laid the primed grenades on the sandbags in front of him.

As the first waves of kilted soldiers loomed out of the darkness, the German rapidly pulled the cords on the grenades to start a five-second fuse and threw them one after the other in an arc. The four stick grenades exploded in rapid succession about 30 metres or so in front of him from his right to his left. There were flashes of light and a deafening roar as smoke, fragments and splinters tore the air apart and half a dozen soldiers from the Seaforth Highlanders fell dead or mutilated to the ground.

Willie saw the bursts of light and heard the sounds from the grenade explosions further up ahead of him and rushed to get to the trenches before the bomber could throw again, but when he jumped over the parapet he found the enemy trench empty. The Germans had disappeared! More and more Seaforth Highlanders arrived at the German front line and were equally astonished by the enemy's absence.

Suddenly, rifle fire started being directed towards them from destroyed buildings beyond the front trench, on the outskirts of the town itself. A Highland sergeant yelled at the men to move on and several dozen men started climbing out of the German trench.

Willie was following the sergeant up out of the trench when he heard the thud of a bullet hitting flesh and looked up to see the NCO falling backwards towards him. He ducked as the sergeant crashed dead onto the wooden floorboards of the trench behind him. He glanced at the sergeant lying on the bottom of the trench with a gaping bullet wound in his chest and was overcome with

---

121 *Stielhandgranate (modell 24)*

fury. William raced up to the first pile of rubble that was once a house and started looking for enemy targets at which to shoot.

Meanwhile the large German corporal had reappeared from a tunnel a short distance away and was throwing more grenades with lethal effect. The attack was beginning to falter because these strong points were proving time consuming and costly to overcome. In the half-light of an approaching dawn the British could now see that the Germans had created several well-defended positions around the long-deserted village and were probably using a tunnel system to connect them.

As the minutes ticked by, more soldiers joined Willie and increased rifle fire was directed towards one well-defended German position. The German grenade-thrower meanwhile, surrounded by an officer and half a dozen soldiers, was doing an admirable job of keeping the enemy at bay. Even so the tide was turning in the favour of the British as a second wave of South African support troops swept in and took up flanking positions surrounding the bunker.

Then a British officer had a bright idea. '*Sprechen sie Englisch?*' he shouted to the Germans.

'*Ja*, what do you want?' came an answer as the battlefield in this location grew quiet. The British officer explained that the Germans were being outflanked and soon they would be overrun. To avoid further bloodshed, the British were offering quarter with a guarantee that the enemy soldiers would be treated honourably.

After a moment's silence, the German officer replied, 'I and my men have orders to defend this position with our lives. German soldiers know how to obey orders. We thank you for your offer, but we die where we stand.'[122]

Every British soldier within earshot was impressed. Nevertheless, if it was their wish to die, then so be it. There was a rush of British

---

122 This incident is quoted in '*Deville Wood*', by Ian Uys (Uys Publishers, Johannesburg, 1983), page 54.

and South African soldiers to the bombed-out building where the German officer had spoken so eloquently only moments before, but as the men stormed over the rubble into the defensive position no Germans were to be seen. They had disappeared again. Suddenly to their left in another destroyed building came the sound of a German machine gun, rifle fire and exploding bombs.

'Shit,' someone swore beside William, 'they're popping up everywhere like bloody rabbits.' Instantly William knew what had to be done. As with the ferrets they had periodically possessed as boys, 'rabbiting' expeditions always involved sending the animal down into the burrow. Today, it would be up to him to get into the hole and flush the enemy out. In this case the first hole was 50 metres away across broken ground where the Germans were spewing death again. The German soldier from the forests of Thuringia had primed more grenades to launch yet another spray of bombs, when he suddenly saw a lone kilted soldier come out from behind some house rubble and rush forward. There was a moment of admiration in the German's mind as the brave Scottish warrior ran towards him, but the fleeting thought was replaced with the pull of a cord.

Willie saw the stick grenade fly through the air towards him and threw his right hand up instinctively in a subconscious action to protect his face. Then the air was suddenly split by the sound and fury of ammonium nitrate exploding close by and everything went blank. Willie did not see anything. Willie did not hear anything. It felt like a runaway horse had slammed into the side of his face and torso. His entire body was numb.

Decades later, Willie would regale his grandchildren about being on his knees and looking down at a strange object which was dangling from his face in front of him. He would tell them that at first he did not know what it was, but then it slowly dawned on him that the small egg-like object was in fact his own eyeball hanging loosely from his fractured face. He described how, without thinking, he tried to place it back into his head, but for some reason it would not reattach. He would explain that at the time he did not know the bones around his eye socket had been smashed. With a mixture of awe and disbelief his young audience heard how all he succeeded in doing was stuffing the gaping hole in his face with mud, dust, blood and tiny slivers of shrapnel. Then it was, according to Willie, that as the violence raged around him, he lost consciousness and slumped to the ground.

After he had lapsed into unconsciousness, subsequent waves of British soldiers fought bravely to secure the rest of the town, but the fighting in the woods beyond was still raging. Reinforcements had been thrown into the engagement to hold on to the advances and during the brief lull in fighting before the anticipated German counter-attack; stretcher bearers from the British lines scoured the battle field retrieving dead and wounded soldiers in their hundreds. Private William Cranston from the Seaforth Highlanders was located, and his webbing was removed and discarded to reduce weight. Then he was evacuated from the front line.[123]

When Willie regained awareness, he was lying in a bed at a British Casualty Clearing Station several kilometres from the front line. He had been one of the lucky ones. In many other sections of the front, the massive British offensive had been repulsed by the Germans without any ground being gained, and wounded soldiers were left to die where they fell because the Germans would kill

---

123 In 2011, the author located a First World War British soldier's brass webbing buckle beside the German front line where William was wounded during the Battle of Longueval. There were several other soldiers killed and wounded at the same location on the outskirts of the village and their webbing belts would have been removed too. There is a one in twenty chance that the brass buckle in the author's possession actually belonged to William. It has become a family treasure.

anyone reckless enough to venture forth into no man's land to save them. Some say it took days for the sobbing, the crying and pitiful calls for help to finally cease.

Willie did not feel lucky. He noticed the medical staff pointing in his direction and whispering among themselves whenever they talked about him. He vaguely remembered one young New Zealand nurse fresh to the horror of war peeling back the bandages that covered his face and immediately vomiting down the side of the bed at what she saw.

At least there was one thing Willie could be thankful for: he did not feel any pain. The orderlies kept pumping morphine into him and Willie was not sure if days or even weeks had gone by since he had been retrieved from the battlefield. Everything was a fog.

He was transferred again, this time to a large Allied hospital near the sea at Le Havre, and after a short number of days moved yet again to England via a hospital ship. At every move, Willie could remember his sergeant telling the lads about wounded soldiers one time: 'The further back you are sent from the front lines, the nearer you are to getting out of the war. However, the nearer to death you have to be too!'

What he did not know at the time was that the stick grenade thrown by the German corporal had exploded in the air about 17 metres away from him. It was close enough to seriously wound him, but not quite close enough to kill him. When the canister containing 200 grams of explosive detonated, a shockwave of metal fragments and wood radiated out at such force it blew off three fingers on Willie's right hand. It also fragmented his right eye socket, smashed his eye, lacerated his face and peppered the right side of his body with a dozen small puncture wounds.[124]

By the time Willie arrived at the military field hospital at Le

---

124 A grandson proudly possesses William's Seaforth Highlander kilt, which still bears faded bloodstains to this day.

Havre the surgeon could see that there was no hope of saving the eye itself. The eye socket was too badly shattered and the risk of infection too great. The best he could do was clean out the wound and remove the eye altogether. What remained of the right side of Willie's face was just a pulpy mush of bone and flesh. His hand and face were swathed in bandages, the puncture wounds on the body washed and dressed and Private Cranston was sent further away from the front for long-term rehabilitation.

The next thing Willie could remember was arriving at First London General Hospital, in the commandeered premises of St Gabriel's College, Camberwell. Because of the morphine, Willie was unaware that it had in fact been more than a week since he had been evacuated from the battlefield in France, but at Camberwell the medical staff gradually reduced the dosage of painkillers and he slowly emerged from his drugged state. Fully conscious, Willie was able to inspect the damage to his hand and realised he would no longer be the premier fiddler he once was. The loss of his prodigious musical ability affected him deeply. No more concerts or *ceilidhs*.[125] No more sessions in pubs for money and drinks. No longer would he be the most popular person at the party.

Quietly, alone in his iron hospital bed, Willie began to realise his life would never be the same again and he felt a blackness overcome him. He had become used to the free drinks and the public admiration when his fiddle-playing entertained people. Now he wondered whether he would ever play again.

For the first time a surgeon spoke to him about his injury. The captain in the Medical Corps had dealt with hundreds of patients like William. He was efficient and caring, yet his bedside manner was brisk and authoritative.

'Private, your wounds may look bad to you at the moment, but

---

125 Traditional social gathering involving Scottish and Gaelic music, folk dancing and sometimes story telling.

they are not life-threatening. We will sew your face back together and that should heal nicely, but you'll have to wear an eye patch for the rest of your life. I'm told that men with an eye patch look handsome and as you're single I'm sure you'll have no trouble attracting many women.'

'Women!' thought Willie, realising it was the first time he had thought about Pat or his mother since the battle, 'I must get in touch with them.' He asked an orderly to notify the two most important women in his life that he was all right and to give them his whereabouts.

Willie may have been one of the older Cranston sons to go to war, but because he was a widower, his 'next of kin' on the official enlistment papers was still his mother, living at St Martin's Gate. A few days later, Sandy Pow, the postman in Haddington, had finished his morning rounds and, as was increasingly the case since this horrible war had started almost two years earlier, his next duty was delivering messages from the War Office personally to the next of kin.

Mr Pow knew the Cranstons well. He had delivered mail to a succession of their homes in Haddington over the years. He had watched the pale, withered shape of the father Alec as he shrank and died from cancer over a painful four-year period. He had silently shared in the eldest daughter's joy of marriage in 1912 and her subsequent departure shortly thereafter to Australia. He secretly admired the Cranstons. They were a hard-working, close-knit typical Scots family that were trying to better themselves. Yet they were finding it very difficult without a breadwinner and everyone in the family had to pitch in to make ends meet. Sandy thought these good folk were much better than some of those living in what was the poor side of town. He had a strong work ethic too, another quality he admired in the Cranstons, and therefore could not abide the unkempt, slovenly people who lived wanton lives around them.

As Sandy Pow delivered his half-dozen notices from the War Office around town he observed that there was a buff-coloured envelope with Elizabeth Cranston's name on it. He also knew that this was not the first piece of bad news concerning her sons' service in the war. A few months earlier son James had died of consumption contracted while on service with the army. Sandy got off his bicycle and adjusted his blue serge uniform. He satisfied himself that he looked official and then he walked up the external stairs at the rear of the two-storey tenement. He approached the front entrance to the flat and knocked. Presently the door opened and he was surprised to see that it was not Lizzie but her daughter Mary who answered. He had seen her occasionally peddling her way to St Martin's Gate from where she lived and work at Tyne House, but still he was not expecting to see her today. Sandy could see by her red eyes that she had been crying.

'I'm sorry tae bother you Mary, but is your Ma at home?' he said in a warm and friendly manner.

'No,' replied Mary, 'Ma's at the Guild Hut. Can I help?' she sniffed wiping away stale tears with a handkerchief.

'I truly am sorry miss, but I have this notice to deliver,' said Sandy holding the envelope in his hand. Mary suddenly realised why the postman was standing at the door. She burst into tears all over again and cried out, 'Oh no, not anither one. I cannae tak' much more.'

Through the sobs and gasps for air, Mary told the postman that only days before yet another brother had died in uniform. This time it was Ian. He was the 'rock' of the family, she said, yet this rock had been blown up by a stray bomb while in the trenches over in France. With fear and trepidation, Mary took the envelope from the postman and opened it in front of him.

There was an intake of breath from Mary, 'It's Willie,' she said barely able to control herself, 'but he's no deid. Thank God he's only wounded.'

At the same time in London, Willie Cranston did not feel like thanking God for anything.

A few days later, another postman in the small rural village of Binsted, Surrey delivered a postcard to Pat Arnold. The postcard was from the staff at 1st London General Hospital informing her that Private William Cranston was currently a patient at the hospital suffering from severe injuries to the head and hand. The note went on to say that Willie had asked to see Pat and finished with the following ominous warning, 'If you do come, we insist you see the hospital staff before you visit Pte Cranston'. Someone had underlined the word 'before' for emphasis.

Pat was smart. From the postcard she knew the man she had fallen in love with was seriously wounded, but more importantly, he needed her. Without a moment's hesitation Pat informed her parents she was leaving immediately for London, a city she had never visited before.

Prior to her departure, Pat's father Samuel took her aside to give her some sound fatherly advice. He said that both parents were very happy that Pat had fallen in love with this gifted and handsome Scotsman. But then the tone of his conversation changed and Samuel, looking at the only daughter he had, said, 'You know he won't be the same man you remember. He probably won't even look the same. Be careful girl. That's all I have to say.'

With these cautionary words still playing repeatedly in her head, Pat departed. She travelled the two-hour train journey from the local train station at Alton to Loughborough Junction Railway station in London and then took a cab the short distance to the hospital. When Pat arrived at the front desk of the hospital she was directed to the third floor of the east wing and told to report to the ward sister in charge of that section.

A few minutes later, the busy ward sister took the postcard from Pat and read it. As she did her attitude softened and she explained in a kind way that Private Cranston had already undergone two operations with more to follow. At the moment half his face was covered in bandages and his right hand was fully encased in gauze dressing.

'He is in a serious condition,' the sister said sympathetically, 'but what's making his condition worse is that he is feeling very sorry for himself. He needs some cheering up and I suspect you're just the ticket. Follow me.'

Pat walked behind the nursing sister into the ward where dozens of men were lying on iron beds positioned against the side walls and facing each other. There was a wide corridor through the middle of the ward and Pat obediently followed the sister as she purposefully marched down the aisle directly to Willie Cranston's bed. There, wrapped in a tight swathe of bandages that covered half his head, was the man she had loved ever since they first met at a Regimental social nearly two years earlier. Pat hesitated. She was unsure whether to approach, but the sister announced her arrival to Willie before she had a chance to decide.

William Cranston slowly turned his head towards her so that he could see Pat with his good eye. He did not know what her reaction would be to the change in his physical appearance. Would she turn and run in horror? He stared at her speechless for a few moments unable to formulate the words that swirled around his mind. He began to mouth something, but nothing came out. This once cocky, outwardly self-assured Scotsman was uncharacteristically mute for the first time in his life. He gazed at Pat with a pleading look of a man who was completely helpless.

Pat saw the look on his face. She recognised it at once. It was the look of innocence, of naked vulnerability that she had seen many times from newborn animals on the farms surrounding her village back in Surrey. The man in front of her lying on the hospital bed needed someone to take care of him. Without a second's thought she instinctively moved forward to hold Willie in a protective embrace.

He cried. She cried and at that moment they both knew that for as long as they both should live, they would be inseparable.

Another operation and three weeks later, Willie was strong enough to obtain leave to journey by medical escort to Pat's home village with his personal possessions including his beloved violin. In the presence of her parents as witnesses, he married Martha (Pat) Arnold in the Holy Cross Church. She was 26 years of age at the time; Willie was 31 and lucky to be alive.

Two months had passed since his wounding in France and Willie had not played his beloved violin once during that time. The bandages on his hand had been replaced by a leather glove to protect the three missing fingers, but Willie had still not tried holding a violin bow.

His honeymoon was not a passionate one, for in truth he was still recovering from his physical injuries, though it was enjoyable and loving as the couple took strolls around the small rural town and Willie slowly regained his strength.

They stayed in the Arnold household for their honeymoon and Pat's parents gave them as much privacy together as the tiny two-bedroom cottage would afford. Every time Willie passed the fireplace in Pat's bedroom he would glance at her violin perched on the mantelpiece, yet he would say nothing.

At the end of the first week of their stay in the house, the family were seated quietly around the dinner table having just finished their evening meal when Willie excused himself. In the silence as both parents looked questioningly across the table at their daughter the sound of a violin being tuned was heard from the bedroom.

By the time the family had assembled to listen, Willie had finished tuning the instrument, but he was struggling to hold the bow. It was difficult even with the leather glove as the stumps still produced short stabbing pains when touched. The Arnolds waited patiently at the bedroom door as Willie slowly gained some control over his bowing action and the warm up gradually grew more pleasant to the ears. When Willie was satisfied that he had mastered the bowing he paused and let his right hand drop limply to let the small audience know that he was ready to play. He coughed once, tucked the violin a little tighter under his chin and brought his bow hand up to play the first notes. The first tune he played was one his father had taught him many years earlier. Willie's dad had told him it was the tune that brought him and Lizzie together at a dance in Edinburgh over 40 years previously.

The Arnolds had never heard the 'Barnyards o' Delgatie' and therefore did not recognise the tune. But they were able to instantly discern the proficiency of the playing. With a burst of pride, Samuel Arnold turned to his daughter and whispered, 'This lad can play a right royal tune on your violin, lass.'

'No, Dad', replied Pat, seeing her violin was still on the mantelpiece behind her husband. 'It's not my violin he's playing. It's Willie's fiddle.'[126]

Agnes Cranston read and re-read the letter from Australia that had dropped through the letter box of Sunnybank Cottage. It was from her namesake Agnes McDowall, the sister-in-law whom she had never seen.

12 September 1916

It is with deep sympathy I write you having just heard of Ian's death. I cannot think he is dead. It's too awful. I am so

126 William Cranston's fiddle originally belonged to his father. It came into William's possession in 1911 on the death of Alec.

very sorry for you and the dear children. It's dreadful and I'm heart sorry for you.

I only trust the wee bairns will be a great comfort to you even though they can't bring you the comfort that you want.

I'm all nerves just now, but I felt I must write as I always felt so proud of all the boys. I don't know if this is much sense as I've got a feeling I don't know what I'm doing. I do nothing but cry and think of the old days. This is a dreadful war.

I'm sure you will be at a loss to know how much you will miss him, but God always opens a door somewhere that will make your burden easier to bear. With love to yourself and the bairns, your loving sister, Agnes.

Clearly the words had been painfully written from the heart and Agnes had already almost consigned them to memory. She placed the letter in her knitting bag with the other two pieces of paper which she had come to cherish passionately. Impulsively, she grabbed all three and rushed from the cottage, seeking the solitude which was almost impossible to find in the house. She sat on a large tree stump and briefly wondered if perhaps Ian had felled the once majestic tree that had grown there. A tree struck down in its prime. Agnes carefully unfolded the cutting of the *Haddingtonshire Courier* dated 22 June and once again read the words:

Sergt.-Major J.B. Cranston, Bathgate. (D.C.M.) Hero killed.

Company Sergeant-Major J. B. Cranston of the 7th Battalion, The Cameron Highlanders, whose wife and two children reside at Sunnybank Cottage, Bridgend, Bathgate, was killed in action on the 17 July.

He had completed his arrangements for the safety of his

men when a shell smashed the entrance and the gallant soldier was killed.

Sergeant-Major Cranston was one of six brothers, whose mother resides in Haddington, who joined the army. Of the six who served, two have given up their lives for their country. [127]

Sgt.-Major Cranston was a soldier prior to the war, and when the hostilities threatened, being on the reserve list, he was called up on 4 August, and was among the first of the regiments to dam the tide of the German advance.

In October 1914, he was wounded, and for several months was in hospital. He was last home in May 1916, and during this leave he was at the funeral of a brother who had died. Had he been successful in getting through July; he was on the list for home duty as an instructor.

As we noted in these columns several weeks ago, Sgt.-Major Cranston was recommended for a D.C.M., and this honour, it is expected, will be given to his widow.

A Distinguished Conduct Medal! How Agnes had rejoiced when she first heard about the proposed award. Now, however, she would gladly trade in his medal for the prospect of having her husband back home with her. She reached for the last piece of paper. It was Ian's final letter to her, written barely three weeks before he was killed. She opened the letter which she had read many times before.

My dear wife,

Just a few lines trusting you are keeping well, also the children. I am quite well and doing fine myself.

---

127 The following year a seventh brother, Robert, enlisted to fight.

Well I dare say you will have seen in the *Times* that I was Mentioned in the Dispatches. Very nice too.

I have in my name to get home as an instructor. The Commanding Officer put through my name seeing I have been so long out here. In fact I have more Active Service than any other man in the Regiment, so I will stand a good chance of getting home perhaps the matter of a month or so. However, I am not building up my mind in getting home for I may get a fall.

I had a letter from my Colonel, which I enclose. I want you to take special care of.

I will now close with love to you all at Sunnybank, not forgetting yourself.

I remain your loving husband

John

PS: Kisses to you, Greta and Sonny.[128]

She ran her fingers slowly and lovingly across the paper, gently lingering over each letter of her husband's name. With that simple action, Agnes started to cry. At first it was quiet sniffs, which were replaced by muffled sobs and then like a great gush of anguish from the depths of her soul came forth wails of sadness. Minute after long minute she moaned at the loss of her beloved Ian. The tears and the hurt kept flowing.

A while later and still seated on the log clutching the now soggy letter, she clasped her hands in prayer and softly said, 'Dear God, you have seen fit tae call my Ian tae your side. I cannot ken your reasons why, nor will I ever understand your divine providence, but I must let you know how I feel about his passing. Ian was more tae me than just a husband. He was everything tae me. With

---

128 The letter is in the proud possession of Ian's grandson.

his support and love I felt that I could do anything, take on any challenge and succeed. He was my rock and I dinna ken what I'll do without him. There is an aching hole in my heart at the moment and I hope that over time you will be able to fill it, but in the meanwhile I just don't know how I will have the strength to look after my children, my parents and my poor wee sisters. Please bless me with your spirit and strength, Oh Lord. Please be my rock from noo on.'

As she lowered her head into her hands and began to sob again, she felt her hands fill with a spongy, stringy substance. She pulled her hands away to reveal that they were holding several clumps of her hair. 'Oh God,' she cried to herself, 'must I lose my hair as well?'[129]

Adam had looked magnificent at the end of his basic training and had enjoyed his leave back in Haddington. Any ambivalence he may have felt on his initial conscription was well and truly behind him and he felt more than ready to join his brothers at the front.

Soon, he was on a ship and across the English Channel to France. When he arrived at the headquarters of the 1st Battalion, Royal Scots Fusiliers it was September 1916 and the regiment was a long way behind the front lines training for a night-time assault. The Somme battle had already been going for three months and had cost hundreds of thousands of British lives, yet the generals were planning even more operations. The next offensive would involve the 1st Royal Scots Fusiliers and other units of the 3rd Division of the British Army. Everyone confidently said this was going to be the huge assault that was finally going to break through the

---

129 Within a few weeks, all of Agnes's hair fell out. For the rest of her life she always wore a wig when leaving the house.

German lines. Adam believed in this optimism, even though every other offensive on the Somme so far had failed to achieve any breakthroughs at all.

The untested Private Cranston was pleasantly surprised by the grit and determination shown by his fellow soldiers in the 1st Royal Scots Fusiliers. He was also impressed by their spirit and sense of pride. At this stage of the war, the 1st Battalion had been reinforced many times by men from the reserve battalions, from the volunteers in territorial battalions, and from early 1916, by men like Adam who had been conscripted. There was hardly a soldier still in the 1st that had been there at the start of the war. Yet somehow the rich, proud traditions and the fighting prowess of this regiment going back over 200 years were being maintained at the highest level. Adam warmly embraced this esprit de corps and began looking forward to the inevitable clash with the enemy which all knew would come soon.[130]

In October, the 1st Battalion along with the rest of the 3rd Division came back from training and took its place in the front lines opposite the heavily fortified village of Serre in northern France. This was the same sector that had proved impregnable for both the French and British forces since the start of the War.

Adam was thankful that none of his brothers had been involved in any of these previous failed attacks. The bodies of hundreds of French and British soldiers had been left to rot in no man's land throughout the summer and autumn as neither side allowed the other to retrieve them.

On 13 November 1916, Private Adam Cranston and the 1,000 men of 1st Battalion, Royal Scots Fusiliers slowly rose out of their trenches in silence at 05:30 hours on a dark, moonless night. The battalion's objective was to capture the village of Serre, 400 metres

---

130 The following events are based on the Unit diary of the 1st Battalion, Royal Scots Fusiliers. Archive Reference No. WO95/1422 National Archives, Kew, London.

up an incline from their own front line and defended by five rings of heavily fortified German trenches.

The tactic used this night was one of surprise. The normal policy of a heavy preliminary bombardment had been replaced by a short five-minute barrage that the generals hoped would not alert the Germans to the imminent attack. The weather conditions were no help; they were atrocious. Heavy snow drifts and fog managed to mask the movement of soldiers who were slowly beginning to enter no man's land. However, the fog was so thick, with visibility down to one or two metres, that the orderly lines of attack which the battalion had practised many times in training started to break up.

Adam's heart was pounding. This was his first engagement of the war and he was scared and thrilled with anticipation at the same time. The soldiers reached the lightly defended German front line with relative ease, but as Adam and his fellow soldiers began to cross over this trench, German machine guns cut through the silence. This was swiftly followed by a prolonged and devastating artillery barrage from the Germans that cut down the exposed soldiers. Within seconds, men started falling around Adam, yet he pressed on to the Germans' well-defended second line and straight into a vicious entanglement of impenetrable barbed wire. Adam Cranston could not move forward, nor could he find his way back through the thick disorientating morning fog. He was last seen struggling to extricate himself from the clutching embrace of barbed wire, having never fired a single round in anger from his rifle.

Within a half an hour of going 'o'er the bags', the attack in this sector was a complete shambles. While some men bravely staggered on, others turned back but many more lay dead or dying in the fog, the mud and the snow.

When some soldiers eventually stumbled back into their own trenches, no one knew if Adam and 200 other missing soldiers from the Royal Scots Fusiliers were dead, dying or had been captured. It was the same situation all along this sector of the front. The Serre Offensive had failed on its first day with thousands of British casualties, including Private Cranston whose disappearance could not be officially categorised at the time.

What no one on the British side knew was that the Germans had been busy adopting new tactics to listen to the enemy. Without the British suspecting a thing, the Germans had, over the previous months, tunnelled underneath no man's land to within several metres of the British front line at Serre. There, they had established listening posts where soldiers armed with stethoscopes and listening sticks could hear what the British were doing above them.[131]

On the day of the attack, a young German observer named Paul Hubschman from the 169th (8th Baden) Infantry Regiment had heard the movement of British soldiers leaving their front line trenches above him. He then relayed the information back to his superiors via field telephone.[132]

German machine gunners waiting in the heavily defended German second line of trenches had months to sight their weapons and fine-tune their fields of fire. They only needed to squeeze the triggers to know that they were causing enormous casualties on an unseen enemy. At the rate of about 400 rounds per minute the German machine guns hit the soldiers as they struggled through the freezing conditions only to be trapped in a maze of barbed wire.

A kilometre further to the rear of the German front lines,

---

131 In 2010 a German listening tunnel was discovered at the exact location where the Royal Scots Fusiliers commenced to cross no man's land. It had remained undisturbed for over 90 years and was only accidentally discovered when the tunnel's roof collapsed causing a farmer's goat to fall in. It was excavated in 2010 at the invitation of the French authorities by The Durand Group, a highly regarded organisation of subterranean military researchers and their report and findings were kindly offered to the author.

132 At Christmas, 1916, Paul Hubschman was again at his listening post deep underneath the British front lines, when he scratched the following graffiti on the wall of his tunnel, '*Paul Hubschman, aus Nürnberg* (from Nuremberg). *Weihnachten* (Christmas) Ano 16 (Year 1916)'.

German artillery were alerted also. When they opened up with a barrage of high explosives, the British caught out in the open did not stand a chance.

A few days later Maggie Cranston[133] was notified that her husband had been posted as 'Missing, Presumed Killed in Action' on 13 November 1916, but for the next few months no further information was received from the authorities.

'Dinnae forget lass,' said Lizzie in the days leading up to Christmas, 'we'll be having an extra guest for Christmas denner.'

Mary was puzzled. How did her mother know that? She was in the process of collecting and storing the food in preparation for Christmas and knew exactly how many people were coming. She had been scrubbing, cleaning and preparing the house in the odd hours snatched from her working days at Tyne House during the previous fortnight.

Now Ma was telling her there would be one more. It was tempting to dismiss her mother's prediction out of hand. Was she somehow expecting one of her dead sons to turn up? Knowing how her mother sometimes seemed to think these days, it appeared a distinct possibility, but Mary said nothing. She had long known to take her mother's intuition seriously. It was one of those things that bound them together.

In common with their friends and neighbours, the Cranstons routinely celebrated Christmas in a restrained fashion. For most, Christmas was just another working day with, for some, the possibility of attending a church service in the evening. Those

---

133 Once Adam had been conscripted, his family could no longer remain in the 'tied' flat owned by his employer. Maggie and the infant child relocated with the mother-in-law, Lizzie, into 46 St Martin's Gate.

living in the town would try to get together and every effort was made to provide a hearty meal. Bedtime would be at much the same time as ever, however, as the following day would be a normal working day. As elsewhere in Scotland, the celebration proper would be held over for another week until Hogmanay when drink would be taken, friends visited, resolutions made (and broken) and dreams dreamt.

This year Christmas would be even more subdued. This was the first Christmas since James and Ian had died for their country and Adam had been declared missing in action only a month earlier in November. Adam's wife, Maggie, desperately wanted to believe that the Red Cross would notify her at any moment of his incarceration as a prisoner. Although no one else really believed Adam was still alive, they tried to appear optimistic. Maggie needed to cling onto her belief because she had a two-and-a-half-year-old child to feed and she yearned for her man to come home.

Then there was Willie, who had suffered his horrific wounds several months back. His rehabilitation had been made easier through the love and care of his new bride, Pat. But everyone knew his recovery would take years and even then he would never be the same man again. Only Sandy and Doddie remained at the front and were still alive thankfully, but the net effect of so much warfare and death was that nobody really felt like celebrating Christmas.

Although Mary had not stayed in the family home for many years it seemed to her that she was expected to contribute more and more to the small household in St Martin's Gate. She was always willing to do more than her fair share and shortly after the beginning of the war had returned to Haddington specifically to help out. But even so at times she could be forgiven for thinking that not all the sacrifices in this bloody war were made on the battlefield.

In particular, she was puzzled as to how her mother who had

long cared for a large and growing family now appeared to find the care of a much smaller household to be beyond her. The once house-proud mother seemed to stumble from one simple task to another apparently unable to finish what had once been routine. Mary accepted that her two youngest brothers, Angus and Robbie, would be of little use on the domestic front. As with all the Cranston male folk, and indeed the Scottish man as a species, it seemed that their talents lay elsewhere. From her sister-in-law, Mary might have expected more, but Maggie was immersed in worry over her missing husband and in any case did not find it easy to share household tasks with her preoccupied mother-in-law.

Mary desperately wanted to change the dark mood that had taken hold of Ma and the rest of the family. She would have also welcomed the opportunity of analysing the reasons behind her mother's declining mental state, but with all the pressure of working for Dr Wallace-James and caring for her own family, there simply was no time for this indulgence. It was sufficient for Mary to know that her mother was sad, nervous, confused and unfortunately getting worse.

She recalled seeing an advertisement in the *Haddingtonshire Courier* one day in September, for an upcoming attraction at the local picture house in Haddington. The proprietors were advertising a war propaganda film produced by the British War Office which was designed to give comfort and strength to a nation shocked by recent losses from the Western Front. It was called *Battle of the Somme*, and Mary thought it would be a good idea for Ma to see it and that maybe it would lift her spirits. Perhaps she might even see some justification in the sacrifice of her two boys and reach some inner peace at their loss.

The Cranstons had rarely been inside a picture house. Indeed they were still a novelty across Scotland. Mary was hoping that the excitement and unusual nature of the occasion would work as a tonic for her mother. The film was meant to instil the population with a sense of pride and nationalism, but it was the first documentary in the world to show the reality of war. Many citizens and not a few soldiers on leave found the images too confronting. The climax of the film was the soldiers readying themselves for battle, at which time the pianist stopped playing and the audience was invited to fill the silence with their own thoughts.

At this point of the film Lizzie started crying uncontrollably. She jumped to her feet and shouted, 'My God, you're killing my boys.' Mary had to remove a visibly upset Elizabeth from the cinema as Lizzie screamed, 'Ma boys! ma boys!' all the way out. The outing had been a disaster.

On the way home Mary struggled to find a subject that mother and daughter could discuss. Then it dawned on her that Yule time was just around the corner and she asked, 'Ma do you think we should have apple pie or dumpling for Hogmanay this year?' Lizzie, who had been most agitated only moments before, paused slightly and calmly said, 'Oh, I don't know Lassie, you're so guid a cook, anything you make will be lovely.' And just like that the crisis was averted, at least until the next time.

It was now a few days before Christmas and while Mary was busying herself both in the small Cranston flat and at work in Tyne House, a young Canadian infantryman was taking his leave and heading north to Scotland. He went to visit one set of relatives in Edinburgh first and then on Saturday 23 December, he caught the afternoon train to Haddington to visit another family of relatives, the Cranstons.

He arrived unannounced, which was not unusual at the time, for servicemen often did not know their leave arrangements in advance and the postal service was expensive. All he had in his possession was an address hastily scrawled on a scrap of paper but no idea where the residence was. He asked the stationmaster for directions but between this person's broad Scottish accent and the young man's Canadian drawl, the instructions were only partially understood.

The young man walked through the town in his Canadian uniform and because it looked so similar to the usual British army khaki, no one gave him a second glance. He crossed over the Victoria Bridge as per the instructions he had interpreted from the stationmaster, but when he got to the far side of the river crossing he was completely lost. Around him were open fields, a run-down orchard and horses huddling against the cold in a paddock. There was a small collection of houses about 200 metres away, but the soldier was uncertain if he should go in that direction. Standing tall beside the road next to him was a five-storey mill of some kind. It was the largest building he had seen so far in Haddington and the sweet smell of freshly ground grain coming from it informed him it was a flour mill.[134]

There was some activity taking place at the mill, which was more than the Canadian could detect anywhere else. But as he was about to cross the road to get further directions, a postman came peddling his bicycle towards him. He asked him if he knew where the Cranston family lived.

'Of course I do,' he affirmed. 'If you come with me, I'll take you there directly. What's your name?'

'Jim Weir from Ontario Canada and I'm pleased to make your acquaintance.'

'Sandy Pow. And I'm very glad you're going to see my friends. They could certainly do with a visitor to cheer them up.'

Typical of the mine of information which he most assuredly

---

134 The site and some of the buildings date back to 1180. In 1916 the location was known as the Bermaline Flour Mill though today it is a malting mill for Pure Malt Products Ltd. (Ref: www.puremalt.com)

was, Sandy managed to remember some useless trivia he had read a long time ago about Canada.

'Do you know the first person to ever survive a fall over Niagara Falls was a woman in 1901?' he said.

'No,' replied Jim, who was nonetheless impressed that anyone in this quiet backwater would know anything about his country of birth.

At the end of a narrow unpaved street that appeared to lead nowhere the two men parted company amicably. As instructed by the postman, Jim Weir walked around the building to the rear and climbed the outside iron stairs to the metal landing along the second storey of a tenement building. Making final adjustments to his uniform he knocked politely on the heavy wooden front door at No. 46 St Martin's Gate. In the gloom of late afternoon, Jim was greeted by a young male who, after introductions, invited him into the household. What Jim found inside the flat disturbed him a little. The young lad he met was called Angus and he was one of two males living in the house. Then there was Maggie, the wife of another son who was missing at the front and who also resided there with her infant child. But what was unsettling was the mother, Lizzie, who seemed emotionally disturbed.

Lizzie Cranston could, however, hold a conversation and during lucid moments comprehend what was happening around her. She understood who Jim Weir was and his distant connection to the Cranston family.[135] She invited Jim to stay with them for the next few days he had on leave, including having Christmas dinner. Tomorrow would be Sunday and Lizzie insisted he accompany the family to the 11am Sunday service at St Mary's Parish Kirk after breakfast and chores. There would be a little surprise she informed him. Her 24-year-old daughter Mary would be joining them.

---

135 Jim Weir's grandfather married the late Alec Cranston's aunt.

The following day was Christmas Eve and at about 10.30am Jim heard a noise at the front door. He looked up to see Mary Cranston enter. Behind her, the low winter sun was bathing her hair in a warm golden glow. She was dressed in her Sunday best, a cream, frilly blouse and a dark beige skirt. Jim was mightily impressed. Suddenly the prospect of a long Scottish sermon seemed rather more exciting!

Mary was a little startled at finding a stranger in her family's flat but before Jim could introduce himself Lizzie called out from inside the flat, 'Hello lassie, he's the guest I told you aboot.' As Private James 'Jim' Weir from Ontario Canada stood to shake Mary's hands, he smelt her freshly washed skin and the aroma of crisply laundered clothes.

After church, Jim escorted Mary back to her work along the Tyne and found out that she had arranged some time off from her employer to cook the family Christmas dinner the next day. Jim could not wait for the time to pass. Sunday afternoon was spent pleasantly wandering the streets of Haddington with both Cranston lads acting as official guides. But in truth Jim was impatiently waiting for Christmas Day, so he would be able to see Mary again.

None of the Cranston family had heard the distinctive drawl of a Canadian farmer before and it fascinated them. The entire family instantly took a shine to this exotic distant cousin from Ontario. His looks, his confident manner, his laconic use of language and his sense of humour set Jim Weir apart. The Cranston women were attracted to him and the two teenage Cranston boys admired him.

Robbie and Angus Cranston reminded Jim of his own two younger brothers, Willie and Tom Weir. He felt comfortable with the Cranston boys and the feeling was reciprocated. Jim Weir was only a decade older than Robert and as far as the boys were concerned he quickly became a substitute older brother. Jim had a few days to observe the Cranston family and his attention was drawn to the youngest male, Angus. He had an intensity about him, which was a little disturbing Jim thought.

First, Angus had an insatiable appetite to know everything about the military. He wanted to know what training was like in Canada; had Jim killed anyone and what would Jim feel like when he ran his bayonet through the stomach of a German? Later, Angus blurted out triumphantly that he had shot at a Zeppelin which had passed over the town several months earlier. Jim did not know whether to believe the 15-year-old or not. Finally, Angus told Jim he could not wait to join the army and get to the front. When Jim asked him why he was all fired up to go to war, Angus just looked at him with a burning intensity of a fanatic and said, 'Revenge.'

The death of Ian and the uncertain fate of Adam within the last few months had done nothing to improve the mental state of Angus. Of the two deaths (for everyone except Maggie was now convinced that Adam was dead), it was the loss of Adam that affected Angus the most. He was seven years closer in age to Angus than Ian and whenever he looked on his distraught sister-in-law Maggie he found his anger welling up.

At this stage of the war several dozen soldiers from Haddington had already died in the service of their country, which meant that many local families had either suffered losses directly or knew of others who had. Christmas 1916 was not a time for thanksgiving or goodwill to mankind. It was a time of intense sadness, culminating in fervent prayers for those still in uniform to survive the slaughter and come back alive and intact.

To Mary, the sadness of the time was all the more reason to produce a Christmas dinner everyone would remember and enjoy. The Scotch broth provided little challenge for Mary, although the ingredients changed slightly each year depending on what was available. The clootie dumpling was altogether more difficult since the rich ingredients were almost impossible to come by in wartime, but Mary felt she had produced something of which everyone would approve. About the main course, she felt distinctly uneasy. She had been almost resigned to making do with a couple of over-priced or ill-begotten rabbits or whatever cheaply priced cuts of meat just happened to be available in one of the butcher's shops. But that was a long shot.

It was then that Angus appeared to save the day at the last minute. The goose that he had rather shamefacedly handed over a couple of nights previously would scarcely have merited a second glance in the years prior to the war, but now with the nation undergoing severe food shortages, it seemed fit for the King himself. Lizzie had surprisingly asked no questions and Mary decided that was perhaps for the best, for she had heard from her kindly employer of the murky trade in wild fowl that was becoming commonplace in the town.

Some put it down to the increasing availability of the bicycle. Edinburgh was readily accessible by this form of transport, the roads were invariably quiet and the Duddingston Loch was on the eastern outskirts of the town, on the edge of the King's Holyrood Park. Until recently it had been the home of hordes of semi-domesticated geese, but their numbers were rapidly decreasing. With the country being severely undernourished this seemed hardly surprising. What did surprise Mary, an enthusiastic smoker of Will's Woodbine cigarettes for many years, was the method apparently used by the hungry poachers to deprive the King of his wildfowl.

The procedure was devastatingly simple. A lit Woodbine would be attached to a fishing hook and line and cast in the vicinity of the geese that were huddled together on the shore. In the dead of night the glowing cigarette often proved irresistible. And a couple of successful catches made the long bike ride back to Haddington well worthwhile. This was the kind of ruse which might have resulted in the perpetrators being hanged in the previous century, and would be very harshly dealt with even today, but two years of war had started to create food shortages and desperate times called for desperate measures. Mary noted that the neck of the goose she had received was, along with the head, missing and guessed that this was a wasteful but necessary ploy to disguise how the unfortunate bird had met its death.

Jim had brought a small bottle of cranberry sauce to have with what he thought would be the traditional Christmas turkey, only to find out people in Scotland at that time ate goose or fish instead. He quietly handed over the bottle to Mary without making any fuss and Mary thought him kind and thoughtful. Jim liked the bird that the family consumed as the main centrepiece of their Christmas meal. It was rich, fatty and deliciously succulent. Not only was Mary a stunningly attractive woman, but she was an excellent cook too.

A thought was beginning to take seed in Jim's mind that he and Mary might consolidate their newfound friendship by agreeing to write to each other. When he finished his meal Jim crossed his knife and fork the way they did in North America at the time. Then he saw everyone else position their utensils side by side instead, the way they do it in Britain. Slightly embarrassed, he glanced nervously at Mary who smiled reassuringly and a feeling of complete acceptance filled Jim. These distant relatives in a faraway land might have strange customs and etiquette, Jim thought to himself, but while he was in Mary's presence it did not matter at all.

Lizzie had put on a brave face while the handsome young Canadian soldier had been visiting, but with his departure there was no reason to pretend. In the brief window between Christmas and Hogmanay, Lizzie had time to reflect on the year that was. And what a cursed year it had been: two sons dead, a third missing on the battlefield and a fourth in hospital lucky to be alive. In the quiet recesses of her mind, grief and desolation mixed with hopelessness as her once stable and happy world fell apart. She found herself wandering about the cold, dark flat in the middle of the night for no particular reason. Was she looking for something? She could not remember. At least her daughter Mary was comforted that it was almost the end of the year and surely nothing else could happen. But she was wrong.

On 29 December news arrived from Edinburgh that Lizzie's mother had passed away the previous day.[136] Margaret was 81 and had died from a heart condition. But it was not her age or cause of death that affected Lizzie. It was the fact that her last connection with the past had been severed. The relationship between mother and daughter had always been strained. All Lizzie ever wanted was to be loved by her, but with her mother's death it was now too late. With some of her family gone and others facing an uncertain future, something finally snapped. No past, no future, only a bleak, awful present.

'Thank God you're here, Effie,' said 17-year-old Robbie Cranston, whose compulsory enlistment was less than a year away. He had

---

136 Margaret Buchan (nee McLeay) died of cardiac valve disease at 3 Arthur Street, Edinburgh on 28 December 1916. (Reference: Scottish Registry Office www.scotlandspeople.gov.uk)

grown up quickly over the last few years, but tonight he looked like he was still a schoolboy. It was six o'clock in the last evening of the year, but no one felt like celebrating. 'She's barricaded hersel' in her bedroom, and refuses tae listen tae reason. She seems tae think the Germans are on their wye tae this very hoose and she says she's ready for them!' For the first time, Effie became aware that Angus was also in the room. He muttered darkly, 'They'll nae be back, nae efter last time. They'll a' be giving Haddington a wide berth I can assure you.'

Angus often thought back to his potential moment of glory almost a year ago when he had fired at a passing Zeppelin, but his comments did not help the current situation. Lizzie had a sturdy wooden chair jammed up hard against the inside door knob of the heavy bedroom door and was completely ignoring her sons' appeal to reason. The boys had tried to open it several times but it would not budge.

'Well, I'll see what I can do,' commented Effie, who until that moment had been rather subdued herself. She stood a little taller, which in her case was still rather short, and cleared her throat.

'Whitever happened tae the legendary Cranston hospitality, Lizzie you auld bugger?' she cajoled. 'It's the first Hogmanay that I hav'nae got a warm welcome at the Cranstons! Whit on earth's got intae you?'

Lizzie's reply was in most part inaudible, but after a string of muffled words through the thick barrier, Lizzie came closer to the door and said, 'Oh, Effie whitever's happening tae my laddies?'

Caught off guard, Effie briefly reflected on the secret which she had never shared with anyone. Her own two sons who were of fighting age might well have been in France, but then again they could be in Macmerry just a few kilometres away or on the far side of the moon. Since her marriage had broken up all those years ago, she had never heard from them. But there was no time for self-pity, she reproached herself. Effie realised that her friend was in a bad way and urgently needed her help. Over the past few days, she had been staying in her room for hours at a time while mumbling incoherently to herself. But this was the first time Lizzie had barricaded the door.

She thought momentarily about breaking down the old, solid door but realised she would probably come off second best in the encounter. Perhaps guile might be a better approach. But what would arouse Lizzie's interest? Then it struck her, the feature article in the local *Courier*, of course.

'Lizzie, have you seen this week's *Courier*?' she said chattily. 'You and your laddies are the star attractions. They've got a bigger spread than the Provost and the hale Cooncil put taegither! Come on Lizzie, you're gaun tae like this. They a' get a mention.'

A few seconds later, the barricaded door slowly inched open. 'I'd better hae a look, then, but I'm warning you, Effie Fairgrieve, if this is a trick, I'll—'

But it wasn't a trick. The *Haddingtonshire Courier* dated two days earlier carried the following article in a most prominent position:

A NOBLE HADDINGTON RECORD – THE SERVICE OF SIX BROTHERS

Intimation has been received that Private Adam Cranston, aged 23, Royal Scots Fusiliers, son of the late Mr Alexander Cranston and of Mrs Cranston, St Martin's Gate, Haddington, has been missing at the front since November 13. In civil life, Private Cranston was in the service of Haddington Co-operative Society as a baker, and was greatly liked and esteemed. Naturally the intimation now received raises grave anxiety as to his fate.

The event adds another fact to a noble family record. Six

brothers in all have joined the colours,[137] and within the past six months death has claimed two, while, in addition Adam has now been missing since November 13.

In May, Private James Cranston, R.E., died from a chill, just as he was about to leave for the front. In July, Company Sergeant-Major John Cranston, Cameron Highlanders, fell on the field after a magnificent record, he having gone out at the beginning of the War, and having undergone all the terrible experiences then involved. He passed through the great retreat from Mons and the struggle on the Marne, coming right down to Loos, through which battle he passed with only a scratch. He was to be released for recruiting and other services at home, but was killed in what was to be, for a time at least, his last week of active service.

Private William Cranston, Seaforth Highlanders, has also seen much fighting. He has been in hospital since July, suffering from serious wounds in the head involving the loss of an eye, he also having other injuries.

Lance-Corporal Alex. Cranston, R.E., after having been for some time in hospital, has again returned to the front.

Lance-Corporal George Cranston, Royal Scots, was seven months at the front, and was invalided home, his health having broken down from trench hardships, thus rounding off for the time being a truly remarkable record of patriotic devotion. Much sympathy is felt with Mrs Cranston in the new and grave anxiety regarding the fate of Adam.[138]

Deeply moved, the two women clung to each other with what was for them, an unusual show of affection. Lizzie dried her eyes.

---

137 The seventh son to enlist, Robbie Cranston, was conscripted the following year in September 1917.
138 *Haddingtonshire Courier* 29 December 1916, sourced at the East Lothian Archives.

'Oh Effie, it's so beautiful, they've done a' my laddies sae prood. Imagine the Cranstons getting a spread like that in the *Courier*.'

The emergency was over for now, but everyone knew that Lizzie could have another 'turn' at any moment. Effie told the boys to remove the chair and any other items that could be used to obstruct the door from her room. It may have been Hogmanay for the rest of Scotland, but Lizzie Cranston was not going to celebrate it.

1917

War had become 'total' with aircraft bombing cities and unrestricted submarine warfare sinking an unprecedented tonnage of shipping. One major military power (Russia) left the war and one major industrial power (America) entered it.

Along the Western Front, generals still continued to wage war using 19th-century tactics, which proved futile when pitted against 20th-century technology.

Yet elsewhere, in the Balkans, the Alps and in the Middle East, Germany's partners were beginning to crack under unrelenting and increasing Allied pressure.

.... On Saturday night I travelled to the fine old town of Haddington, where I stayed at the home of Mrs Alex. Cranston, having my Christmas dinner at her house. The late Alex Cranston was a cousin of Mr George Binnie, also of Mr and Miss Cranston of Dornoch.[139] Mrs Cranston has six sons

---

139 Dornoch is a small community not far from where the Weir family lived in rural Ontario. It was named after a town in the Scottish Highlands.

in the army, two having lost their lives within the last few months, one missing, one losing an eye, the other two still on active service. She is the proud possessor of a letter from the King expressing his appreciation of the patriotism of her sons.

But that does not atone for their loss and there are few homes over here that have not suffered through the War.

Thus wrote Private Jim Weir in the January edition of the Ontario *Durham Chronicle* about his fateful trip to Haddington. Perhaps he was already aware of its significance.

Looking back on that Christmas visit he could only vaguely recall the details. All he remembered was the angelic face of Mary Cranston whom he had greeted at the door and the undeniable fact that from the first moment he saw her he felt a strong attraction. Jim remembered asking Mary if he could write to her on a regular basis and while he could not recall her exact answer, she certainly indicated her consent. In the meantime, there was a war to be fought.

In March 1917, Jim's much-loved 147th Battalion (the Grey County Battalion) arrived in France and was immediately disbanded as a consequence of the entire Canadian Expeditionary Force being restructured. Individual soldiers were absorbed into various other battalions and in Jim's case he was sent to reinforce the 4th Battalion of the Canadian Mounted Rifles (4CMR). He deeply regretted the breakup of the 147th Battalion and being separated from his pals who had all come from the same area of Ontario and had been together for over a year. In Jim Weir's opinion, the 147th was one of the finest battalions Canada ever produced and it was a great shame they never got to fight together under this unit's banner.

Regrets aside, Jim and the rest of the soldiers knew that they had to go where they were needed and Jim arrived at the

4CMR just in time to participate in the first major Canadian offensive of the war, the attack on the previously impregnable Vimy Ridge.

The British and French had tried to capture this ridge three times in the past two years, but had been repelled on each occasion. The total loss of Allied lives so far in these unsuccessful attacks had been estimated at more than 100,000. However, the battle plan of the Canadians was brilliantly prepared and perfectly executed and between April and May 1917 the troops achieved a remarkable victory. Thousands of German troops and guns were captured and the Canadians achieved all their objectives.[140] The high point of the battle was a fixed bayonet charge up the steep incline of Vimy Ridge in the face of withering German machine gun fire with thunderous artillery overhead and against skilled, battle-hardened Germans. In the ferocious hand-to-hand fighting as the Canadians reached the top of the ridge, boys from the Canadian colonies turned into men. And they would never be the same again.

Thankfully, Canadian casualties were relatively light compared to previous major Allied offensives, but nevertheless more than 10,000 Canadian soldiers were killed, wounded or missing out of the estimated 50,000 Canadian troops that took part in the battle. Specifically, the 4CMR suffered 51 killed, 181 wounded and 12 missing in the month of the offensive. Jim Weir was one of those invalided from the field.

Leading up to and during the battle, Jim suffered a marked exacerbation of his goitre,[141] a pre-existing condition which grew

---

140 It has been said since that Vimy Ridge is to the Canadians what Gallipoli is to the Australians and New Zealanders. Both battles forged a sense of 'coming of age' as nations. The major difference with this analogy is that Vimy Ridge was a significant victory whereas Gallipoli was not. The Battle of Vimy Ridge was in fact the single most successful Allied advance on the Western Front to that date.

141 Goitre is a chronic enlargement of the thyroid gland in the neck.

worse the more he trained, drilled and exercised.[142] During the Battle of Vimy Ridge all the Canadian soldiers were called upon to endure physical hardships none had experienced previously as the fighting at times was hand-to-hand and exhausting. Jim Weir was removed from the battlefield suffering extreme shortage of breath, choking and difficulty swallowing.[143]

During his long convalescence, which started in France and subsequently moved on to England, he performed light duties, which involved no heavy exertion. Typical work for Jim and others classified as unfit for front line service would have been clerical in nature, or tending gardens to produce fresh vegetables for the troops in the front line. Jim wrote constantly to Mary in Haddington and when he was finally well enough to travel, he obtained leave to visit Scotland where he asked Mary to marry him. Mary accepted.

It was February 1917 and Sandy Pow was uncharacteristically reticent as he saw yet another buff-coloured envelope from the Ministry of War addressed to the Cranston home. Since this terrible war had started he had not socialised with this family as much as before.

It was his deliberate choice. Sandy had delivered many buff-coloured envelopes from the Ministry of War to grieving families

---

142 During the Great War, medical authorities in both Canada and the USA noticed an unusually high incident of goitre in recruits from the Great Lakes and Pacific Northwest areas, resulting in many young men being rejected from service on medical grounds. It was discovered that the main reason for the appearance of goitre was the lack of iodine in the diet. Minute quantities of the chemical were then added to table salt and in less than a year, the incidence of goitre was greatly reduced. (Ref: Joseph B. Schiel, Jr. and Anita Joan Wepfer, Distributional Aspects of Endemic Goitre in the United States, *Economic Geography*, Vol. 52, No. 2, (April 1976), pp. 116–26)

143 Taken from the service record of Jim Weir, Canadian Archives.

in Haddington. Too many he thought. He knew more than most citizens of the suffering that many families in the town were going through, especially the Cranstons. Sandy did not want to see them face-to-face again so soon after delivering the notice about Adam being missing. Once, the Cranston family had filled him with joy, now every beige letter to them filled him with dread.[144] Sandy Pow therefore slipped the letter through the slot of the front door of the flat and made a hasty retreat in case one of the Cranstons happened to open the door on him. A short time later Maggie returned home from shopping. As she opened the front door she stopped dead in her tracks.

There on the floor along with one or two innocent items of mail was an envelope from the Ministry of War. Inside the flat she could hear Lizzie in the kitchen muttering to herself repeatedly. This was clear evidence that she was not having a good day. Perhaps she has seen the letter but had chosen to ignore it. Maggie put down the groceries on the floor and picked up the envelope. She turned it over to read the addressee and momentarily stopped breathing. The letter was addressed to her, so it had to be about Adam and not one of Lizzie's other sons.

Shaking with fear, she tore open the envelope and read the following words typed on Army Form B 104-82 from the Ministry of War:

Madam, it is my painful duty to inform you that a report has this day been received from the War Office confirming the death of 40808 Private A.M. Cranston, Royal Scots Fusiliers who had previously been declared Missing in Action on 13th November 1916 with the B.E.F. in France.

---

144 Each envelope carried four possible notifications for the next of kin, all of them negative. The serviceman was wounded, missing in action, had been taken prisoner by the enemy or worst of all had died.

I am to express to you the sympathy and regret of the Army Council at your loss. The cause of death was Killed in Action.

Any application you may wish to make regarding the late soldiers effects should be addressed to 'The Secretary, War Office, Whitehall, London SW' and marked 'Effects'.

I am Madam, your Obedient Servant, Colonel R. S. H. Theobald, Officer in Charge of Records

Standing in the entrance to the small flat, Maggie felt utterly alone as the emotions of grief and loss started to rise within her.

Since receiving the earlier notice from the Ministry of War in November 1916 that Adam was reported 'Missing in Action' she had been hoping, believing, praying that Adam had been captured, not killed in the Battle of Serre. A few of his fellow soldiers had indeed been taken prisoner by the Germans: why not Adam? But as the months went by it became harder to keep the illusion going. Other wives and mothers had long ago received official confirmation that their loved one had been taken prisoner, but she had received nothing.

Now this letter destroyed any remaining hope she might have had. Crushed, she knew she had to tell her mother-in-law before the rest of the family came home. Holding the letter and fighting back the tears, Maggie walked into the kitchen to see Lizzie wiping an already dry plate with a tea towel. She put the plate down only to pick it up again and start the process of wiping all over again.

'Ma,' Maggie interrupted, but Lizzie did not look up or stop mechanically wiping the plate. 'Ma,' Maggie repeated, this time a little firmer. Still no response. Maggie then walked over to her mother-in-law and gently touched her on the arm.

'Lizzie, I need to talk to you,' she said insistently. Lizzie Cranston stopped and shook herself out of her ritualistic behaviour. She turned to her daughter-in-law and saw the letter in her hand.

'It's aboot Adam isn't it?' she said. 'Please tell me he's coming home, please, please.'

With her bottom lip quivering and her eyes welling up with tears, Margaret Cranston, widow of Adam Cranston, looked into her mother-in-law's eyes and said with a trembling voice, 'No Ma, Adam's deid.'[145]

Death appeared to have the Cranston family in its sights and it was no respecter of age. In April 1917, Lizzie's 10-month-old grandson James, whom she had never seen, died in Musselburgh from acute bronchitis.

In a cruel twist, the death of this child meant that at least she was able to see her eldest son, Sandy, who had been given a fortnight's leave to attend his young son's funeral. Even though funerals were strictly men's business, Lizzie insisted on taking a batch of freshly baked scones to her daughter-in-law Annie to help her out. Mary insisted that Angus escort Ma and gave him strict instructions not to misbehave. On the train to Musselburgh, Lizzie tried to think when she had last seen the whole family? Could that have been at her daughter's wedding to that fine stonemason from Ayrshire? What was his name again, she thought? When was that wedding again?

Lizzie had always been convinced that Sandy would have made an excellent soldier, just as he had been a dutiful son, but the Sandy who greeted her arrival was not the Sandy she had long known. How he had changed! Surely he was too old to be in the thick of battle?

---

145 Adam's body was recovered in late February 1917 when the German army on the Western Front retired to a new defensive position several kilometres to the east known as the Hindenburg Line. After several failed attempts by the Allies and the loss of thousands of lives trying to capture Serre over the preceding eight months, the Germans in the end yielded the village to the British without a fight.

In fact Sandy had been badly affected by this war: an injury the previous year, which his mother knew nothing about, and in particular the staggering casualty list of his brothers had affected him deeply. Ever since the end of 1916 there had been a sense of dread growing stronger every day in his mind.

Back at the front, he had dealt with this in the only way he could. He had tried to put it out of his head and concentrate on the job at hand. He worked so hard and so diligently that his commanding officer promoted him to Sergeant with the promise of more home leave. As much as he tried, he simply could not shake the belief that his time was up. Everywhere he looked, death was stalking the Cranston family, and his leave, when it materialised, did little to help.

It was during this compassionate leave that Sandy found himself taking his eldest daughter for a walk across the old so-called 'Roman' bridge spanning the River Esk at Musselburgh.[146] Without warning, he suddenly blurted out to Ann, then aged 13, 'Lass, if anything happens to me, you have to look after your mum and help her bring up the bairns.'

Doddie Cranston was never a strong man. In fact he could be accurately described as small and sinewy, but at least he was always quick with a smile and a joke. His brothers called him the 'runt' of the litter in good-natured fun. If truth be told, Doddie was something of an extrovert, but all that changed after he had spent six months recovering from the hell of Festubert in May 1915. He had become much quieter and even his actions were a little slower. But there was one aptitude the shell shock did not

---

146 The bridge itself was constructed in the 16th century, but became known as the 'Roman' bridge because it was built near the site of an ancient Roman military camp.

affect: he was still an expert marksman. When he was discharged from hospital he was absorbed into the newly formed Machine Gun Corps[147] and given a new service number. Reluctantly, he had to hand back his Glengarry of the Royal Scots to wear the standard issue khaki service cap of the Corps.

Lance-Corporal George Cranston learned to use the Lewis machine gun with deadly effect and he, along with hundreds of other machine gun teams, was placed throughout the British front line wherever the action was the fiercest. However, two matters took place involving Doddie that changed his life in the army yet again.

The first incident had occurred when he was on manoeuvres in the bitterly cold winter a few months previously. The battalion was obliged to cross a frozen river in France. There was some hesitation from the ranks, but the officers insisted it was safe. They ordered the soldiers to 'break step' and space themselves farther apart than normal, thereby reducing the pressure on the ice. Soldiers started to cross but when it was Lance-Corporal Cranston's turn, he baulked. In his mind he had returned to that fateful day in Haddington in the winter of 1902 when, as a 10-year-old, he had followed his older brothers Willie and James to work. They were repairing a curling pond beside the River Tyne near a bend in the waterway and the river was partially frozen. The older brothers had wisely walked along the bank, but Doddie decided to take a short cut across a bend in the river to catch up with them. He got halfway across when the ice broke.

Doddie did not remember much after that, but was informed Willie and James heard the ice crack and turned around to see their young brother plunge into the freezing water. As the weight of his wet clothing pulled him in under the ice sheet, it was only

---

147 Formed in October 1915 to produce soldiers specialising in the use of the Lewis machine gun.

the desperate intervention of the older brothers that saved him from certain drowning. However, that incident left Doddie with an overwhelming fear of crossing any water that was covered in ice. Since that day he had never ventured onto an ice rink or stepped onto a frozen lake and he was not about to break that habit now. First, his sergeant told him to move onto the ice, but Doddie refused. Then an officer appeared and issued Lance-Corporal Cranston with a direct order to advance onto the ice, again he refused.

When two strong NCOs grabbed hold of him and tried to manhandle him over the frozen river, Doddie panicked and started throwing punches. He was eventually subdued and charged with 'Insubordination' and 'Fighting'.

Later that afternoon, minus his cap and belt to demonstrate he was being disciplined, Doddie was paraded before his commanding officer. After a brief hearing, the colonel stripped him of his rank and ordered forfeiture of one month's pay. In addition, he was required to perform extra guard duty for the following month.

The second matter took place almost concurrently. By this stage of the conflict many British infantry units were so dangerously depleted after the five-month long Somme offensive that they required reinforcements urgently. Despite his handy skills with a Lewis gun, Doddie was needed elsewhere and as 1917 began he was transferred yet again, this time to the Cameronians (Scottish Rifles). At least he had the concession of wearing a Glengarry bonnet again on his head, which this time proudly displayed the regimental badge of a five-pointed star within a thistle wreath above the stringed bugle horn of the light infantry. He was also given yet another service number.

Newcomers at the front were surprised to find that life was not always about unrelenting warfare. For every year of the war the British soldier spent an average of only 100 days at the front. For the rest of the time he was in reserve, on work details, training, resting or on leave. When on leave in 1917, Doddie tried to use these statistics to allay the concerns his mother and siblings had for his safety.

'It's nae a' fighting you ken,' he assured them. 'We sometimes get oot o' the trenches and intae the long grass which has been dried by the sun. There we would enjoy a warm hour or two smoking, bletherin' and reading letters frae hame. Even if the sector does get a wee bit hairy wi' the Hun shelling us or taking pot shots at us, I'm amazed that as soon as the din dies doon, we can hear the skylarks singin' in the air and the soft sound o' wind blawing ower the grasslands. Aye, sometimes it can be a bonnie place tae be.'

Nobody believed his reassurances off course; the idyllic imagery did not match the reality of the hundreds of new deaths published each week in the papers. It certainly did not square with the fact that Doddie had already lost three brothers and a fourth, Willie, was so badly wounded he would never fight again.

The old doctor looked at the woman in front of him in the Guild Hut. She was not his patient or at least this was not an official consultation. It was an all too infrequent tea break and a chance to momentarily take the weight of his feet. He had willingly stepped in to fill a vacancy when Dr McIntosh had volunteered to work for the Ministry of War, but this conflict was lasting much longer than he had imagined. Here he was back in harness almost 10 years after he had retired.

'Mrs Cranston,' he ventured, after a split second taken to remember her name, 'yesterday, you were serving tea at Amisfield House, on Monday you were working on the laundry at Newton

Port and here you are today at the Guild Hall. Could I suggest that you might be overdoing it a little? This is the first time I have seen you sit down all week and I am sure you have a home to run when you finish here.'

But Lizzie was no longer sitting down. She had gulped her own tea while it was still almost scalding hot, had whipped Effie's unfinished cup from her hand and was now hobbling impatiently in front of the old doctor in an effort to get him to drink up. She would need to make a fresh pot before the man with the gramophone announced the last dance. Lizzie had no desire to discuss her situation with the old doctor.

'You might have noticed, Doctor,' she replied with just a little less deference than she usually used when speaking to her 'superiors', 'that there's a war oot there to be won and we won't win it sitting here passing the time of day when there's work to be done. Now excuse me.'

The doctor was fighting a losing battle: 'The sister of my housekeeper has been telling me about a trip her church is organising to Longniddry for some of their older members. I understand there is a seat or two available.' He was on shaky ground. 'I'm sure I could pull a few strings. These ankles of yours look as if they could benefit from a nice ride in the train.'

'I would thank you Doctor to leave my ankles alone,' was Lizzie's haughty reply. 'Do you read your papers? Hundreds o' fine young men are being killed and wounded every day. There will be nae train rides tae Longniddry or anywhere else as lang as these b..., b...' – she hesitated, reddening slightly as she searched for the right word, 'boors' she concluded, 'are trying tae kill a' my laddies!' The doctor looked flustered, but Effie came to the rescue. 'I think she meant 'bastards' doctor, but she's no one for swearing.'

It was September 1917, a month after Robbie had celebrated his 18th birthday, and his call-up papers had duly arrived. They were entirely expected and came as a surprise to no one. Lizzie had not been well of late but her response to the letter could not have been anticipated by Robbie.

She became hysterical, wild with anger and consternation. In one breath she called upon God to smite the Germans who by this stage of the war she hated with a pathological loathing. But she also called God to strike down the British generals who kept calling for ever-increasing numbers of men to sacrifice in the battles of France.

'I'm no having it, dae ye hear,' she screamed to no one in particular when she read the official notice. 'You bastards have had enough from this family. It's no fair and I'm no goin' tae stand for it.'

With that uncharacteristic lapse into swearing, she raced off to see her best friend Effie Fairgrieve who by this stage of the war had also become her chief counsellor and minder. When Lizzie showed Effie the notice the two of them flew into a white hot rage and strode off to the minister of the local Parish Church of Scotland to demand his help.

The Reverend George Wauchope-Stewart, BD, was a fastidious man who had a love of music. He was also used to delivering complex lectures about religious philosophy on his Sunday sermons at St Mary's Kirk in Haddington, one of the oldest parish churches in Scotland. In short, he was a man of learning, distinction, considerable intellect and a powerful sense of self-worth. But when two women burst into his manse with anger burning in their eyes and hair wildly unkempt he reasoned that discretion and conciliation was the wisest and safest course for him to take.

He knew Lizzie Cranston well. He had even arranged for the family's sacrifice to be written up in the *Courier*. Some said he was also responsible for writing a report on the family to Buckingham Palace that resulted in a 'King's Letter' being dispatched to Lizzie in 1915 thanking her for five of her sons (at that time) going to war. With Lizzie waving a fresh call-up notice in front of him, the Reverend Wauchope-Stewart was acutely aware that Robbie would soon be the seventh Cranston son to enlist.

He sat quietly behind his rich mahogany desk while her friend Effie Fairgrieve outlined the reason for their hasty and emotional visit. They wanted his support in writing a letter to the recruiting office in Haddington to save the seventh Cranston from being drafted into the British Army. Effie spoke forcefully, rationally and compellingly. The Reverend Wauchope-Stewart quietly reflected what a powerful force this woman was and made a mental note to never get on her wrong side in the future.

Yet as reasoned and logical as the plea was to exempt a parishioner's son from conscription, George Wauchope-Stewart knew he could not comply with what these formidable women wanted. He believed in the war and Britain's involvement in it. He had never doubted from the very moment war started that God was on the side of Britain, France and their allies in a war against forces of evil who would destroy civilisation if they won. In the Reverend's mind it was therefore necessary for every able-bodied man to do his Christian duty and fight for God, King and Country. However, he also knew that the Cranston sacrifice had far exceeded that of any other family he knew. There were limits to duty, which this family had manifestly surpassed. As he thought about the conundrum a vague compromise came to mind.

A week later Effie and Elizabeth insisted on accompanying a very embarrassed Robbie to the local recruiting office in Haddington, where they reported to a sergeant from the Black Watch Regiment.

The recruiting sergeant, originally from Dundee, had already seen three years of war, firstly in Gallipoli and finally in France where he had taken shrapnel in his right leg. He had faced Turks and Germans, but he had never faced the sheer indomitable force that was presented to him this day in the form of two middle-aged women. He was convinced they would eat him alive if he said the wrong thing!

Effie Fairgrieve instantly fell into her accustomed role of speaker, while Lizzie Cranston stood muttering incoherently to herself and swaying rhythmically back and forth on her feet. The sergeant had seen more than his fair share of 'shell shock' victims in France. From what he saw in front of him, it looked like this lady was suffering something similar. The sergeant knew he had to process dozens of lads who were turning up this day and the two agitated ladies in front of him would only cause the day to stretch out until late afternoon. By then his badly damaged leg would be screaming in pain and he would need yet more tincture of opium to cope. So he tried the official line first.

'Madam your King has demanded that your son join the glorious British Army...' But the words had barely left his mouth when Effie retorted, 'She's already received her thanks from the King in a letter for sending five sons to the war. Last year a sixth joined. He disnae need a seventh!' she yelled in his face in as good a voice as any parade ground sergeant-major he had heard.

'But it's the law,' he said somewhat less forcefully. Suddenly, Elizabeth Cranston rushed in with her eyes wild with emotion.

'You're no having him,' she screamed, pushing Robbie protectively behind her. Dealing with a disturbed woman was something the sergeant was not experienced or trained in. He was starting to have second thoughts about what he should do. Effie stepped in to defuse the tense situation and said, 'We hae a letter here that might be of interest to you, Sergeant.' She pressed an envelope that bore the hallmark of St Mary's Kirk, Haddington into his hand. Stepping back, he opened the letter and read its contents to himself.

To whom it may concern.

Mrs Elizabeth Cranston is a fine upstanding citizen of Haddington. She is also a devout Christian and tireless worker in the community for those less fortunate than herself. Since this war began, this lady has seen six of her sons join the colours. Each son bore arms willingly.

You need to be aware that three of those sons have already given their lives for this great and noble cause and in addition another son has been seriously wounded. The two remaining sons are fighting in the thick of it on the Western Front. In my humble opinion, this patriotic family would benefit from your sensitivity when it comes to the enlistment of seventh son, Robert Cranston.

Robert is completing his apprenticeship as a joiner and might I respectfully suggest that his skills could be more usefully applied in a branch of the Armed Service that is in desperate need for skilled men such as he. I am referring to the Royal Flying Corps.

I would deem it a personal favour if you would assign the young man you have before you to the Royal Flying Corps for ground crew training.

I am your humble servant

Rev. George Wauchope-Stewart BD

Minister

Ten minutes later Robert Cranston was officially an airman conscripted into the Royal Flying Corps, instead of an infantry battalion to which the sergeant had been about to allocate him.

On their way home, Effie believed it was her oratory that kept her best friend's son out of the trenches. In a rare lucid moment, Lizzie Cranston thought the minister's appeal had probably swayed the sergeant. But back at the recruiting office awaiting transfer to a training camp, Robbie had no doubts what force had saved him from becoming more 'cannon fodder'. It was the Roman coin given to him by his brother Ian that he kept fingering in his pocket.

In Australia, Agnes regarded 1917 and the events surrounding it with mixed emotions. On the one hand, raising a young family and physically helping her husband build their home were among the most enjoyable and rewarding experiences she had ever had. However, the death and wounding of her dear, dear brothers caused her great pain and sorrow.

Sometimes she found herself holding some insignificant object from Scotland and then spontaneously bursting into tears. Her emotions were a roller coaster and even her sensible, reserved husband sensed she needed the occasional lift to her spirits. One of the last items John made and added to the interior of their living room were two large dark-stained plate rails.

'What are you doing that for?' asked Agnes who was still astounded that her husband had built a stone cottage out of the bare ground.

'Just you wait and see, lass,' was his enigmatic reply.

When the rails were finally installed, John went out to the original building which had now been turned into a wash house. He came back with two large flat rectangular brown paper packages. He carefully unwrapped both items and Agnes saw that they were large photographs each in thick wooden frames. One was of the Cranston family taken in 1908 and the other was of Agnes and John's wedding in 1912.

He moved about the room inspecting each wall to determine the best location for each framed photograph. After what seemed to be a deliberately long build-up of suspense, John positioned the pictures at opposite ends of the room facing each other across the sitting room.

'There,' he said with both hands upturned as if asking a question, 'what do you think?' Agnes recognised the effort that John had gone to. She smiled sweetly to her thoughtful husband and realised that even though life was not good, she still had a lot to be grateful for.

Later that day she dipped her pen in the ink well and gazed at the blank sheet of paper in front of her until the ink had all but dried up. It was the umpteenth time that she had done the self-same thing. She was uncertain even as to whom to address the letter. It seemed obvious that it should be to Ma but then again she could never be certain that it would be read. Mary though, could be relied on to read it to Ma and would eventually reply with the latest news from home. Agnes wanted to share the good news about the home being finished, but felt constrained. As much as she wanted to share good news, it was only bad news that seemed to be coming from Scotland. She was beginning to dread those letters which had once been a source of so much joy.

It seemed so stupid to have to write a Christmas or New Year's message in November, but even then it could not be guaranteed to arrive in time. The post was uncertain in these days of war. Should she tell Ma how well they were doing in Australia and how pleased they were in their new home? If only she could see it. Perhaps she should mention Drew and how busy he was – better not mention the cough, though. Should she ask how Robbie was getting on in the Royal Flying Corps? One thing was sure: she was not going to enquire about Sandy or Doddie. It seemed like every time in the past she had asked Mary about them, Agnes had been informed they had been wounded again. Writing home had become so difficult.

Agnes stood up briskly and replaced her pen in the ink well. It could wait for another day. The portrait of her beloved family taken all those years ago in Haddington seemed to look down on her expectantly and she found herself muttering the 'Cranston' prayer under her breath.

May fortune smile upon ye
Wherever ye may be,
May all your days be happy days
And many may ye see.[148]

As 1917 drew to a close, bitterly cold winter winds started to creep their way into Lizzie's two-bedroom flat again through the many gaps in the doors and windows. Even the old stone walls now felt cold and damp to the touch. Pretty soon, thought Lizzie, the water pipes would freeze like they did every winter. But on this particular bitter night it was not the thought of cold in the future that really bothered Lizzie. Her concerns were more immediate. The fires in the house had almost gone out for lack of fuel and the internal temperature was dropping rapidly to unhealthy levels. Yet the external coal bins, located underneath the steep stairs which led to the second-floor landing and her flat, were thankfully full.[149]

---

148 Thirty years later, Agnes wrote these words in a letter for her granddaughter to memorise. The note is now a treasured artefact of the family.

149 At this stage of the war, coal rationing was being progressively introduced across Britain, but it had not extended to Scotland yet.

However, that was not the problem. The issue was that none of her boys were available to fetch the fuel.

Throughout her married life, a man had always performed the exhausting task of bringing fuel inside the home. It may have been offcuts of wood or lumps of coal, but it had always been a man's job to carry it into the house. But tonight, the only son still residing with her was not at home. Lizzie felt a sudden jab of regret as she realised that out of nine sons only Angus was still living with her. Even though he normally performed this task willingly, on this particular night as an apprentice plumber, he had been called out on an urgent task.

Slowly, she rose from her chair and grabbing the old iron coal bucket from beside the living room fireplace, she went down the outside metal stairs to the ground. Several times she had to use her hand to steady herself on the iron railing as she descended and could feel the intense cold instantly penetrate the joints of her arthritic hand.

Underneath the flight of steps Lizzie opened the lid of the coal bin and filled up her bucket with as much coal as she could carry. With the extra weight of the coal, her ascent up the stairs was painfully slow. By the time she had returned to the flat the 62-year-old widow was shivering with cold, her hands were aching and she was at the point of exhaustion.

Too tired to stoke the fires properly she managed to place only a few lumps of coal on the living room fire before falling back into her favourite chair and wrapping herself in shawls and blankets.

'Where are ma boys?' Lizzie mumbled to no one as her breath condensed to fog in the near freezing room, 'It's no like 'em to no bring the coal in. I'll talk to Alec the morn.'

As the room's gaslight flickered in the freezing night air, Lizzie suddenly felt very alone.

1918

*F*aced with an average of 150,000 American troops freshly
arriving each month on the Western Front and Allied generals
(especially from Canada and Australia) implementing successful
new tactics, the Germans knew the war had turned against them.

With a million men available from the east after Russia signed
a peace treaty, the Germans launched one last desperate offensive
along the Western Front in March. It was their last throw of the
dice and it came perilously close to succeeding.

After the German failure, the Allies went on the offensive
everywhere and unrelenting pressure caused Germany's partners
to collapse internally. Bulgaria and Turkey were the first to sue
for peace. When Austria-Hungary signed an armistice, Germany
was left isolated, weakened and without the supplies to continue.

Riots and mutinies spread across Germany and the commanders
realised there was no point in continuing the war. On 11 November
1918, the German leaders signed an unconditional surrender and
the First World War was officially over.

Mary Cranston knew every inch of the magnificent, oak-lined dining room in Tyne House. It was now almost three years since she had first been employed by Doctor and Mrs Wallace-James in what to her was their mansion. It was separated from her family's inadequate flat in St Martin's Gate by a short walk and the entire length and breadth of the class system in Great Britain.

Mary was renowned for her flexibility, and although an experienced cook she had become intimately acquainted with every inch of the floorboards on which she now stood, as she had whiled away her spare moments with a scrubbing brush. In truth, it was a task that she quite enjoyed. But Mary Cranston, 27, would never scrub that floor again, because when next she entered the familiar room she would be Mrs Weir. It was 4 February 1918, her wedding day and she was very contented.

It was not, and never could be, the wedding that she had long dreamt of, a wedding like that of her sister Agnes some six years before. Apart from her dear Pa, that was the last time the entire family had all been together. How things had changed. Very few family members were able to be there and nowadays such get-togethers were invariably strained. Her youngest brother Angus, 10 years her junior, was present to give the bride away. A few years earlier, any one of her older brothers would have gladly stepped in to escort her down the aisle, but war limited her options.

Thank goodness for the scattering of family friends who seemed genuinely happy for her and for Molly her workmate who had been slaving since early morning to make the day a memorable one. And memorable it most certainly would be. The Wallace-James's gesture of giving over their magnificent dining room to the wedding party had taken Mary completely by surprise. It was hardly the kind of action typical of a master to a servant and was clearly an unselfish demonstration of the esteem in which she was held in her employers' eyes. The childless couple perhaps regarded her as the daughter they never had.

She glanced at the man she was about to marry, a distant relative, Private Jim Weir, a 29-year-old Canadian whose family could obviously not be present. He was looking well despite having been invalided from the battlefield in France 10 months earlier. Mary's courtship had been carried out largely by correspondence. It may not have been all that conventional, but in wartime this was becoming increasingly common.

Looking back at her life so far, Mary realised that like her sister and mother before her, she in reality had been working before she was old enough to read and write. Of course it was unpaid labour helping Ma manage a busy, bustling family of rambunctious boys who were rapidly maturing into men. She thought of the prizes she had won at school: two medals and ultimately a brooch, for an unprecedented five years' perfect attendance. She was the first to admit that she was not particularly academically gifted, but wondered what she might have achieved if things had been different. That was never to be. There had been chores to be carried out early in the morning and then more jobs waiting for her after she returned home from school.

As she prepared to make the short walk down the makeshift 'aisle' with her handsome husband, the soon-to-be Mrs Weir could be forgiven for thinking that she was the only Cranston lately on which fate had chosen to smile.

The chill of spring on the Somme filled the air as Sandy sat on an upturned box of empty jute bags. Surrounding him was the strewn rubbish of a storage depot being emptied in a hasty move. It was March 1918 and the Germans had broken through the British line to the southeast of them.[150] The division had just received orders to relocate as quickly as possible to defend a breach in the line which threatened to split the British Army around Rosières in northern France.

The task of Sandy's unit – 84th Field Company, Royal Engineers – was to assist the 20th (Light) Division establish new defensive positions throughout this area. Specifically, Sandy was part of a working party of Royal Engineers ordered to repair a bridge over the Somme canal that another company of Royal Engineers had partially destroyed near the town of Ham. As frustrating as it might have been to the ordinary soldier, Sandy knew that in the rapidly changing circumstances of a major offensive such as this, bridges that were considered expendable one minute, could become vitally important the next.

The repair detachment was lead by a lieutenant, but Sandy was the next senior soldier in rank and the more experienced of the two. To ensure the wagons were loaded with as much construction material as they could carry and be ready to leave at midnight, Sandy ordered the troops to begin loading at around 21:00 hours and by 23:00 he could see that they were ahead of schedule.

For the first time that day, Sandy had somehow managed to have a little time to himself to start his next most important task – writing a letter home to his wife Annie. However, surrounded by the loud, confused noise of people finishing off the provisioning of the wagons, he first had to compose himself and his thoughts. It was not the first letter he had written to his wife. In fact since being called up in June of 1915, he had written a regular letter once every two or three months back to Scotland.

But far less often he had also written 'special' letters; letters that soldiers sometimes write to their loved ones on the eve of

---

150 The events in this chapter are based on the Unit diary of the 84th Field Company, Royal Engineers. Archive Reference No. WO95/2107, National Archives, Kew, London.

a significant battle. It was in those letters that a soldier wrote about things which really mattered, about the love for his wife and children, about their future together if he survived the forthcoming battle, about dreams and last requests. Sandy had written only three of these 'special' letters since first being on the Western Front almost three years ago. This would be his fourth.

When Annie had received her first 'special' letter, during the Battle of Loos in 1915, she had been quite shocked at the candid nature of the words. Normally Sandy would not communicate with such frankness, but when she received another similarly personal letter that coincided with the Battle of the Somme in 1916, she was able to see a pattern and therefore the motivation behind these rare pieces of correspondence. On the one hand, she treasured receiving what she had come to secretly call these 'special letters' from Sandy because they offered her an uncommon glimpse into her husband's innermost thoughts. Such acts of candour were unusual enough for any Scotsman, but they were exceptional for a Cranston. On the other hand, she also feared these letters, for they meant that he was about to engage in a very serious battle that Sandy thought he might not survive. At first she was confused: Sandy was with the Royal Engineers and he had promised her that he would never be placed in the thick of battle. His unit, the 84th Field Company of the Royal Engineers, was mainly concerned with building and maintaining roads, railways, water supply, fortifications and bridges.

Sandy had reassured Annie several times that there was nothing for her to worry about, hoping that he could convince her.

But Annie was wiser than that, and by the time she had received her third unusually personal letter (during the Battle of Passchendaele in 1917), she suspected that Sandy had been required at times of great peril to enter the thick of battle and fight like any other British infantry soldier. This forced her to realise that he could die like one too. What Sandy had not told her was that he had been trained in the use of explosives, specifically Amatol,[151] and when he was not engaged in carpentry he had become something of a specialist in mining, and setting explosive charges.

It was becoming increasingly difficult to keep his activity with explosives a secret from Annie, especially when a small mishap with a charge of Amatol in December 1917 caused him to be hospitalised in France for a month.[152]

Sandy thought about where to begin the letter. Time was short so he could not write the story of his life. He thought about his wedding to Annie in 1901 when he was just 22 and she was still a teenager. Then he considered talking about the seven children they had together and he remembered how Annie had made all the clothing for each child. When times were tough, as they invariably were, this hard-working wife of his would take on dressmaking jobs for money to augment the family's meagre income. Before the wedding, Annie was employed as a seamstress and in the 17 years since they had been married she had always found time to continue her craft and make a little money out of it as well.

Should he mention 1916, the most horrible year his family could ever have endured? Of course Annie knew the details well enough although he had played down the extent of his own injuries, which had been serious enough to earn him a 'Blighty'[153] and six months convalescing in a hospital in England. However, hard as it was to imagine, he was the lucky one.

151 Amatol is an explosive made up of TNT and ammonium nitrate and was used extensively by the British in the First World War.
152 Reference: Service Record of Alexander Cranston, Royal Engineer, Service No. 103604.
153 During the Great War a 'Blighty wound' referred to an injury that was serious enough to require medical evacuation to Britain from the various theatres. Blighty is soldiers' slang for Britain, originally from an Urdu word meaning foreign.

Doddie had literally had the stuffing knocked out of him with shell shock and then there was William. He had a mental image of Willie's badly mangled hand and fractured eye socket and he shuddered. Sandy wondered how Willie was really copying with the loss of the two best talents he possessed – his good looks and his superb skill with the violin. In the two years since 1916, he had seen for himself how the family's casualty toll had affected other members of the Cranston family. His mother had clearly become increasingly anxious and mentally unstable. The last report of her from Haddington mentioned that she was becoming confused and absent-minded. On leave in 1917, Sandy had seen for himself how she was obsessively dwelling on the loss of her dead sons.

Robert had recently been called up and was eager to do his bit for God, King and Country, but it was Angus the youngest brother that bothered Sandy the most. He was so filled with anger and hatred towards the enemy that all he said he wanted to do was join up as soon as he turned 18 so that he could kill Germans.

The widows and children of James, Ian and Adam were finding it tough and the miserable widow's pension paid by the British Government was barely putting food on the table. The Cranston family had always been poor, but at least they had usually been happy. Now, all he saw was a family that was shattered, confused and angry. The Cranston family was beginning to disintegrate.

Sandy dismissed the idea of sharing these feelings with Annie almost as soon as the thoughts entered his head. Of course he would not burden Annie with her in-law's catastrophes, it was something the Cranston family should endure silently, individually and stoically.

He had written to Annie before about their marriage and their family, so this time he would write to his wife about something that was so important to him that he had never even spoken to

Annie about it at all. However, he decided to start the letter with a trivial family report and see how it flowed from there.

To Annie Cranston
50 Hercus Loan
Musselburgh
Scotland

From Sgt Alexander Cranston
Somewhere in France[154]

Dearest Annie

It has been a wee while since I wrote to you last, but I am at a bit of a loose end right now and thought I would scribble you a few lines while I can. First of all I am still keeping fine since my leave with you and the bairns in Musselburgh last year. I had a bit of a cold during the middle of winter, which was quite chilly here, but that's long gone and now that the days are getting warmer I feel quite chirpy. By the way, thank you for the wee bottle of rum that you sent me for Hogmanay. What a braw idea to hide it inside the black bun. It must have cost you a lot so keep making clothes for the bairns and taking in paying orders.

I managed to get to see our Doddie a month or so back. He's with the Royal Fusiliers from London, but the truth is he seems to be in a different Unit every time I hear about him. He's seen more fighting in the last four years than any person I ken. He seemed fine pleased to see me and we had a braw time in the nearby town sharing a few drinks and memories. He is now quite grown up, although a little tired and drawn.

---

154 It was forbidden for soldiers to write specific locations in any correspondence, in case the information fell into enemy hands.

To think I had already left school when he was born and now, here we are, brothers in arms. It seems like just yesterday that he was a young lad and I was teaching him some football skills in the gas-light outside our front door in Haddington. Now he's slogging it out in the trenches, helping us win the War.

He told me that he had managed to get over to Vermelles Cemetery last year and pay his respects to our Ian. He said it was a small cemetery in the middle of the town, but Doddie felt honoured to be the first Cranston to visit the cemetery since Ian was buried there. I must try to get over there myself if I can.

'Sergeant ... Sergeant!' broke through the voice of a young corporal, 'We've loaded all the tools and wood in the wagons, what next?' Sandy shook himself back to the present and focused on the loading at hand.

'We're repairing a bridge, Corporal, do you nae think we micht need concrete?' he barked back. 'Put half a dozen bags of cement onto each wagon.'

The corporal was a 26-year-old from Ross-shire in Scotland's far north and had previously been awarded the Military Medal for gallantry on the battlefield. In stark contrast, his sergeant – Sandy Cranston – had once found him drunk in Amiens after failing to return from leave. He should have lost his corporal's stripes for the offence of being 'Absent Without Leave', but Sergeant Cranston did not press charges. When he eventually sobered up, he still had his rank and his reputation as a brave soldier remained intact. And now he regarded Sandy as the 'big brother' he never had.

'Right you are, Jock,' said the corporal, breaching strict military protocol in not addressing his superior officer by rank. But in appropriate circumstances, Sandy allowed his corporal this indulgence because he knew that behind his back everyone else in the 84th Field Company of Royal Engineers called him 'Old Jock', including Major Symes the Company commander. Obviously Sandy was not the only Scotsman out of the company's 130 officers and men. But at 39 Sandy was the oldest Scot in the company by a good 10 years.

After the corporal had scampered away, Sandy drifted back to the pressing task of letter-writing. Would he discuss the fact that he had paid half his parents' rent in Haddington for years while he and Annie struggled financially to raise their own young family in Musselburgh? He decided against it.

Annie had never raised any objections, despite their own tough economic circumstances. She seemed to understand and accept that this sacrifice was exactly what the eldest son should do. She never once raised the matter with him. But helping out his parents and the financial strains this created on his own family did lead to the biggest decision Sandy had ever made in his life to date, to work in America. This was certainly a subject that he had wanted to discuss with Annie for quite a while, but up to now he had shied away from raising the matter with her. He had undergone a change in the USA and he wanted to tell her about it, but the words were difficult for him to compose because he had rarely spoken so candidly before.

If this letter was going to be his last as he feared (although he would not share that piece of information with Annie), he wanted to make sure she knew exactly how he felt. He picked up his pencil and began to write again.

When I was in hospital that terrible year of 1916, I got to doing a bit of thinking and I sorted a few things out in my head. You ken how it was a distant cousin of mine, William Cranston of San Francisco, that invited me to America, all those years ago.

1918

What I maybe never told you was how impressed I was by him. Before the earthquake and fire of 1906, he was doing very well for himself, building and selling houses, but the catastrophe ruined his business completely.

Yet, in the middle of all this destruction, he was still optimistic about his future and that of his adopted country.

He even said that one day he would see to it that one of his family would go in for politics. Politics, Annie. Can you believe it?[155]

I ken no other country where a man can come from nothing, make a fortune, then lose it and still think he's worthy of being elected to the council or whatever it is called ower there.

What's more, he was the same age as me and before the quake he lived in a big two-storey house with four bedrooms that was all paid for, whilst we were in two small rooms in a tenement, paying rent. Ten years on, nothing's changed for us but we hear that William's done so well he's moved into a great big mansion.

Then came Ma's instructions to come hame as Pa was dying. As the eldest son, of course, I had no choice, I had to come back but at the time I had just started making good money. As it turned out Pa's ill health was to go on for three more years. Ah well.

Thinking about all this on the train back to New York, I was struck by how our lives had grown along different paths.

We were both from the same Scottish stock, yet America had provided William with more opportunities than Scotland could ever have presented me. The truth is I fell

---

155 Sandy was referring to William MacGregor Cranston of Palo Alto, California (1879–1953), whose prediction was fulfilled by his son Alan MacGregor Cranston (1914–2000) becoming one of the longest-serving Senators in the US Government (1969–93) and unsuccessful candidate for the US Presidency in 1984.

in love with America. There, I've finally said it after staying silent all this time.

Annie, if I ever get out of this bloody place alive, I want to take you and the bairns to America to start a new life for us all. If America's not to your liking, maybe we could go to Australia instead, where my sister Agnes went and seems to be getting on just fine. I just feel that Scotland's no longer the place for us and the bairns.

I've got to close now lass – the boys are ready to move out, but I want to finish by saying how much I love you and miss being with you and our bairns. Once again, when I get home, I want us to leave Scotland for a new life abroad.

Until then, dearest, I love you and miss you very much.

Suddenly, an officer's whistle pierced the evening's activities and NCOs started barking orders to assemble the work party and move off. While Sandy and his group would move east, the rest of the Company of Engineers would dismantle the camp and establish a new base farther to the west. This move had a sense of real urgency about it and Sergeant Cranston's mind quickly returned to the immediate job at hand. He signed the letter and folded it into an army brown envelope upon which he hastily wrote the address. As he walked past Company Headquarters, itself in the throes of being dismantled, he slipped the letter into the outgoing mailbag that was hanging from a tent pole.

All night the band of 20 Royal Engineers from the 84th Field Company pushed ahead through darkened country lanes. The engineers rode in silence, distributed evenly among the six wagons full of construction material. The only sound coming from the wagons was that of the draft horses breathing, the crunch of steel-rimmed wheels crushing the gravelled road underneath and the occasional clink of metal from the harnesses, but no one noticed them as they passed through tiny villages and hamlets.

What the Engineers and everyone else could hear quite distinctly was the ominous sound of artillery fire getting louder as they closed in on the rapidly changing front line. There was definitely some heavy action taking place near to where they were heading. Sandy hoped that his detachment would get to the bridge in time to make some sort of a contribution. Every one of his soldiers knew that the front line had to be stabilised soon to stop the succession of withdrawals that had begun two days before.

As the force moved across the darkened landscape, Sandy could see groups of French civilians streaming back from the ever-approaching Germans. They passed a temporary British camp near the town of Dury, which had been abandoned earlier in the night for an unknown reason. Equipment and munitions were scattered everywhere in the haste to leave. As the Engineers' wagons filed past the scene one by one, it looked as though the 'fighting withdrawal' they had been told about was turning into a retreat.

They pushed on down into the flood plain of the Somme valley for another kilometre or so until they reached a small stone bridge over the Somme canal.[156] It was now about 03:00 hours on the morning of 23 March and they had finally reached their objective. As the soldiers jumped down from the wagons, Sandy surveyed the scene in front of him. It was surprisingly peaceful at the canal crossing and except for the bridge itself, which was moderately damaged by explosives, there was no evidence that four years of warfare had ever visited this place. The concrete bridge was raised on stone footings so that barges could easily pass underneath.

---

156 The Somme Canal, or Canal de la Somme, joins the northern grain region of France with the English Channel. Construction started in 1770, but was not completed until 1843.

On either side the banks were filled with poplars that were full with luxuriant spring growth. The trees were gently swaying in the cool night breeze making a soft, rustling sound. Sandy could also hear the sound of flowing water coming from underneath the bridge and for a moment thought this would be a wonderful place in the daylight to have a summer picnic.

The road that they used to approach the damaged bridge continued over the crossing and then in a straight line across the countryside toward the tiny village of Ollezy; the direction from which Sandy and his officer had been assured the Germans would be coming. There were no other crossings over the canal for some distance in either direction, which made this particular bridge vital for both sides.

Sandy studied the road and noted satisfactorily that he had unrestricted views down the road all the way to Ollezy about half a kilometre away. He could even see one or two faint house lights twinkling from that direction. At least he would not be caught by surprise when the Germans finally arrived.

As always, the Engineers placed their weapons close at hand in case they were needed and then they set about clearing away the rubble and broken sections of the bridge. Expertly, these men replaced gaps in the road with heavy planks of wood they had transported with them. The bridge had been sturdily constructed decades before and the half-hearted attempt to hastily demolish it had not seriously threatened its integrity.

As well as repairing the bridge, the officer ordered Sandy to turn his attention to erecting defences to protect the crossing, in the unlikely event that they needed to defend the bridge. Sandy and a team of engineers started filling the empty jute bags as quickly as possible with soil from a farmer's field next to the road. Then they placed a few bags of concrete at the two cardinal points on the side of the bridge facing the expected approach of the Germans from Ollezy. The filled sandbags were placed around them and across the road to make a barricade that they hoped would be at least half a metre high and offer the soldiers minimum protection, if they needed it. Before Sandy had left the storage depot the previous night he had made sure that a minimum of 10 boxes of empty jute bags were loaded onto the wagons. As each box contained 25 bags, Sandy reasoned that 250 sandbags would be enough for any job. But as he inspected the finished barrier he ruefully concluded he needed twice that number. It simply was not high enough. However, he still had one more way to slow the enemy's advance.

Sergeant Cranston, two corporals and a dozen Sappers then took planks of wood, corkscrew pickets and reels of barbed wire and hastily erected entanglements 20 metres or so beyond the makeshift firing line. It was while the barricades were nearing completion that a lone British rider on horseback suddenly appeared. He was leading four packhorses that were carrying heavy loads in their saddlebags. Sandy could see that horses and rider alike were sweating profusely and there were also flakes of white foam on the horses' flanks and mouths. The officer on horseback breathlessly informed the lieutenant in charge of the repair party that the situation had deteriorated dramatically in the last few hours and the enemy had broken through some kilometres away.

The bridge was no longer an asset but a liability and the lieutenant's new orders from headquarters were to destroy it so it would not fall into enemy hands. The saddlebags on the pack horses contained enough amatol to demolish the bridge completely. Further, the majority of the working party was ordered to withdraw with the lieutenant leading them. A much smaller party of men would be left behind to set the explosives and destroy the bridge.

Because of Sandy's experience with explosives he was ordered to stay behind with three other soldiers to complete the task of demolishing the bridge. The officer on horseback informed Sandy that he had about two hours at most before the enemy was expected to arrive, so his orders were curt indeed.

'Don't dawdle. Blow the bloody thing up quickly and withdraw westwards. Understand?'

As the main body of Engineers departed back the way they had come, Sandy understood better than most that when told he had two hours to destroy the bridge, it probably meant he only had one. In Sandy's mind, it was going to be a very close affair. It was now 09:00 hours and with the Germans expected at any moment, nobody needed any encouragement to complete the task at hand.

All four men pulled satchels of Amatol from the saddlebags and secured them to various points of the bridge under Sandy's supervision. Then they inserted blasting caps (detonators) into each bag and attached slow-burning safety fuses to these detonators. These fuses were trailed to a central point on the Dury side of the bridge. Two Sappers jumped over the concrete railing and started attaching more bags of explosives to the underside of the bridge. They returned trailing long leads of fuses back to the already established central firing point. Sandy was impressed that everything had been accomplished in such a short time and now all he needed was to light the fuses and withdraw back towards the British lines.

'Jock, behind you!' shouted the corporal suddenly. Sandy and the others turned around as one and saw the first heads of German foot soldiers cresting a rise about 300 metres away. The fact that they were lightly armed and equipped was all it took for him to know that these were the much vaunted *Stoßtruppen* (Stormtroopers) the German Army had created only one year previously. These soldiers were highly skilled, lightly provisioned and worked in small numbers designed to penetrate enemy lines, wreak havoc and rapidly move on to the next objective.

The worst part for Sandy was that these Germans were not approaching up the road as expected from Ollezy, but were coming over the top of a hill behind them, on the Drury side of the canal! The tiny troop of Engineers on the bridge were about to be cut off.

'Hold them off,' shouted Sandy as he saw more heads starting to appear over the hill in the late morning light. By the time the four Royal Engineers had obtained their rifles and crouched down behind the concrete railing the first rounds of rifle fire started whizzing towards them. The Germans had mastered the difficult technique of firing on the move and were rapidly closing the gap from the hill to the bridge. A quick look showed Sergeant Cranston that there were now a couple of dozen stormtroopers bearing down on them with more arriving every second.

'This is going to be a close thing,' Sandy growled to his corporal who seemed to be shadowing his every move. The first Germans were now approaching the bridge itself when Sergeant Cranston shouted, 'Gi'e the buggers hell!' Four rifles opened up in unison and one or two Germans collapsed to the ground. But the rest ran on to hide among the poplar trees beside the canal to his right and direct their fire at the poorly protected engineers on the bridge.

Sandy saw several more stormtroopers race across the field to the trees on his left. The air became thick with bullets that were coming from both the left and the right hand sides of the road to Dury, fizzing overhead. '*Shit*', Sandy thought, '*we're trapped!*'

From out of the corner of his eye, Sandy saw a stick bomb which had been thrown from the direction of the trees on his right suddenly appear through the air. The grenade landed on the roadway far enough away from him and went off with a rush of hot air, deafening noise and the whistle of dozens of small projectiles contained within the weapon connecting with hard surfaces and soft tissue in all directions. One of Sandy's tiny force lay dead on the roadway. At any moment the Germans would rush the three remaining soldiers and secure the bridge for a vital crossing point.

As Sandy's hearing returned, a strange thing happened. Usually his head would be filled with a jumble of competing thoughts, but as the noise of battle returned Alexander Cranston, Sergeant of Engineers, became surprisingly calm and determined. He reasoned there was only one thing he could do in the circumstances. He must detonate the explosives to deprive the Germans of this important crossing, even if that meant blowing himself and his men up with the bridge.

Sandy coolly stood up oblivious to all the mayhem around him and the sound of enemy fire that had now been focused in his direction. He strode a few metres over to the collection of fuses and without a moment's hesitation impassively lit them. The spaghetti of fuses spluttered to life and started on their separate ways to the individual explosive charges. Sandy knew he had to hold off the Germans for the next 30 seconds. But the Germans had also seen what Sandy had just done and they knew they had to extinguish the fuses immediately or lose the bridge.

A dozen stormtroopers rushed the crossing with their bayonets fixed to their rifles. Sergeant Cranston swung his rifle into position and fired at the charging stormtroopers. So did his tiny force of Royal Engineers, who by now all knew what action their sergeant had taken, had accepted it without question, and joined in the fight to deprive the enemy of the bridge.

A grey uniform came running at Sandy with his bayonet pointed directly at his heart. Sandy parried the weapon away and rammed his own bayonet into the German's side as he went past. The soldier's forward momentum pulled the rifle butt out of Sandy's hands. As the German crumpled to the ground the bayonet was still embedded in his chest and Sandy could not get it out. It was stuck fast and Sandy was unarmed.

Another German appeared, but as the stormtrooper brought his bayonet up to strike, a rifle discharged loudly next to Sandy. The German slumped to the ground, dead. Sandy turned to his corporal on his knees beside him with blood pouring from several fatal wounds.

'That's for Amiens, Jock,' were the last words he said.

Sandy looked around on the bridge to see that the fuses were within seconds of reaching the detonators. The enemy could not stop the demolition now. It was too late for everyone. As he turned back a young German private rushed up to him.

Half in anger at the death of his comrades and half in fear at this being his first 'kill' the well-trained but inexperienced private looked at the defenceless sergeant of Engineers in front of him and squeezed the trigger of his rifle. The last thought Sandy Cranston had was that the young man who shot him seemed to be about the same age as his own son.

The Germans swept onto the bridge just as the lit fuses reached the blasting caps. There was a slight 'bang' as the first detonators went off, followed instantly by a huge roaring explosion as satchel bags full of amatol ripped the bridge apart. A spectacular eruption of concrete, stone and body parts flew from where the bridge once stood.

When the smoke and dust cleared there was nothing left of the crossing over the canal and nothing left of any of the people who were on it.

Over the next few days the 84th Field Company moved at least seven times, from Le Quesnal, to Roye, then Mézières-en-Santerre, Onvillers, Faverolles and Dancourt-Popincourt in quick succession. The company finally came to rest exhausted at Fresnoy-en-Chaussée. Everyone hoped that the little working party at the bridge would somehow find their way back to the Company, but after three days it was no use pretending and a roll call was finally taken to officially determine casualties.

Days later, Annie Cranston of Musselburgh received a letter from the War Office, informing her that Alexander was officially declared missing on 26 March 1918 and presumed dead.[157] His body was never recovered and all that signifies his passing today is his name inscribed high up on a memorial stone wall of a war cemetery in Pozières, France.[158]

At about the same time in Germany a mother received a notice from the German Ministry of War which said that her stormtrooper son was missing at a bridge on the Western Front and also presumed dead. His body was never recovered either. Unlike Sgt Cranston and the other British soldiers who died on the bridge that day, his name does not appear on any memorial to signify his loss to the Fatherland.

It had been a strange morning altogether, thought Robbie.[159] An unseasonal thick pea-souper blanketed the aerodrome at Azelot, near Nancy in France's north-west. This had prevented the British planes from No. 99 Heavy Bomber Squadron Royal Air Force

---

157 Even though the death of Sgt Cranston and other Engineers at the bridge occurred on 23 March 1918.

158 Corporal George Ross, Sapper William Strathdee and Sapper Harry Wickham from the 84th Field Company of Royal Engineers were also officially declared missing and presumed dead on 26 March 1918. Their names are inscribed on the walls of the Pozières memorial, as well as another 14,000 British and South African soldiers who lost their lives during the German Offensive in this sector of the front. None have a known grave.

159 The following events are based on the Unit diary of 99 Squadron Royal Flying Corps/ Royal Air Force. Archive Reference No. AIR 1/176/15/198/3 National Archives, Kew, London. Also Sqn Ldr Pattinson, *History of 99 Squadron, RAF. March 1918 – November 1918*, Naval and Military Press (2004).

(RAF)[160] from taking off to bomb Stuttgart again. But it had given Robbie the opportunity of carrying out further inspections on these disappointing planes for which he and the other ground crew were responsible.

Everyone in 99 Squadron agreed the Airco DH9 was a 'dud',[161] with its unreliable engine and lightweight frame, yet there was nothing else available until the new and improved DH9A they had been promised became available in a few months' time. In the meantime accidents, mechanical failures and the Germans – with their superior machines – were combining to cause an alarming loss of aircraft and the men that flew them.[162]

The adjutant had summed up the situation succinctly when he addressed the ground crew saying, 'Patch them up as best you can and keep them flying. Until we get the new aircraft, that's all we can do.' And that is exactly what Robbie and the other ground crew did, every day.

He would usually rise early and conduct a daily inspection of the frame and rigging of the aircraft, which had been allocated to him specifically. He ran his experienced eye over the struts and ailerons[163] in particular, as these were the likely weak points of the plane's flimsy construction. If needing repair, and many of them did, Robbie would patch fresh pieces of cotton cloth over the torn or bullet-holed section and fix the new piece with strong adhesive glue.

On this unusual day, Robbie was stitching some cloth onto the fuselage of the bomber when the sound of a single-engine plane

---

160 On 1 March 1918, the Royal Flying Corps, which had previously been under the command of the army, evolved into a separate entity of its own and was renamed the Royal Air Force.

161 Pejorative slang term for something defective or useless.

162 According to official statistics, between May and November 1918, two squadrons on the Western Front (Nos. 99 and 104) lost 54 DH9s shot down, and another 94 written off in accidents out of a normal complement of 48 planes. (Reference: Mason, Francis K., *The British Bomber since 1914*. London: Putnam, 1994.)

163 Hinged flaps on the trailing edge of each wing to stabilise the plane in flight.

came circling the aerodrome high above the fog. At first the few airmen who were up thought that it must have been one of the new American planes that had lost his way in the fog. Therefore no one was concerned as the unseen plane circled the aerodrome. But then the plane came lower as if to land and the unmistakable German 'Iron Cross' insignia could be seen on the wings of the enemy two-seater biplane.

An airman half-dressed returning from the ablution block was stunned to see an enemy fighter coming in low across the airfield. He raced over to an iron hoop hanging outside the headquarters building and begun furiously hitting the object with a metal clapper.[164] The German pilot was just as surprised. Having recovered from almost landing at an enemy aerodrome, he considered a quick strafing run or two might make up for his foolish mistake before disappearing back into the safety of the fog. Below him he could see a squadron of British bombers lined up unprotected in neat rows on the ground. The planes were parked in a line and extremely vulnerable to enemy strafing, even though it was not expected. Several ground crew raced across the grass field to move the precious planes out of the pilot's path. Robbie, who was already working on his plane, got a head start in pulling it free from the line. For all its weight, the Airco DH9 Heavy Bomber was in fact quite manoeuvrable when resting on the ground, if unloaded.

Out of the corner of his eye the German fighter pilot saw one of the British planes being pulled out of line. This was an opportunity too good to miss. He changed the direction of the plane slightly, ignoring the irritating chatter from the one or two British anti-aircraft guns that had commenced firing.

From the far side of the airfield, he targeted the plane and the lone ground crewman who was slowly pulling it to safety.

---

164 This incident is recorded in the War Diary of 99 Squadron for 29 August 1918 and the German plane was identified as a Hannover two-seater escort fighter (Hannover CL.II).

Low and flat he came on at a steady 130kph over the airfield not veering or changing his altitude a metre.

Robbie, busy pulling the plane away, heard the unmistakable roar of the biplane growing louder behind him. He turned around to see it. The German fighter was heading across the field directly at him and the plane that Robbie was moving alone.

He stood facing the oncoming plane knowing that these were possibly his last moments on earth. He was terrified. Without thinking he thrust his right hand in his trouser pocket and there he found his treasured Roman coin. It had brought him luck ever since brother Ian had entrusted it to him back in 1914. Perhaps it would again? He started rubbing it for what might be one last time. The German pilot saw the British crewman stand his ground and calmly put his hand in his pocket.

Outraged at such impertinence, he reached up and primed the single fuselage-mounted Spandau machine gun by pulling back on the loading hammer. With a firing rate of over 500 rounds per minute the machine gun would obliterate the lone British crewman as well as the plane he was standing beside.

The gap between plane and target rapidly narrowed – 250 metres …200 metres … and 150 metres, which was the optimum distance to fire. The German fighter pilot squeezed the trigger. Nothing! The gun had jammed. By the time he had reached up and reset the weapon again he had already overshot the target.

As he looked down and was contemplating another run, several shots from the two operating anti-aircraft guns came whistling past the plane. He realised that the British gunners were beginning to get their aim and if he hung around the field for much longer his luck might run out. He decided against another run and turned away to fly back to his base.

On the ground Robbie Cranston was left shaking uncontrollably. It was a miracle that he had escaped certain death. He pulled the object of his miraculous survival out of his pocket and caressed it once more for luck.

For Doddie, 1918 really started in March when he was discharged from hospital in England to rejoin the effort at the front. At the end of the previous year, he had again suffered a 'Blighty' wound. On this occasion the *Haddingtonshire Courier* reported he was 'wounded in France by shrapnel in face, head and hand'.[165]

This time when he recovered he was transferred once again, to the fourth unit in which he would ultimately serve. This time, it was the Royal Fusiliers, which was unofficially known proudly as the City of London Regiment. By this stage of the war, the Regiment had grown to more than 40 battalions and was taking replacements from anywhere in the United Kingdom. Battalions of the Royal Fusiliers were serving in every theatre of the war.

Private George Cranston had regained some of his confidence that had been completely shattered three years earlier at Festubert. Even so, he would never be his former extrovert self. But there was still one way he would draw attention to his extraordinary service. It was there for all to see on the left sleeve of his uniform jacket.

British soldiers were entitled to wear 'wound stripes'[166] and 'good conduct' and 'overseas service' stripes.[167] This system clearly identified the faithful few who went to war from the very start of the conflict and had been subsequently injured in battle. To see

---

165 He had been admitted to the Lord Derby's Hospital in Winwick, Lancashire. The hospital was originally built as an asylum, but had been converted to a military hospital with 2,160 beds in 1916 when the need for beds escalated dramatically during and after the Somme.

166 A wound stripe was a 4cm gilded bar pinned to the left sleeve of the soldier's jacket by means of a backing plate and a split pin. It was positioned lengthways down the sleeve. There was no limit to the number of wound stripes that a soldier was allowed to wear.

167 One cloth blue stripe for every year of service, and one red cloth stripe if the soldier went overseas before 31 December 1914.

a soldier with the full complement of overseas stripes was a rare thing.[168] To see a soldier wearing overseas service stripes as well as one wound stripe, even rarer still. Private George Cranston was wearing the full set of service stripes, plus *two* wound stripes.

Upon entering any *estaminet*[169] on leave, a hush would descend as the soldiers who observed his left sleeve gave him the respect a fellow comrade like him deserved. He had merely to point to one of his wound stripes, mention the name of the battle in which he was wounded and for the rest of the night his drinks would be purchased by others. Soldiers would be drawn to him, just to be in his presence. Many could only imagine the horrors that he had survived, yet they hoped that by being in his company, it would somehow bring them luck too.

But one final, cruel turn of the dice awaited Doddie Cranston.

In the last two months of the war, when the British were pushing the stubbornly resisting Germans back through the Artois region of northern France, Doddie was exposed to mustard gas and evacuated from the battlefield yet again.[170]

It is hard to accept that a young man who had survived four years of war and had already been hospitalised twice with serious injuries should succumb to a gas attack in the last weeks of the war.[171] He was evacuated back to Britain for an incredible third

168 By this time of the war, out of many millions of British soldiers serving in France, there were perhaps fewer than 50,000 soldiers wearing the full complement of one red stripe and four blue stripes. The rest of the 120,000 or so who went to France between August and December 1914 had either died or been invalided out of the war.

169 A small French café selling coffee, tea, alcohol and snacks.

170 Mustard gas had only been introduced into the war by the Germans in July 1917, yet it caused more British casualties in the last year and a half of the war than all forms of gas had in the three years previously (165,000 British soldiers killed or non-fatally affected July 1917–November 1918, versus 22,000 in the previous 30 months).

171 According to the War Office Report, *Statistics of the Military Effort of the British Empire during the Great War 1914–1920* (published 1922), 3,229,701 soldiers, sailors and airmen of the British Empire were wounded or died in the war out of 8,689,467 who served. A ratio of more than 1:3. On the Western front a soldier was considered to be a 'veteran' if he survived just one battle.

time and spent an unknown length of time in a military hospital trying to recover from the agonising effects of the gas.

Doddie's war was over but peace and contentment for him would prove stubbornly elusive.[172]

Then suddenly, the war was really over. In any event, the guns fell silent. At 05:00 hours on Monday 11 November, the Armistice was signed and Germany surrendered unconditionally. The fighting and dying was to continue for another six hours until 11:00 hours. This was to give time for the order to cease firing to reach every unit, Allied and German along the entire 700 kilometres of the Western Front, which extended from the Channel coast to the Swiss border.

In London, an announcement was made in Parliament. Then both Chambers adjourned for the day and paraded *en masse* to church. This set the tone nationally and as the news filtered through to Haddington the atmosphere seemed strangely muted as surprise mixed with overwhelming relief competed with sober reflection to help subdue any excesses of celebration. While some citizens did celebrate with unrestrained jubilation, many more, like the remnants of the Cranston family, chose to remain behind closed curtains focused on their own thoughts and prayers.

For Angus it was a time of unsurpassed turmoil. By this time he realised he had developed into a vastly different person from the one that had been at school three years previously. This had nothing to do with his physical appearance, which had altered too: it was his attitude to life he was thinking about. It had changed

---

172 John Singer Sargent, a famous war artist, painted a haunting image of British soldiers blinded and burned by gas in the same sector and at about the same time as Doddie was affected. Even if George Cranston was not present in the actual painting, his gassing would have produced an equally horrific sight. The painting is simply called 'Gassed'.

totally, growing progressively harder with the death of each of his older brothers in war. He surprised everyone by going straight home from work after news of the German surrender had spread across town to spend the evening brooding moodily alone.

For over four years Angus had lived and breathed the war and was hurt deeply each time tragedy visited the family. His oft-stated ambition was to reach the age of 18 and avenge his fallen brothers by killing as many Germans as he possibly could. Now, five months before he could officially enlist, these ambitions had been cruelly thwarted.

But it was not quite as straightforward as that. Uppermost among the emotions felt by young Angus as the bells started to ring out across the land, was one of immense relief. This reaction was totally understandable to everyone else, but to him it was an indication that his posturing of the last four years had been a sham. He pretended that he was bitterly disappointed by the Armistice, but deep down he was relieved, even grateful. These mixed emotions only fuelled the feelings of guilt which already dominated his life.

The first few days after Armistice came and went and for once, Lizzie was not out and about all day long. As a result she missed the church services rapidly organised on the day following the announcement because she had not heard about them. Instead, she stayed indoors and prayed for her many sons who had died or been wounded.

It was an incensed Angus who strode into the family home on Friday night brandishing a copy of the *Haddingtonshire Courier*.[173] The *Courier* was read in nearly every home in Haddington and was a great favourite of the Cranstons following a number of highly praiseworthy articles about the family that had been published during the conflict.

---

173 *Haddingtonshire Courier* Friday 15 November 1918.

'Ma, I'll never read this bloody paper again. Never! Dae you see whit they have got on their front page? On the very week that we won the war!'

Every week since the paper started publishing almost 60 years earlier, the front page had consisted entirely of tightly packed advertisements with no hint as to the contents inside. It was a tried and tested formula that seemed to appeal to advertisers and readers alike. Angus, however, was furious and had the complete attention of Ma and his sister Mary. With the newspaper held aloft in his left hand he pointed angrily at certain advertisements at random.

'Ladies Underwear for Winter Wear, Split Firewood, whatever that is!' His voice broke uncontrollably, '...and a lost collie dug! You've got tae go in tae the centre o' it tae read about the Armistice under a headin' ca'd Peace.' He was losing any semblance of composure.

'Ma, I've lost the four best brithers a man could ever wish for and as far as this damned rag is concerned – they're worth less than a bloody collie dug!'

The women were alarmed since they had seen signs of Angus's temper in the past, but thankfully, on this occasion his grievance was not with them. He threw the paper down in disgust and stormed out the front door, saying over his shoulder, 'Stuff this cairry on. I'm aff tae the Lang Bar!'

The *Courier* also told of the forthcoming combined service of thanksgiving that was to be celebrated by all the local clergy that Sunday. A day later when Mary saw Effie Fairgrieve the two agreed that come what may, they would make sure that Lizzie Cranston was there. For Effie, this was a big commitment. Being raised a Catholic, she had never set foot inside a Protestant church in her life, but as the local priest was also attending she felt the Pope could not possibly object.

Lizzie, who had spent the intervening few days in solitary

contemplation, seemed quite ready to reappear on the Sunday and make her way with the others to the huge gathering. Although semi-ruined since the Reformation,[174] St Mary's Parish Church is one of the biggest in Scotland and that day played host to what was described as possibly its largest attendance ever. Several members of the clergy took turns to address the combined congregations while Lizzie, Mary and Effie huddled together on a groaning pew well towards the rear. Effie was sceptical, Mary distraught and Lizzie concentrated hard on being attentive.

The Reverend George Wauchope-Stewart entered the pulpit and those who had heard him before braced themselves for a lengthy and difficult-to-follow tirade. He had never been in any doubt that the British forces had been fighting on God's behalf and that therefore eventual victory was inevitable.

'We meet today,' he declaimed, 'under a profound sense of gratitude to God. The thick cloud which cast such a deep shadow on our national life has at last been rolled away.'[175]

Mary nodded in agreement. Lizzie, head down and hands clutched tightly together, voiced a silent prayer. Only Effie seemed critical of the Almighty. She addressed her friends with a sidelong glance: 'Whit took him sae bloody lang?' she muttered.

---

174 Partially destroyed by the army of Henry VIII in 1548–49 and finally restored to its full splendour in the 1970s, after more than 400 years.

175 From a report of the service published in the *Haddingtonshire Courier*, 22 November 1918, which quoted Reverend Wauchope-Stewart directly.

1919/1920

*T*he 'war that will end war' came to an end in November 1918
and it was time to count the cost. Empires that had lasted
centuries were wiped away in the fighting. While the victors
squabbled over the spoils of war, reparations were imposed on the
defeated that were so excessive they would contribute to another
global conflict less than a generation later.

In total, an estimated 68 million soldiers, sailors and airmen fought
each other over four long, bitter years. It is believed approximately
10 million combatants died, while another 21 million were wounded
and a staggering 8 million remained unaccounted for.

Scotland, with a small population of only 4 million, sent away
more than 700,000 men in uniform to fight. Of that number
approximately 125,000 died and more than twice that number
were wounded. This is regarded as one of the highest casualty
rates out of any of the countries that fought. But statistics alone do
not give a true indication of the extent of losses. Across Scotland,
towns and valleys lost husbands, sons, fathers and brothers.

Everyone was affected. But the dying did not stop when the guns fell silent.

Even as the Great War was coming to a close, another more deadly scourge was circling the globe. The influenza pandemic (1918–20) would kill another 20 million people worldwide.

It was now almost a year since Mary Cranston's wedding and with the war over it was becoming easier for her to envisage her long-term future with husband Jim. A future that she had always known would not involve Scotland.

After the briefest of honeymoons, Jim had returned to Surrey and the headquarters of the Canadian Expeditionary Force. There he was attached to a Labour Battalion until the end of the war when the Canadian soldiers were repatriated.

Prior to his marriage, Jim had sent half his pay home to his mother in Canada. After the wedding, Jim redirected that portion to Mary. Over the first year of their marriage, Mary received approximately £120 as 'separation payments' from the Canadian Army, a very acceptable amount in Scottish terms when the average annual wage was less than half that.[176] As a married woman, Mary could no longer work as a domestic servant (the domain of girls and single women). But the separation allowance enabled her to return home to St Martin's Gate in some degree of financial comfort and look after her mother full-time.

By now the repatriation of all Canadian soldiers had begun in earnest. Servicemen were sailing back home at the rate of nearly 50,000 per month.[177] But for Mary, there was much unfinished business in Haddington. Her brother Doddie was finally discharged

---

176 Rubinstein, W.D. (1977), 'The Victorian Middle Classes: Wealth, Occupation, and Geography'. *The Economic History Review* (Issue 30, 1977: pp 602–23).
177 Nicholson, G. W. L., *Canadian Expeditionary Force 1914–1919*. Ottawa: Queen's Printer, 1964, pp.503–506.

from a military hospital, but when he returned home, now a civilian, he was in extremely poor health. His journey back to the remnants of his family in Haddington was a long and painful one.

Mary had no warning that Doddie was about to appear on what was an already fraught January morning. The past few months had not been easy.

Mary fought back her frustration as Lizzie plucked endlessly at the buttons of her cardigan, which showed evidence of several earlier meals she had failed to clean up. 'Tinker, tailor, soldier, sailor,' Lizzie muttered distractedly to herself as she fumbled with each button in turn. 'Rich man, poor man, beggarman, thief!'

With a great deal of effort Mary bit her lip and said nothing. The war had taken a heavy toll on her mother and now though it was over, the damage was irreparable. 'Tinker, tailor, soldier,' she began again and for Mary the sound of someone at the door came just at the right time.

At first, it looked as if Lizzie was unaware of the person's presence in her kitchen. His face was covered in blisters, his demeanour, that of a broken man. But a flicker of recognition appeared in the old woman's eyes and her meaningless rhyming came to a stop. Slowly she reached out her hand towards the pathetic ex-soldier: 'Oor poor wee Doddie!' Her eyes had filled with tears. 'Whitiver is gaun tae become o' us?'

Time was running out for Mary with Canada beckoning any day now and she wrote to her sister Agnes in Australia for what was to be the last time from Scotland. Increasingly, the task of keeping Agnes and her family updated with snippets from home had fallen to Mary. Over the past years she had written about her wedding and the enlistment of their seventh brother Robbie. Later she broke the news about Sandy's death and how difficult it would be now for his widow, Annie, to raise six children on her own. In Australia, Agnes shuddered at the thought.

Equally disturbing, were the continual references to Ma's declining mental state. Of course, Mary did not use the terminology of a qualified psychiatrist, but she left her sister in no doubt that their mother's behaviour was becoming increasingly erratic.

Mercifully, shortly before she was due to sail, younger brother Robbie returned home. The timing was perfect. In the short time before her departure, Robbie the joiner hastily made his sister a sea chest for the journey and listened with awe and consternation to her report of the family's disintegration. Mary said her farewells to a now shattered family in Haddington in March 1919, joined her husband in England and left Scotland for ever.

The week-long voyage over the ocean was cramped and uncomfortable. The Canadian authorities had intentionally squeezed as many war brides as possible into the SS *Melita* to save money on each trip. As near as Mary could figure there were at least 500 other war brides on the vessel, most were accompanied by a husband and in many cases with infants.[178]

Mary felt better on deck than down in the confined quarters in steerage. There, she would stroll around the open wooden deck arm in arm with Jim while the cold and biting April winds blew in from the northern Atlantic. She overheard other ladies talking and was drawn to the many Scottish war brides on the ship. Most were looking forward to a life in a new land; nevertheless, all were sad at leaving their families behind.

When the steamship docked at Saint John harbour, New Brunswick, in April 1919, the Army Paymaster was waiting for Jim and the other soldier-husbands to come ashore. Amid a crowd of disembarked passengers at the dock, including the occasional crying baby, Jim and the other soldiers were discharged from the Canadian Expeditionary Force. He was handed his final separation

---

178 It has been estimated by the Canadian Government that over 32,000 mainly British war brides were transported for free to Canada in one of the least known post-Great War migrations.

payment of 100 Canadian dollars, thanked for his service to King and Country and then summarily told he could be on his way.

He conceded it was not much to show for three years' service, but he promised Mary that as soon as they were settled they would start building a new life for themselves as farmers in Ontario.

Jim sent a telegram to his parents from Saint John informing them that he and Mary would spend a few days resting in the port before completing the final leg of the journey back to the family property in Varney, Grey County, Ontario. He gave them details of their expected arrival at the Varney railway station on the Wellington, Grey and Bruce Railway line and politely requested someone to collect them at the station.

A few days later, Jim was surprised to see that a goodly number of people were waiting to greet the couple at the rail siding of Varney. It was not a small thing for people in Ontario to travel so far on roads and lanes that in the current spring season could often be a considerable challenge to man and beast. After warm greetings all round, those gathered soon led off in a line of assorted horse-drawn conveyances. The family farm was several kilometres away. Mary drank in all the sights and sounds around her. She was finally going to meet her in-laws.

Over the noise of the horses, harnesses and wheels squishing in the mud, Jim pointed out local sites to Mary, including the one-room school house he had attended, as well as the church. But it was heavy going through the slush and mud. When the procession finally arrived at the homestead, Jim's mother was the first to embrace the couple. Fighting back tears, in a long hug for Jim she tried to make up for three long years all at once. Jim's father, also named John, formally shook the hands of his son and daughter-in-law, but did not show any emotion. He never did.

Inside the small farmhouse there were a large number of visitors all anxious to welcome back their neighbour, friend and in some cases fellow soldier. As the party got underway Jim introduced his new bride to everyone. She was reserved; they were welcoming. Finally, John Weir, the father, called everyone to order and in a slow, deliberate delivery typical of the farmers in this region of Ontario he spoke.

'My son Jim's been away from us for a while. He volunteered to be a soldier and do his bit for the Empire. He fought bravely, but has suffered some injuries. Unfortunately, many of his pals suffered an even worse fate. We're glad he's now back with us and hopefully will continue his recovery.' The father paused while those present remembered the other casualties from the area, then shuffling his feet out of nervousness he continued.

'But our soldier has not returned to us alone. We are delighted he has found a beautiful bride of sound Scottish stock. I've been informed she is a wonderful cook and so we look forward to many favourite meals from home.' John then said, 'Let us pray' and led them in a heartfelt prayer of thanksgiving. After which, those gathered sang the family hymn 'O God of Bethel', a hymn which had been sung at every family gathering since John's Scottish ancestors had arrived in Canada a generation earlier. The father wanted to say something special to finish off the welcome.

'Ladies and gentlemen,' he said with a display of eloquence rarely seen from him, 'after an absence of more than three years, please welcome back into the bosom of this family, my son the soldier and his war bride.'

Robbie Cranston returned to Haddington in February 1919 and faced a family situation that was critical. War's end in November 1918 did not mean an immediate recall of all troops from the front; some units were needed to stay in place for logistical and administrative reasons. Such was the case for Robbie's 99 Squadron.

The squadron flew daily missions over Germany to verify that the ceasefire was still holding and report any infractions to authorities.

Then in January 1919, news was received that the entire squadron was to be transferred to India to patrol the troubled Waziristan region on the North-West Frontier. All conscripted airmen in the unit were asked if they wished to stay on, or be sent home and demobilised. This included Robbie, who was young, single and freshly promoted to Airman 2nd Class. It seemed like a wonderful opportunity to continue with the RAF and even see exotic locations as his older brother Ian had done. But he had received further news from Mary about how poorly the family was doing back in Haddington and he knew where his real duty lay, and it was not in uniform in a far away location. He turned down the once in a lifetime offer and was discharged from the RAF, returning home to Scotland on 7 February 1919, by which time Robbie had been away from home continuously for 15 months.

What he found waiting at home shocked him. His mother was now deeply traumatised at the loss of so many sons. Doddie was a pitiful sight. Skin was blistering and peeling from his groin, neck and arms where the gas had seeped through his clothes and into his skin. To make matters worse, his younger brother, Angus, was also causing Robbie considerable concern.

Angus started blaming himself for not being able to serve in the army and for being left behind when his more deserving brothers went off to fight. He blamed himself for not dying in place of his brothers who, in his opinion, were all better than he. He became convinced that if he had gone to war and died in battle, it would have saved his braver, better brothers from suffering the same fate.[179]

---

179 This mental condition was officially recognised for the first time in the 1960s and was called 'survivor guilt'. It derives in part from a feeling that the person did not do enough to save the others who perished and in part from feelings of being an unworthy relative to those who died. Some blame themselves when loved ones die tragically or traumatically, as in warfare. Today it is considered a subsection of Post Traumatic Stress Disorder.

Big decisions awaited Robbie, but his first task was very much of a practical nature – to get a job. Luckily, as a joiner by trade, he was able to secure employment at James Stark & Sons who carried on a high-class joinery and cabinet-making business only 100 metres from the flat in St Martin's Gate. The joinery shop was located in a dilapidated old building where among the many items being manufactured were bespoke coffins for local undertakers. Hence the building was known locally as the 'coffin house'.[180]

The Spanish flu was sweeping its way across Scotland at the time and Stark's were struggling to keep up with increasing orders for coffins. They were grateful to take on an extra hand, especially as he lived so close that he could stay back late and do extra work.

Thus it was, in his own time and using discarded offcuts lying around the 'coffin house', that Robbie hastily made a sea chest for his much-loved sister, Mary. It was not a thing of beauty, but it was strong and sturdy enough to handle the journey across the Atlantic.

With spring in full bloom, Robbie assessed the situation further and visited the widows of Ian, Adam, James and Sandy. He quickly realised that Ma was being more of a hindrance than a help to them. Once, when visiting William and Pat in the Borders, she had wandered off and had to be rescued by neighbours. Robbie looked at the situation from all angles and sat down to write a letter to his sister in Australia.

In Australia, Agnes received all letters postmarked Haddington with a sense of unease. For several years now, they had contained

---

180 In the 1950s, before he became a famous actor, Sean Connery worked at Stark's, which was still operating from the same 'coffin house' in St Martin's Gate. Connery was employed as a French polisher for a time. It was said that if he missed his bus home to Edinburgh he would make himself comfortable in a coffin for the night.

mainly bad news. It was with no sense of satisfaction that she realised that the only pieces of cheerful news that had lately been exchanged between them had come from her own pen.

Her brother Drew had moved into his own flat in the inner western suburb of Stanmore and was doing well for himself. And now that the war was over, he had bought a butcher's shop in partnership with a mate he had worked with for years. Agnes was pleased for Drew and it seemed that he was making his way in the world. The other item of good news was that she had given birth to a third son in 1919, named John Buchan ('Ian') McDowall in honour of her fallen brother.

In contrast, the news from Scotland was invariably tragic and she found it difficult to absorb. She needed someone or something to blame for this calamity and her focus turned easily to the Germans. Agnes had never harboured any ill will towards Germany or its people before the war. In reality she had never really thought about them at all, but over a time span of just four short years she developed a profound hatred of everything German.

With Mary now in Canada, Agnes had wondered how her mother and brothers would cope without a woman to look after them. The answer came from an unexpected source, her second youngest brother Robert. The last time Agnes had seen him he was only 13, but now he was a man who had experienced life at the front. And his letter was straight to the point.

Robert outlined the terrible state of affairs the Cranston family was in and gave particularly grim accounts of the worst affected individuals. He did not hold anything back and Agnes was impressed at how her young brother had matured into a clear-thinking, responsible adult. The purpose of the letter was clear. Robert was asking, in fact pleading, to relocate the family to Australia and initially at least to live under Agnes's care.

It was a huge decision for Agnes to make and one that she

was not prepared to take alone. Agnes called a family conference with husband John and brother Drew to discuss their Scottish family's plight. It was going to cause an upheaval in the McDowall household, but Agnes felt she had no choice. As a good and loyal daughter and sister, she felt duty bound to accept the burden of caring for the shattered Cranston family. Only Willie would stay in Britain and it saddened Agnes to realise she might never hear his wonderful fiddle-playing again.

Her decision was never in doubt. Several weeks later Agnes sat down and penned a letter to Robert accepting her role as carer and inviting four extra Cranstons to come and live in Australia. Towards the end of 1919 came a reply informing Agnes of the date and time of their arrival.

Robert with the other immediate members of the Cranston family arranged to leave Scotland on 31 March 1920 on the TSS[181] *Euripides* for new lives in Sydney. Robbie was only 20 years old at this time and effectively the head of the family. Out of the 12 children born to Alec and Lizzie Cranston, only Willie was to remain in Scotland.

The Saturday before the family left Haddington for Australia, Angus visited his favourite watering hole one last time. The evening's air was still quite cool as he warmed himself by the log fire drinking steadily in the Long Bar. As usual it did not take him long to get drunk. It seldom did these days; his tolerance for alcohol was already impaired, at the age of just 19. But it did not bother Angus, because he reasoned he could sober up on Sunday[182] and be more than ready for the big journey on Monday.

---

181 turbine steam ship
182 At the time there was no Sunday pub trading in Scotland.

It was getting close to the recently relaxed closing time,[183] but Angus was in no hurry to leave. The usual Saturday night crowd in the Long Bar was being augmented by the arrival of the occasional person coming in for a drink before going home. A stranger approached the bar and stood beside Angus. While this person waited patiently to be served, Angus decided to strike up a conversation. He told him, 'You know in battle, I'd follow the pipes into the very gates of Hell.' The other customer seemed impressed with this war-time recollection, but a regular at the pub jumped in and called him a fraud.

'My boy was only 17 when he went off the war. You were a year older, but stayed at home'.[184]

Angus, already heavily affected by alcohol, was now incensed that he was not only being called a liar but by implication also a coward. The publican interrupted and tried to restore some calm before matters escalated further. Even at such a young age, Angus had gained an unenviable reputation around town for being a violent drunk and the publican did not want another fight in his establishment caused by this hothead. As soothing as he could be the hotelier said, 'Think aboot all the men who really died, Angus, especially your own brothers.' Angus hesitated momentarily, swaying slightly on his feet.

'It's one of your last nights in Scotland,' the publican continued 'let's no' be havin' any fuss. Why don't you have a drink on me?' The prospect of a free drink was attractive to Angus and resulted in him calming down marginally. But the publican sadly knew

---

183 During the war the closing time for public hotels throughout Britain was progressively lowered to 9pm and it was only raised to 10pm in 1919 after the war had ended. (Ref: Arthur Shadwell, *Drink in 1914–1922, a lesson in Control*, Longmans, London, Green & Co., 1923)
184 An even more extreme example would be that of Private James M Marchbank from Newbattle, near Dalkeith, Midlothian Scotland. He served in the same Battalion as Doddie and was only 14 when he went off to war in August 1914. During the conflict he was awarded the Military Medal for bravery. James survived four years of war and returned home in 1919, still only 18! (Reference: Newbattle at War www.freewebs.com/eltoro1960/boysoldier.htm)

from his recently healed black eye that a combination of alcohol and unresolved issues caused Angus to become a belligerent and aggressive drunk.

Angus was staring vacantly at nothing in particular when his attention was drawn to another man who had just entered the bar. In his intoxicated mind this new stranger looked vaguely familiar. But who could it be? For an instant, he thought he had recognised his beloved brother Adam. He lurched over to the man and clutched drunkenly onto the lapels of his overcoat. Angus stared unfocused into the startled man's face and exclaimed, 'I should have gone instead of you. Adam, dae ye no hear me!'

The man in the overcoat did not understand why he was being called Adam, as it was not his name. The stranger struggled free of Angus's grip and exited the pub in a hurry. Witnessing the exchange, the publican concluded that he had finally had enough of Angus for the night. As sympathetic as he and most of the regulars were to the plight of the Cranstons, he still wanted Angus out of the pub before he started another fight. Even though this was his second last night in the country, Angus was refused service yet again and ordered to leave the premises.

As he stumbled out of the hotel, ashamed, angry and still feeling guilty about not saving his siblings, he turned back to the customers and with alcoholic spittle spraying from his mouth, shouted at no one in particular, 'It should hae been me, I tell ye. It should hae been me.'

Two days later, on Monday, 29 March 1920, the carter's horse, with all that was left of the Cranstons' worldly goods tied to the cart behind it, slowly quenched its thirst. It knew that it had passed the Railway Hotel and that the trough from which it now drank greedily was the last before the railway station itself. It was a journey it had made many times before. The old lady perched precariously between the carter and her son Robbie on that crisp afternoon had also made the journey in the past.

'Bide close tae me Robbie,' she said to her son 'and we'll see your brothers soon enough.' But Lizzie was not at the railway station to welcome her boys home from the war. She was there to leave Haddington for ever. When she climbed the stairs to the platform, she was surprised to see a number of family members there to greet her.

'Och,' she said to no one in particular, 'they must be here to meet ma boys as weel.'

But her boys were already there. Standing on the platform in their Sunday best were Doddie and Angus and there was Willie too.

'That muckle patch on his e'e maks him oot tae be a richt manly laddie,' Lizzie announced. 'That English wife of his has struck it lucky with Willie.' Further down the platform Lizzie saw a figure; surely that was 'oor Ian?' Then Lizzie remembered the awful truth and cried out loud, 'No, no, it cannae be oor Ian.' Robbie held his mother's hand and did his best to reassure her and explain why she was really at the railway station.

Bags and boxes had already been stored in the goods section of the train and people were mingling on the platform to say their final farewells before the Cranstons departed for ever. The many children jumping about belonged to Jim's widow Annie. She still lived in Haddington and the station platform was barely 400 metres from her flat in Court Street. The Plough Tavern, where Annie now worked as a barmaid, had generously given her the afternoon off and the school had given the children permission to be away too. As the headmistress said, 'We're proud of James and his brothers. They all went to this school and their names will be honoured on a memorial we've commissioned for those ex-pupils who served in the Great War.'[185]

But the children did not care about such concepts as honour, duty or sacrifice. For them it was simply a day off school and they celebrated it by running and playing all over the platform.

Sandy's widow Annie could not get away from Musselburgh, but she had previously sent her best wishes along with those of her six children. She was kept busy working full time as a seamstress and Musselburgh was far away. There was little time for socialising. Unfortunately Willie's own wife Pat could not attend as she was looking after two-year-old Betty and was heavily pregnant with their second child. Ian's wife Agnes had long since moved back to her parents' home in Bathgate where she was raising two children under seven and valiantly taking care of her blind mother, her bedridden father and two sisters, who were both unable to work.

Willie was patience personified, organising matters and comforting Ma. Did she remember Maggie, Adam's wife? Of course Lizzie thought she remembered. Where could the pair of them have got to? Then she suddenly really did remember.

'Taking hersel' back tae Slamannan in Stirling as soon as the war was finished. Still maybe it was just as well, it wis gey hard tae share a kitchen wi' your in-laws.'

The station was full of noise and bustle. People were getting on the train, goods and parcels were being carted about and even the train was noisily producing steam, which wafted in great plumes across the assembled people and occasionally shrouded them in white smoke. It was time for the family to complete their farewells.

But not everyone on that platform was family. Dressed in her Sunday best and looking almost as wide as she was tall, Lizzie's best friend, the usually bubbly, larger-than-life Effie Fairgrieve, hung

---

185 This Roll of Honour can still be seen today hanging in the entrance of Haddington Infant School, which relocated in 2012.

slightly back, her complexion beetroot, her breathing laboured from the walk from her home. She had come to say her 'cheerios' to Lizzie Cranston, her best friend of more than 15 years. Eventually their eyes met. Lizzie was not quite sure what was happening, but seemed aware that she was going away and leaving her best friend behind. Effie, at 70 years of age, was under no illusions that she would ever see Lizzie again. With tears streaming down her face, Effie seemed uncharacteristically lost for words.

'Tak' care,' she wheezed, 'Oh please, tak' care. Now be aff wi'you before I mak a spectle o' mysel' in front o' abody.'

It was the nearest she ever came to expressing her deepest feelings and for just the briefest moment, Lizzie seemed to respond with a flicker of a smile.

As the train pulled out of the station and the town of Haddington began to recede into the distance, the travelling Cranstons settled into their seats in the carriage. Lizzie turned to her son Robbie: 'My grunnie is wanting me in Keith,' she explained.[186]

That day, the first in the Cranstons' long journey to the other side of the world, would be remembered for many things. But foremost in the memories of those present was not the friends and relatives wishing the Cranstons God speed and safe travelling, but the sight and sound of Effie Fairgrieve singing at the top of her lungs to be heard over the sounds of the steam train pulling out of the station. No one could remember Effie ever uttering a musical note before, but there she was in full view of the public without the slightest concern that her voice was clearly out of tune. With tears streaming down her ruddy plump face, she was standing in the middle of the platform and singing lustily:

Will ye no come back again?
Will ye no come back again?

---

186 Elizabeth's grandparents (John and Janet McLeay) both died of old age at Keith in the 1880s.

Better loed ye canna be;
Will ye no come back again?[187]

The following day Effie burst into the office of the *Haddingtonshire Courier* and through the sheer force of her indomitable spirit, arranged for the following article to be written in the newspaper:

It is with feelings of regret that we parted with our esteemed friend, Mrs Cranston on Monday, who, with three of her sons were to leave Waverley Station with the night train for London with the expectation of sailing for Australia on Wednesday.

Mrs Cranston has been long well known in Haddington. She came with her late husband and took up residence in the town forty years ago and had a large family, who were mostly grown up when she was left a widow ten years ago.

The family consisted of nine sons and two daughters. The daughters are both married – one in Australia and the other in Canada. Of the nine sons, seven of them joined the colours in the early stages of the War, three of whom fell on the battlefields of France[188] and more badly wounded.

Mrs Cranston's long stay in Haddington was that of great activity and hard work and many who knew her can testify to her unselfish and noble life in seeking to help and serve others with little or no thought that she too required rest, which she was often deprived of in attending the sick.

We wish her safe voyage to the distant land, where we trust she will have many happy days to spend in peace and tranquillity.[189]

---

187 'Will ye no come back again', words by Lady Carolina Nairne (1766–1845), set to a traditional Scottish folk tune. Originally intended as a plea for Bonnie Prince Charlie's return, by the early 20th century it had become more widely used as a traditional Scottish song of farewell.
188 One more, James, dying at home of illness contracted during training.
189 *The Haddingtonshire Courier* (2 April 1920)

PART THREE

(1927-9)

A PLACE
OF SAFETY

It was 1 July 1927 and the Cranston family huddled in the windy corridor outside the old sandstone court in Darlinghurst, Sydney, waiting to present their case. It was a very traumatic day for everyone, except, that is, the very person who was the subject of the court proceedings.

The family was standing outside the Lunacy Court of New South Wales and were about to take the unprecedented step of seeking to commit Lizzie Cranston to a hospital for the insane.

Since making the ambitious trip to Australia seven years earlier, the Cranstons had celebrated their fair share of births and marriages but a dark cloud continued to hover over them. The premature death of brother Drew in 1923 had stopped them in their tracks and destroyed any vestige of normal functioning in Lizzie, the beloved matriarch known to them all as 'Ma'.

Outside the court John McDowall stayed in the background, smoking his pipe. He was ever ready to support his wife Agnes, but otherwise said nothing. Everyone knew that this was Cranston business and nobody seemed inclined to look the others in the eye.

Robbie was first to speak; like Doddie and Angus he was not accompanied by his wife.

'We've a' tried and failed and God kens, we've a' got families of oor ain tae think aboot. Ma will be a lot happier,' he continued unconvincingly to his siblings and then he cut to the chase. 'The paperwork's right here, including the two doctors' reports. They say it's the only thing that can be done.' The well-built man that was Robbie Cranston shed a single tear.

'But why dae I feel sae bloody awful aboot it?'

A court official called the family inside and they took their seats behind the table facing the bench. Lizzie Cranston was among them with some knitting in hand, but as far as she was concerned she was back in Scotland darning a sock.

The magistrate informed the family he was there to conduct an inquiry into Mrs Cranston's mental competency and if necessary sign an order scheduling her to a mental institution. First he looked at the doctors' reports, compiled separately, which told the magistrate what the family from bitter experience already knew.

Lizzie Cranston was described as being 'disorientated; restless; confused; wanders and often needs to be found by the police; undresses in public; has no knowledge of her age, name, date of birth or country of origin; quite incapable of taking care of herself and talks to imaginary people'.

The magistrate asked the family if they could add anything. Tragically, each in turn acknowledged that the bleak catalogue of symptoms described to a tee the woman that their beloved mother had become.

Agnes broke down and through tears admitted that caring for Ma had eventually proved beyond her and to their credit both Doddie and Robbie along with their wives had taken their turn at one time or another to try and look after her, but everything they had tried was in the end unsuccessful. Finally the magistrate turned to the person in question and said, 'Mrs Cranston do you know where you are?' Lizzie lifted up the sock to show the man and said, 'Guid Borders wool.'

He asked a few more questions which received equally senseless answers and when satisfied, the stipendiary magistrate officially wrote down that Mrs Elizabeth Cranston was 'Insane and not under proper care or control'. The court ordered the poor woman be taken immediately into custody and transported by padded wagon to Rydalmere Mental Hospital, located beside the Parramatta river.[190]

Even though it was what the rest of the family wanted, it did not lessen their feelings of guilt and distress. In particular it broke Agnes's heart.

Was Lizzie Cranston happy in the sprawling, Victorian asylum complex at the mental hospital? Possibly not. As she wandered around the exercise yard or stared blankly at a pair of knitting needles and a ball of wool she was invariably accompanied by anxieties that had her permanently on edge.

In truth, Lizzie gave the impression of settling in at Rydalmere. She ate well and most importantly of all, she was safe. When she talked, she talked about Scotland, in a dialect that was understood by no one. Sometimes she talked about her grandparents, sometimes about a graveyard in Leith, by Edinburgh, and sometimes about somebody called Effie. Occasionally, she would talk about her boys and sometimes she'd mention them by name. But more often she would be silent as if gazing to some distant horizon looking

---

190 Much of this information is compiled from accessing Elizabeth Cranston's mental health file during her stay at Rydalmere Mental Hospital (1927–29), which is held at the New South Wales State Archives, Australia.

for someone that she perhaps couldn't quite put a name to. She loved Queen Victoria and hated the Germans. And gradually the days turned into months. The family took turns to write regularly asking about her welfare. Once Agnes asked:

Kindly tell me how she is keeping in health and if her memory is any improved. I should like to know as it is not easy for me to get away to see her. I'm always wondering if she is any better in mind as she was such a good mother to us.

They also visited when they could. Lizzie would smile at them, eat whatever snacks they offered her and then appear to forget them.

At one time Robert sent a letter to the Medical Superintendent containing the family's explanation of how Elizabeth came to be mentally ill. Robert wrote:

The cause of my mother's illness is due to the War as she gradually became more forgetful and had the habit of mislaying things. She had seven sons fighting in France and four were killed in the short time of two years.

Three of us came home. One with the loss of an eye and I'm afraid the constant worry of it all caused her mind to wander.

The last twelve months she has got worse and it was a hard job to keep an eye on her as she would run away from home. She also had a tendency to undress herself.

She seems to remember a lot about home in Scotland, but as far as Australia is concerned, it's a blank to her.

Every morning she would get up and say that she was going away to see her Grandmother and, as her Grandmother brought her up, she must fancy she is back in childhood.

She was never any-time dangerous. Used to eat well, but

often got up during the night to wander. Since she came to Australia she has lost another son. That was four years ago and probably that has also helped towards her illness.

She has worked very hard all her life having eleven in the family and the loss of her sons at the War is to blame and nothing else!

Hoping that while she is under your care, she will improve in health.

The doctors were convinced they were dealing with a straightforward case of senile dementia. However, the family remembered the horrors of 1914–1918 and the devastation it wrought on their close-knit family. They looked on the pathetic shell that was once Lizzie Cranston and believed that the Great War had claimed yet another victim.

The nurse released her gentle hold on her patient's wrist, checked the second hand of her watch once again and reached for Lizzie Cranston's chart. All her experience told her that the end was very close.

John McDowall woke with a start only to discover he had scarcely been asleep. It was barely ten o'clock on a mild March night in 1929 and his wife had just woken him up with an urgent elbow to his ribcage.

'We have to contact the asylum tomorrow,' she said emphatically.[191] But before John could ask why, Agnes had rolled over and promptly gone back to sleep.

It was early morning in Priceville, Ontario, yet Mary Weir was

---

191 At the time the McDowalls did not have a phone installed, so the couple would have to walk the 20 minutes or so up to Gordon Post Office to use the public telephone.

up and preparing breakfast for her family. She was heavily pregnant with twins, but that did not mean her workload had diminished.

The family had moved from the farm into town six months before, but for the Weirs old habits were difficult to break. Despite the absence of any cows that needed milking, here they were sitting at the breakfast table at something very near the crack of dawn, while the rest of Priceville slept on. She was in the kitchen making porridge as she had done many hundreds of times before. Jim was sitting at the table with nine-year-old Alexander and his young brother Adam as Isabelle, the toddler, screamed insistently from her cot.

Suddenly, the milk jug slipped from her hand and smashed on the floor. Jim, who was not well himself,[192] immediately thought something had happened to Mary's pregnancy. As fast as he could he rushed to her side.

'Whatever's the matter, love?' he asked. Standing in the middle of the floor with milk running everywhere, Mary looked into her husband's eyes and said, 'It's Ma. Something terrible has happened!'

The nurse tenderly moistened Lizzie's mouth with a swab wrapped around her forefinger as her breathing grew shallower. In Lizzie's mind the rhythmic ticking of the wall clock in the ward gradually transformed into the sound of a forester chopping wood.

She saw her husband skilfully wielding his axe as he split timber in one of the woods around Haddington. He stopped, and in her imagination turned to look in her direction. While he smiled other men joined him. First Sandy, then Ian, followed by Jimmy, Adam and finally Drew.

---

192 Jim was so afflicted by 'Creeping Paralysis' that he could no longer continue earning a living as a farmer.

Lizzie's breathing suddenly became silent. In that most crucial of moments, what could only be described as a smile slowly spread across her face. Then the remarkable woman who was Lizzie Cranston was no more.[193]

---

193 Final patient entry reads: '15 March 1929. Patient had an attack in the afternoon and again in the early evening, after which she gradually sank lower and lower until she finally expired.'

PART FOUR
THE AFTERMATH

The Great War started the unravelling of the Cranston family and scattered them around the world. But the story of grief and separation continued for several more decades until the last sons and daughters of Alec and Lizzie passed away.

SCOTLAND

WIDOW AND CHILDREN OF ALEXANDER CRANSTON (SANDY)

After the death of Sandy in 1918, Annie stayed on in the family home at Musselburgh, where she struggled to raise a family of one son and five daughters under 16 years of age. Annie died in 1961 and is buried in the churchyard of St Michael's Parish Church, Musselburgh.

By the time each of the children had grown up many had lost touch with the rest of the extended Cranston relatives and some even with their own siblings.

WIDOW AND CHILDREN OF JOHN CRANSTON (IAN)

Ian Cranston's wife Agnes was left a widow at the age of 25. Not only did she bring up two small children without a husband's support, but Agnes also looked after her own mother who was blind; her father who had become bedridden; her sister Lena who was disabled and never worked; and finally another sister, Jessie, who had learning difficulties. Later in life she even added two grandchildren to the list of people she took care of.

Agnes died in Bathgate in 1977, aged 86, and was buried there by a loving family who always believed she was a wonderful example of how to manage heartbreak and service to others with dignity.

WIFE AND CHILDREN OF WILLIAM CRANSTON

In 1920, when the rest of the family left Scotland for Canada and Australia, Willie was the only surviving Cranston of the original family to remain in Scotland. He had no option. Willie had to stay because his war-related injuries still required regular medical treatment and the British government was only prepared to pay for it as long as he remained in the United Kingdom.

His wife, Pat, died in 1953 at the age of 62 from a cerebral thrombosis and Willie passed away in 1957 from a heart attack at 73 years of age. Music remained a great part of their lives as they raised their three children.

WIDOW AND CHILDREN OF JAMES CRANSTON

Even though Annie received a war widow's pension, she still had to work to earn enough to raise a young family of five, all under eight years of age at the time of her widowhood. Living next door to the Plough Tavern in Court Street, Haddington, made the choice of employment easier. Years later while still working as a barmaid and in her mid-30s, Annie caught the attention of an agricultural contractor, Laurence Wallace, who was staying at the Plough while helping farmers bring in the harvest with his mechanical harvester.

In 1923, they married and raised another family of children. She died in 1958 in Haddington at 73 years of age.

WIDOW AND CHILD OF ADAM CRANSTON

Adam and Maggie had one child, Alexander born in 1914. After Adam died, Maggie returned to live with her parents in Station Road, Slamannan, Stirlingshire, in 1919.

Years later, in 1925, she remarried and the separation from the Cranston family became permanent. Maggie died in 1974, at the age of 85.

CANADA

HUSBAND AND CHILDREN OF MARY WEIR (NÉE CRANSTON)

After the war, Jim obtained a modest war veteran's loan from the Canadian government and purchased a small 50-hectare farm near Priceville, Ontario about 2km away from his parents and family.[194] However, it was located in what is still regarded as poor farming country and the harder that Jim worked, the worse his health became, and his attempts to earn a living from farming ultimately came to nothing. In late 1928 the family moved into the nearby small village of Priceville and the farm was leased out.

In 1932, during the worst financial crisis the world had seen, the Weir family found themselves virtually penniless. Facing financial ruin, Mary suffered a complete mental breakdown. She was admitted to the Hamilton Asylum, Ontario, suffering from

---

194 Information on this and following matters is derived from Mary Weir's clinical file at the Hamilton Asylum, Ontario Canada with permission of the Ontario Archives (Source: Hamilton Psychiatric Hospital patients' clinical case file #37830, RG 10-285, Archives of Ontario).

Manic Depression[195] and spent the next seven and a half years in treatment. Jim's unmarried sister Belle Weir helped raise the five young Weir children and look after her brother, whose health was continuing to decline.

John James 'Jim' Weir died on 24 October 1938 at the age of 50 from asphyxiation due to partial paralysis of his throat muscles as well as 'basal nuclear disease' or what the locals called 'creeping paralysis'.[196]

In 1939 Mary was eventually discharged from the asylum, fully recovered. She died on 12 August 1962 at the age of 71 from a heart attack at the home of her daughter Sheila. Mary was buried alongside her husband in the Priceville cemetery, Ontario, Canada.

---

195 Now known as Bipolar Affective Disorder.
196 Information obtained from Jim Weir's Death Certificate. Basal Nuclear Disease is now known as Basal Ganglia Disease, which is used to describe a number of degenerative motor-neuron diseases, including Parkinson's disease, Dystonia and Huntington's disease.

AUSTRALIA

HUSBAND AND CHILDREN OF AGNES MCDOWALL (NÉE CRANSTON)

The McDowalls maintained a close relationship with relatives in Scotland and Canada until Agnes died. During the 1930s and 1940s the couple were stalwarts of the Scottish-Australian Society, organising balls and attending Hogmanay and Burns nights.

Agnes worked hard all her life. She loved and protected her family with passion and was warm and generous to almost everyone. Yet, she had developed a pathological hatred of Germans and of Germany. Agnes passed away suddenly from a massive heart attack in 1951 at the family home at Gordon. She was only 65 years of age.

John McDowall died in 1972 at the age of 87 and is buried along Agnes at Northern Suburbs Cemetery, Sydney. The family had four children.

WIFE AND CHILD OF GEORGE CRANSTON (DODDIE)

After arriving in Sydney, Doddie could only secure temporary menial jobs, which he could not hold down for long. As a result of the gassing in the First World War, every nine months or so, parts of his skin peeled off exposing raw flesh underneath. During these times he had to remain for long periods submerged in an oil bath to avoid infection. He was finally declared permanently incapacitated in 1928 by the Australian authorities.

Doddie married Matilda 'Westie' West at St John's Church, Milson's Point Sydney in 1924, when he was 32 years of age and she was 37. They had one daughter.

Australian authorities would not grant Doddie a war pension, claiming it was Britain's responsibility. Conversely, the British authorities refused to give him one either, because he had left the United Kingdom. This was the same policy that kept Willie in Scotland.

George Cranston died in 1963 at 71 years of age. Matilda followed a year later.

WIFE AND CHILD OF ANDREW CRANSTON (DREW)

After setting up the butcher's shop in Sydney's inner west with his friend Ted Ball, Andrew spent much time in the company of the Ball family. He fell in love with Ted's young, demure sister, Elsie, and in 1921 at the age of 26, Andrew married Elsie Violet Ball, then 21 years old. Twelve months after their marriage Elsie gave birth to a daughter, who tragically died five days later from injuries to the head sustained during a difficult instrument birth.

While Elsie was pregnant Andrew was diagnosed with pulmonary tuberculosis. His condition deteriorated and he died 18 months later in 1923 at a sanatorium to the south of Sydney.[197]

197 The Waterfall Sanatorium was the only purpose-built facility for the treatment of tuberculosis in the State of New South Wales. The hospital operated from 1909 to 1958. (Source: State Archives of New South Wales)

Years later Elsie married a carpenter, Oliver Watts. Elsie died in Sydney in 1979 at the age of 79 years.

WIFE AND CHILD OF ROBERT CRANSTON

In Australia, Robbie secured employment in the nascent air transport industry thanks to his acquired wartime skills maintaining warplanes. Robbie married Janet 'Jean' Rew in the Sydney suburb of Burwood on 18 December 1926. They had one son. From the early 1930s Robbie worked on planes in both Papua New Guinea and in Sydney, firstly as a mechanic/engineer and latterly as an aviation inspector.

He died suddenly from a heart attack in 1950. Jean died in 1974.

WIFE AND CHILDREN OF ANGUS CRANSTON

At the age of 23, when Angus was a plumber living with his brother Doddie and Westie, he married Annie Pullar Morrison (then 21 years of age). Annie was the daughter of John Morrison, who along with his wife and family had emigrated to Australia years earlier and were still close friends of John and Agnes McDowall.

Despite being a heavy drinker, Angus somehow managed to enlist in the Australian army during the Second World War and saw service from 1940 to 1945. However, more than a quarter of his time in the army was spent Absent Without Leave, or sick, or in the stockade charged with drunkenness or fighting.[198]

He lived out the last years of his life a lonely alcoholic in a rented tin shed in Sydney. Angus died of respiratory arrest in 1951, just nine days prior to his 51st birthday. He was buried in

---

198 There are 39 entries in Angus' Service Record: for being sick (17 entries); Absent Without Leave (AWOL, 12 entries); Drunkenness (5 entries) and Conduct Prejudicial to the Good Order and Military Discipline, a term that usually means fighting (5 entries). The total amount of days ordered in detention, admitted to hospital or absent from the army without leave totalled 497 days out of 1790 days in uniform – the equivalent of 1½ years or 28 per cent of his service in the Australian Army.

a soldier's grave at Rookwood Cemetery, Sydney in accordance with his will.

Annie died in 1980 at 77 years of age. They had three children.

CONCLUSION

*T*he Great War tore apart the fabric of this Scottish family
and scattered them to the four corners of the globe. Family
members gradually lost contact with each other and the story of
this remarkable family's sacrifice was almost forgotten. A century
later, and after much painstaking research, the threads of the
Cranston family have been woven back together again.

BIBLIOGRAPHY

BOOKS AND BOOKLETS

Abrams, Lynn and Brown, Callum G., (eds) *A History of Everyday Life in Twentieth Century Scotland*, Edinburgh University Press, Edinburgh, 2010

A Walk Around Haddington, 4th edition, East Lothian Tourist Board, Haddington, 1994

Angus, George, *Haddington, Old and New*, East Lothian District Library, Haddington, 1991

Banks, Arthur, *Military Atlas of the First World War*, Pen & Sword, Barnsley, 1997

Bennett, Margaret, *Scottish Customs from the Cradle to the Grave*, Birlinn, Edinburgh, 2009

Bevan, George, *Jum's War: Finding My Father*, Murdoch, Sydney, 2007

Buchan, John, *The History of the Royal Scots Fusiliers 1678-1918*, Thomas Nelson & Sons, London, 1925

Cameron, Ewen A., *Impaled Upon a Thistle: Scotland Since 1880*, Edinburgh University Press, Edinburgh, 2010

Carter, Ian, *Farm Life in Northeast Scotland 1840-1914: The Poor Man's Country*, John Donald, Edinburgh, 1979

Cross, Robin, *In Memoriam: Remembering the Great War*, (in association with the Imperial War Museum), Ebury, London, 2008

Devine, Tom, *The Scottish Nation A History, 1700-2007*, Penguin, London, 2006

Dickson, A., and Treble, J. H., (eds) *People and Society in Scotland: A Social History of Modern Scotland in Three Volumes*, Volume III 1914-1990, Birlinn, Edinburgh, 2004

Duff, Duncan, *Scotland's War Losses*, The Scottish Secretariat, Glasgow, 1947

East Lothian Revisited – Then and Now, Whittingehame House Publishing, Haddington, 1992

Ferguson, Niall, *The Pity of War 1914–1918*, Penguin, London, 1998

Gray, W. Forbes and Jamieson, James H., *A Short History of Haddington*, 1986 edition by SPA Books, Stevenage, originally printed by the East Lothian Antiquarian and Field Naturalist's Society, 1944

Green, Charles E., *East Lothian*, William Green & Sons, Edinburgh, 1905

Griffiths, Trevor and Morton, Graeme (eds), *A History of Everyday Life in Scotland 1800 to 1900*, Edinburgh University Press, Edinburgh, 2010

Hart, Peter, *The Somme*, Weidenfeld & Nicolson, London, 2005

Harvie, Christopher T., *No Gods and Precious Few Heroes: Twentieth Century Scotland*, Edinburgh University Press, Edinburgh, 1998

Holmes, Richard, *Tommy: The British Soldier on the Western Front 1914-1918*, HarperCollins, London, 2004

Howard, Michael, *The First World War*, Oxford University Press, New York, 2002

Illustrated London News, 102-page special edition publication of 'The Glorious Reign of Queen Victoria, 1837-1901'

Johnson, Niall P. A. S., 'Scottish flu: The Scottish experience of Spanish flu', *Scottish Historical Review*, Vol. LXXXIII, No. 2, 2004, pp. 216–26

Jünger, Ernst, *Storm of Steel* (tr. Michael Hofmann), Penguin, London, 2004

Lumsden, James (ed.), *The Battles of Dunbar and Prestonpans and other selected Poems*, William Sinclair Publishers, Haddington, 1896

Lynch, Michael, *Scotland: A New History*, Pimlico, London, 1992

Macdonald, Catriona M. M., and McFarland, Elaine W., *Scotland and the Great War*, Tuckwell, East Lothian, 1999

MacLeod, James Lachlan, 'Greater Love Hath No Man Than This: Scotland's Conflicting Religious Responses to Death in the Great War', *Scottish Historical Review*, Vol. LXXXI, No. 211, April 2002, pp.70–96

Manz, Stefan, 'Civilian Internment in Scotland during the First World War', in Richard Dove (ed.), *Totally Un-English: Britain's Internment of Enemy Aliens in two World Wars*, Yearbook of the Research Centre for German and Austrian Exile Studies, The Netherlands, Vol. 7, 2005

Matheson, Peter, 'Scottish War Sermons 1914-1919', *Records of the Scottish Church History Society*, Volume XVII, 1971

Mitchell, R G, *A Hundred Years of Haddington*, D. & J. Croal, Haddington, 1999

Muir, Edwin, *Scottish Journey*, new edn, Mainstream, Edinburgh, 1996

Nicholson, G. W. L., *Canadian Expeditionary Force 1914–1919* Ottawa, Queen's Printer, 1964

National Archives (United Kingdom)

Oliver, Neil, *Not Forgotten*, Hodder, London, 2006

Ontario Archives, Canada

Panayi, Panikos, *The Enemy in Our Midst: Germans in Britain during the First World War*, Berg, New York/Oxford, 1991

Pattinson, L. A., *History of 99 Squadron, RAF March, 1918 – November, 1918*, Naval and Military Press, Uckfield, East Sussex, 2004

Pearson, Stuart, 'The McDowall Family', *The Historian*, The Official Journal of the Ku-Ring-Gai Historical Society, Vol. 37, No. 1, November 2008

Robertshaw, Andrew, *Somme 1 July 1916: Tragedy and Triumph*, Osprey, Oxford, 2006

Royle, Trevor, *The Flowers of the Forest: Scotland and the First World War*, Birlinn, Edinburgh, 2007

Rubinstein, W. D., 'The Victorian Middle Classes: Wealth, Occupation, and Geography', *The Economic History Review*, Issue 30, 1977

Sheldon, Jack, *The German Army on the Somme 1914–1916*, Pen & Sword, Barnsley, 2005

Schiel, Joseph B., Jr, and Wepfer, Anita Joan, 'Distributional Aspects of Endemic Goitre in the United States', *Economic Geography*, Vol. 52, No. 2, April 1976

Scottish Censuses 1891–1921

Smout, T. C., *A Century of the Scottish People 1830–1950*, Fontana, London, 1986

Strachan, Hew, *The First World War*, Penguin, London, 2005

State Archives of New South Wales

State Library of New South Wales

Statham, Craig, *Lost East Lothian*, Birlinn, Edinburgh, 2011

Statham, Craig, *Old Haddington*, Stenlake, Ayrshire, 2007

Tabraham Chris (ed.), *Weel Speed the Plough: A Souvenir*

BIBLIOGRAPHY

Photographic Album Celebrating the 200th Anniversary of the United East Lothian Agricultural Society, D. & J. Croal, Haddington, 2004

Taylor, A. J. P., *The First World War*, Penguin, London, 1966

Uys, Ian, *Delville Wood*, Uys Publishers, Johannesburg, 1983

Valuation Rolls, Haddington 1900–20, accessed at East Lothian Archives

Walsh, Michael, *Brothers in War*, Random House, London, 2007

War Office Report, *Statistics of the Military Effort of the British Empire during the Great War 1914–1920*, 1922

Willmott, H. P., *World War I*, 2nd edition, DK Publishers, London, 2012

Winter, J. M., *The Great War and the British People*, 2nd edition, Palgrave Macmillan, London, 2003

MAGAZINES, NEWSPAPERS AND INTERNET SOURCES

East Lothian Life (quarterly magazine)

Haddingtonshire (now *East Lothian*) *Courier* archives

The Scotsman archives

http://1914-18.net

http://ancestry.com

http://archive.org/details/7thbattcameron00sanduoft

http://eastlothain.gov.uk

http://findmypast.com/passengerlists

http://inthefootsteps.org.uk/Articles/1914-18GreatWar/LifeInTheTrenches.htm

http://johngraycentre.org

http://maps.nls.uk

http://news.ourontario.ca/GHPL/search for digital copies of *Flesherton Advance* newspaper.

http://snwm.org
http://www.awm.gov.au/blog/2007/11/13/the-seabrook-brothers-all-three-killed-at-passchendaele/
http://www.gwc.org.uk/cms/our-school/history-of-george-watsons-college/watsons-war-records/
http://www.cwgc.org
http://www.clevedon-civic-society.org.uk/Content/Records/Military/WW1Casualtiesf.html
http://www.educationscotland.gov.uk/video/n/video_tcm4567273.asp
http://www.freewebs.com/eltoro1960/boysoldier.htm
http://www.golftavernhaddington.co.uk/.html
http://www.nationalarchives.gov.uk
http://www.puremalt.com/
http://www.scotland.gov.uk/Topics/Environment/SustainableDevelopment/funding/communityprojects
7http://www.scran.ac.uk
http://www.thermos.com/history.aspx
http://www.scotlandspeople.gov.uk